TEACHING RELIGIOUS AND WORLDVIEWS EDUCATION CREATIVELY

Teaching Religious and Worldviews Education Creatively offers a fresh perspective on the Religious Education (RE) curriculum. This second edition is crammed full of practical lesson ideas underpinned by cutting edge research authored by specialists in the field. It helps teachers understand what constitutes an effective and creative Religion and Worldviews Education (RWE) curriculum, and challenges teachers to view RWE as a transformatory subject that offers learners the tools to be discerning, to work out their own beliefs and to answer puzzling questions.

This second edition of *Teaching Religious and Worldviews Education Creatively* includes fully updated chapters from the first edition with 11 new contributors and 5 brand new chapters. New topics include:

- Visits, visitors and persona dolls
- The RE Searchers approach
- New ideas about policy, practice and assessment
- Insights into RE in the UK and around the world
- Anti-discriminatory RE
- New and updated practical classroom ideas from practicing teachers

Teaching Religious and Worldviews Education Creatively is for all teachers who want to learn more about innovative teaching and learning in RWE in order to improve understanding, knowledge and enjoyment, while at the same time transforming their own as well as their pupils' lives.

Sally Elton-Chalcraft is Professor of Social Justice in Education and Director of the Learning Education and Development Research Centre, University of Cumbria, UK, researching into RE and anti-racism. Sally is co-editor for the widely used *Professional Studies in Primary Education* (2022) 4th ed London-Sage. Cooper, H. and Elton-Chalcraft, S. (eds)

T0384897

THE LEARNING TO TEACH IN THE PRIMARY SCHOOL SERIES

Series Editor: Teresa Cremin, The Open University, UK

Teaching is an art form. It demands not only knowledge and understanding of the core areas of learning, but also the ability to teach these creatively and foster learner creativity in the process. The Learning to Teach in the Primary School Series draws upon recent research which indicates the rich potential of creative teaching and learning, and explores what it means to teach creatively in the primary phase. It also responds to the evolving nature of subject teaching in a wider, more imaginatively framed 21st century primary curriculum.

Designed to complement the textbook Learning to Teach in the Primary School, the well informed, lively texts in this series offer support for student and practising teachers who want to develop more creative approaches to teaching and learning. Uniquely, the books highlight the importance of the teachers' own creative engagement and share a wealth of research informed ideas to enrich pedagogy and practice.

Titles in the series:

TEACHING SCIENCE CREATIVELY, 2ND Edition
Dan Davies and Deb McGregor

APPLYING CROSS-CURRICULAR APPROACHES CREATIVELY
THE CONNECTING CURRICULUM
Jonathan Barnes

TEACHING LANGUAGES CREATIVELY
Edited by Philip Hood

TEACHING PHYSICAL EDUCATION CREATIVELY, 2ND Edition
Angela Pickard and Patricia Maude

TEACHING MATHEMATICS CREATIVELY, 3RD Edition
Linda Pound and Trisha Lee

TEACHING ART CREATIVELY
Penny Hay

TEACHING ENGLISH CREATIVELY, 3RD Edition
Teresa Cremin

TEACHING RELIGIOUS AND WORLDVIEWS EDUCATION CREATIVELY, 2ND Edition
Edited by Sally Elton-Chalcraft

For more information about this series, please visit: https://www.routledge.com/ Learning-to-Teach-in-the-Primary-School-Series/book-series/LTPS

TEACHING RELIGIOUS AND WORLDVIEWS EDUCATION CREATIVELY

Second Edition

Edited by
Sally Elton-Chalcraft

Routledge
Taylor & Francis Group

LONDON AND NEW YORK

Designed cover image: © Lisa Dynan

Second edition published 2024
by Routledge
4 Park Square, Milton Park, Abingdon, Oxon, OX14 4RN

and by Routledge
605 Third Avenue, New York, NY 10158

Routledge is an imprint of the Taylor & Francis Group, an informa business

First edition published by Routledge 2015

British Library Cataloguing-in-Publication Data
A catalogue record for this book is available from the British Library

ISBN: 978-1-032-42170-4 (hbk)
ISBN: 978-1-032-42169-8 (pbk)
ISBN: 978-1-003-36148-0 (ebk)

DOI: 10.4324/9781003361480

Typeset in Times
by Deanta Global Publishing Services, Chennai, India

CONTENTS

CONTENTS ▪ ▪ ▪ ▪

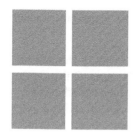

CONTRIBUTOR BIOS

Rebekah Ackroyd is a lecturer in education at the University of Cumbria. She teaches on a range of postgraduate education programmes including on the master's programme as well as teaching RE at undergraduate level. She is a specialist in Religious Education (RE), having studied Theology at undergraduate level before teaching in schools in Birmingham and Blackburn. Her PhD explored how teachers of RE construct and promote mutual respect and tolerance. She is enthusiastic about making research useful and accessible to practitioners and helping young people to learn about religions and worldviews in the classroom and beyond.

Alexandra Brown is a Philosophy, Ethics and Religious Studies secondary school teacher, academic, visiting lecturer, writer and poet whose work focuses on Christian theologies of liberation, Islam within the Black American experience and decolonising issues of social justice pertaining to gender, race, class, disability and sexual identity within the English religious education curriculum. Theologically and philosophically, Alexandra aligns with Black Liberation Theology, Womanism and Afro-Pessimism. She also engages in public speaking, advisory and consultancy work regarding anti-racism and decolonialisation within primary, secondary schools and FE institutions. Alexandra describes her ponderings, reflections, words and ontology as 'residing in liminal spaces'.

Sally Elton-Chalcraft is Professor of Social Justice in Education and Director of the Learning Education and Development Research centre, University of Cumbria, UK. She is convenor of the Religions, Values and Education special interest group for the British Education Research Association. She teaches on undergraduate, graduate, masters and doctoral programmes and publishes in the areas of Religious Education, anti-racism, and professional practice. Currently she is researching different approaches in education including art-based community focused provision and also the relevance of Charlotte Mason's practice for contemporary pedagogy. She has given keynotes in India, Germany, Ireland and the UK. She is co-editor of a widely used teacher education textbook: Cooper, H. and Elton-Chalcraft, S. (eds) (2022) 4th ed *Professional Studies in Primary Education*, London-Sage. Throughout her career as a primary school teacher, teacher educator and academic, she has been passionate about making education accessible, engaging and thought provoking leading to a fairer world.

Kate Christopher teaches RE at a secondary school in East London, and works as a national RE adviser, supporting both primary and secondary colleagues. She manages the website RE:ONLINE and creates CSTG's online short courses for teachers' CPD.

Her work with teachers is in curriculum development and teachers' wider professional identity.

Ruth Flanagan is a senior lecturer in Education, subject lead for Primary Humanities, Programme Director for the Primary PGCE and Race Equality Resource Officer at the University of Exeter. She has taught for over 30 years at primary, secondary, adult education, undergraduate and postgraduate levels. Having lived and worked in India, Russia and Ethiopia, Ruth's research interests are in intercultural communication, the origins and evolution of worldviews and the significance of these on education throughout the world. She has researched and published in the field of religious education, worldviews and education more generally.

Giles Freathy is a senior lecturer at Plymouth Marjon University where he is a Partnership Lead in the teacher education partnership. Having taught RE across Key Stages 1 and 2, Giles also undertook advisory roles in Cornwall. Giles has written materials for projects led by the University of Exeter, including the 'RE-flect Project: A Programme to Foster Metacognition in the RE Classroom'. He is co-creator of *the RE-searchers approach* and has authored and co-authored e-books and chapters in various publications explaining and developing this internationally recognized and award-winning approach (TES, 2014).

Katie Freeman is Chair of the National Association of Teachers of RE (NATRE). She is a serving primary school teacher with eighteen years' experience, she has worked in both community and church schools. Katie is the RE leader at Bickleigh Down CofE Primary School in Devon, a member of the working party for RE with the Church of England and one of the original hub leaders for Learn Teach Lead RE in the Southwest.

Penny Hollander has been a teacher with experience in primary and secondary schools and higher education at the University of Cumbria. Her major teaching interests are effective RE provision in schools and particularly children's spiritual development. She is currently working as a freelance consultant, mainly with Carlisle diocese, in an advisory capacity and delivering training in RE and collective worship. She has recently written some materials for the National Society's Christianity Project. She is also a trained SIAMS inspector.

Imran Kotwal is the founder of Muslim Learner Services and IslamREsources.co.uk. He is a *Hafidh al Qur'an* and can lead Muslims in prayers. Imran supports schools with Islam assemblies, pupil workshops, sessions for parents and staff training. He is regularly invited by SACREs, Diocesan Bodies and MATs to lead Islam CPD for their RE leads. Imran served as head of a highly successful multi-faith chaplaincy team as well as leading Muslim students in Friday prayers at Salford City College for over ten years. He has previously trained and worked as an Ofsted inspector (AI). Imran is the Muslim representative for the Standing Advisory Council on Religious Education (SACRE) in Salford and Wigan.

Fiona Moss is a primary specialist. She has worked for RE Today for over 14 years. Fiona is also the Chief Executive Officer for NATRE and is well-known in this context for her involvement in RE at a national level, supporting teachers, working across key stakeholder organisations and lobbying to the government to support RE. Before joining RE Today as National RE Adviser she was a primary teacher for 15 years and then the RE and SACRE Curriculum Adviser for Leicester City council. She is currently the Editor of RE Today's Primary RE series Exploring religion and worldviews and previously edited 'Inspiring RE', 'RE Ideas' and edited and written for a large number of other publications. She was also one of the writers for the Understanding Christianity resource. She trains hundreds of teachers each year in schools and works with local authorities and dioceses across the country and worldwide.

Janet Orchard is Associate Professor of Philosophy and Religion in Teacher Education and Director of Postgraduate Research at the School of Education, University of Bristol. She is a philosopher of education taking a comparative interest in relationships between philosophy, religion and teacher education. She belongs to AULRE (the Association of University Lecturers in Religion and Education) and the International Seminar on Religious Education and Values (ISREV) and serves on the editorial board of the British Journal of Religious Education (BJRE). She is co-editor of Professional Reflection.

Georgia Prescott started her career as a primary school teacher in London and Cumbria. She subsequently worked as a Senior Lecturer in Primary Religious Education for many years at St. Martin's College and the University of Cumbria. She is currently a member of Cumbria Standing Advisory Council for Religious Education (SACRE). Her teaching, research and publication interests include Religious Education, Philosophy for Children (P4C), and Spiritual, Moral, Social and Cultural Development (SMSC).

Lynn Revell is a Professor of Religion and Education at Canterbury Christ Church University. She has worked as a primary school teacher and as an RE teacher in secondary schools. She is interested in the challenging conversations teachers have with pupils about religion and beliefs and the ways in which religions are often misrepresented in classrooms.

Saima Saleh (SLE for RE) is a primary teacher and head of RE/Religion and Worldviews at Ravenscote Junior School in Surrey, where she has managed the subject since 2013. She is also a member of the NATRE executive where, as Local Groups and Networks Lead, she helps teachers of RE to connect through a variety of local, national and global groups. With over 29 years of teaching experience, Saima has a particular interest in anti-racism and strives to raise an awareness of this through her work.

Linda Whitworth taught Religious Education in both secondary and primary schools and for 26 years lectured in Primary RE in Initial Teacher Education at Middlesex University. She is a member of NATRE executive and co-edits Professional Reflection in RE Today. She is now a consultant for Primary Religion and Worldviews, working with Early Career Teachers. Her research interests include the role of Religion and Worldviews in intercultural understanding and its contribution to interdisciplinary studies across the Humanities.

Jane Yates is the RE Adviser to Cumbrian SACRE and the North West RE Hubs Lead. She is also an advanced trainer for SAPERE – the national charity for Philosophy for Children, Communities and Colleges (P4C). Jane leads on a number of regional and national projects including: SAPERE *Thinking together in Science and RE*; Cumbrian SACRE *Virtual Voices in Religious Education* (VVRE); and the North West region's AREIAC *Young Ambassadors for the Freedom of Religion or Belief.* Central to Jane's life is being a volunteer and facilitator for Anti-Racist Cumbria.

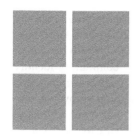

SERIES EDITOR FOREWORD

Creativity in education concerns almost everyone. Parents, carers and teachers all seek to support young people in developing cognitively, socially and emotionally in order that they can thrive successfully in an increasingly uncertain world. Creativity is central to this. It is a crucial twenty-first-century competency which we urgently need to foster in schooling and more widely in our complex, globalised and digital societies. In the last two decades, increased interest in creativity and creative pedagogies has been evident in the work of educators and researchers, and politicians and political systems too have become more aware of the potential need for creativity (e.g. OECD 2018; Lucas 2023). Today, creative approaches to learning are of international interest, and teachers want to expand their repertoires of practice and nurture young learners' creativity.

Recognising that creativity and creative thinking are key skills for 2030's learners. The Organisation for Economic Co-operation and Development (OECD 2018) introduced a test of young people's creative thinking in 2021 in their suite of assessments for 15-year-olds. This Programme for International Student Assessment (PISA) is highly influential on governments worldwide, so as the years unfold, more space and attention will be given to creativity in policy, practice and research.

Other potent factors are shaping this new 'creative turn'. As I have argued previously, the relentless quest for higher standards and curriculum coverage has often obscured the personal and affective dimensions of teaching and learning (Cremin 2015, xi), but in the context of the aftermath of the Covid-19 crisis, educators are as concerned about children's mental health and social and emotional wellbeing, as they are about their learning loss and academic 'catch-up'. The challenge of balancing both requires considerable creativity and a professional mindset characterised by imagination and flexibility, not compliance and conformity. The curriculum needs re-shaping and new priorities are emerging.

> Rebalancing the curriculum now to make creativity, critical thinking, decision-making, critical thinking, problem-solving, collaboration, resilience and adaptability as prominent as English, maths, science, dance, history and philosophy is what we need to do.
>
> (Lucas 2020)

The Curriculum for Excellence in Scotland and the Welsh Curriculum recognise and celebrate the role of creativity, and whilst the English curriculum does not profile it nearly as clearly, the Durham Commission (2019) developed a vision for promoting creativity in education. This collaboration between Arts Council England and Durham University examined the benefits of a creative education for young people from birth to the age of 25, with reference to economic growth, skills and social mobility; community identity and social engagement; and personal fulfilment and wellbeing. To realise its rich vision will take time, but many schools across the UK already seek to develop innovative curricula that interests and engages all children, and many teachers find renewed energy and enthusiasm through deploying creative pedagogies. However, their capacity to do so effectively relies upon a shared understanding of the concept of creativity and demands that the myths and mantras which surround it are confronted. For far too long the misconceptions that creativity is connected only to the arts and confined to a few particularly gifted individuals have held sway. We must move on.

Whilst debates resound about the difference between the 'Big C' creativity of genius and the 'little c' creativity of the everyday, most scholars argue it involves the capacity to generate, reason and critically evaluate novel ideas and/or imaginary scenarios. It encompasses thinking through and solving problems, making connections, inventing and reinventing and flexing one's imaginative muscles in all aspects of learning and life. The OECD view it as:

> The competence to engage productively in an iterative process involving the generation, evaluation and improvement of ideas, that can result in novel and effective solutions.
>
> (OECD Directorate for Education and Skills 2018: 6)

To nurture such competence, teachers need to recognise that knowledge and creativity are two sides of the same coin, not polar opposites, and need to make effective use of creative pedagogies. In a systematic review of the international literature in this area (spanning 1990 to 2018), Kerry Chappell and I worked to understand the nature of creative pedagogies in the years of formal schooling. We created inclusion and exclusion criteria and analysed the 35 finally included peer-reviewed papers from 14 countries. We identified seven characteristics of creative pedagogies, namely: generating and exploring ideas; co-constructing and collaborating; encouraging autonomy and agency; problem solving; playfulness; risk-taking; and teacher creativity (Cremin and Chappell 2019).

The characteristic most frequently evidenced was generating and exploring ideas. Perhaps this is not surprising as making and investigating ideas is often associated with an ethos of openness in which strong teacher–student relationships exist alongside a balance of freedom and structure. In one of the studies, for instance, the researchers noted practitioners breaking conventions and enabling students to learn from their teachers' mistakes (Henriksen and Mishra 2015). The second most frequent characteristic of creative pedagogies was co-constructing and collaborating. This may well challenge the profession to shift from what Vlad Glăveanu (2010) describes as the 'I-paradigm' to the 'We-paradigm' of creative collaboration. In addition, in many of the research studies we reviewed, collaborative activity and teacher-student relationships were seen to be central to the co-construction of creative pedagogies.

Teachers' own creativity also emerged as a characteristic of creative pedagogical practice, with evidence of teachers playfully pioneering their way forwards in lessons, investing time in discussion and sharing their pleasure in creative processes. Such professionals not only recognise, value and exercise their own creativity, but also seek to promote creativity in others (Cremin 2009; Cremin et al. 2009, Cremin et al. 2022). Perhaps, in tune with Eisner (2003), these practitioners recognise that teaching is an art form and that teachers benefit from viewing themselves as versatile artists in the classroom, drawing on their personal passions and creativity as they research and develop their practice. In exploring possibility thinking, which Anna Craft (2000) argued is at the heart of creativity in education, a team of us observed the interplay between teachers and children who were involved in thinking their ways forwards as they immersed themselves in playful contexts, posed questions, took risks, showed imagination, self-determination and were innovative (Craft et al. 2012; Burnard et al. 2006; Cremin et al. 2006). In my own work related to reading for pleasure, I have seen how teachers hold up a mirror to their own practices as readers and learn more about the social and relational nature of reading through reflecting on their creative engagement. As a consequence, they more effectively foster classrooms of engaged readers (Cremin et al. 2022). A new pedagogy of possibility beckons.

However, support is needed to help teachers seize such possibilities and this is exactly what this series of books offers. It accompanies and complements the fifth edition of the textbook *Learning to Teach in the Primary School* (Cremin et al. 2024) and aims to support teachers in developing as creative practitioners. The books do not merely offer practical strategies for classroom use, (although these abound), but far more importantly they seek to widen teachers' knowledge and understanding of the research-informed principles underpinning a creative approach. The 13 texts in the series engage with key areas of the primary curriculum, mediating research evidence and making different theoretical perspectives and scholarly arguments accessible and engaging. In the process, the series seeks to demonstrate the practical relevance and value of research to the teaching profession.

If you aspire to develop further as a research-informed practitioner and creative, artistically engaged educator, then you will find much of value here to support your professional learning journey and enrich not only your pedagogy and practice, but the children's creativity in the process.

ABOUT THE SERIES EDITOR

Teresa Cremin is Professor of Education (Literacy) at The Open University, UK, and co-Director of the Literacy and Social Justice Centre which creates space for research, practice and advocacy to enrich educational opportunities for all. Teresa is an ex-teacher and teacher-trainer, and now undertakes research and consultancy in the UK and abroad. Her socio-cultural research focusses on volitional reading and writing, teachers' literate identities and creative pedagogies. She has published over 30 books, including the popular *Learning to Teach in the Primary School* (with Cathy Burnett, Ed, 4th edition, Routledge 2018) and she edits the accompanying series focussed on teaching creatively across the primary curriculum. Other recent texts include *Reading Teachers: Nurturing Reading for Pleasure* with Helen Hendry, Lucy Rodriguez Leon and Natalia Kucirkova (Routledge, 2022), *Children Reading for Pleasure in the Digital Age* with Natalia Kucirkova (Sage, 2020), *Writer Identity and the Teaching and Learning of Writing* with Terry Locke and

Storytelling in Early Childhood: Enriching Language, Literacy and Classroom Culture with Rosie Flewitt, Ben Mardell and Joan Swann (both Routledge, 2017).

A fellow of the English Association, the Academy of Social Sciences and the Royal Society of the Arts, Teresa is a currently a trustee of the UK Literacy Association, an appointed DfE Reading for Pleasure expert, chair of the Advisory Group of the Paul Hamlyn Foundation Teacher Development Fund in the Arts, a board member of the Reading Agency, and a Great School Libraries Champion. Previously, Teresa has served as president of the UKLA, and of the UK Reading Association, and as a trustee of BookTrust and the Poetry Archive. Teresa is passionate about developing readers for life and leads a research and practice coalition to support the development of children's and teachers' reading for pleasure https://ourfp.org/.

REFERENCES

Burnard, P., Craft, A. and Cremin, T. (2006) 'Possibility thinking', *International Journal of Early Years Education* 14 (3): 243–62.

Chappell, K., Craft, A., Burnard, P. and Cremin, T. (2008) 'Question-posing and question-responding: The heart of possibility thinking in the early years', *Early Years* 28 (3): 267–86.

Craft, A. (2000) *Creativity Across the Primary Curriculum*. London: Routledge.

Craft, A. (2011) *Creativity and Education Futures: Learning in a Digital Age*. London: Trentham.

Craft, A., Cremin, T., Burnard, P., Dragovic, T. and Chappell, K. (2012) 'Possibility thinking: Culminative studies of an evidence-based concept driving creativity?', *Education 3-13: International Journal of Primary, Elementary and Early* 41 (5): 538–56.

Cremin, T. (2015) 'Creative teachers and creative teaching', in A. Wilson (ed.) *Creativity in Primary Education*. London: Sage, pp. 33–44.

Cremin, T., Barnes, J. and Scoffham, S. (2009) *Creative Teaching for Tomorrow: Fostering a Creative State of Mind*. Deal: Future Creative.

Cremin, T., Burnard, P. and Craft, A. (2006) 'Pedagogy and possibility thinking in the early years', *International Journal of Thinking Skills and Creativity* 1 (2): 108–19.

Cremin, T. and Burnett, C. (eds.) (2018) *Learning to Teach in the Primary School* (4th edition). London: Routledge.

Cremin, T. and Chappell, K. (2019) 'Creative pedagogies: A systematic review', *Research Papers in Education*. DOI: 10.1080/02671522.2019.1677757

Cremin, T., Hendry, H., Leon, R. and Kucirkova, N. (2022) *Reading Teachers: Nurturing Reading for Pleasure*. London: Routledge.

Durham Commission Team (2019) *The Durham Commission on Creativity and Education*. Arts Council/Durham University. https://www.dur.ac.uk/creativitycommission/report/firstreport/

Eisner, E. (2003) 'Artistry in education', *Scandinavian Journal of Educational Research* 47 (3): 373–84.

Glăveanu, V. P. (2010) 'Paradigms in the study of creativity: Introducing the perspective of cultural psychology', *New Ideas in Psychology* 28: 79–93.

Henriksen, D. and Mishra, P. (2015) 'We teach who we are: Creativity in the lives and practices of accomplished teachers', *Teachers College Record* 117 (7): 1–46.

Lucas, B. et al. (2023). *Creative Thinking in Schools: A Leadership Playbook*. Carmarthen: Crown House Publishing Ltd.

Lucas, B. and Spencer, E. (2020) *Zest for Learning: Developing Curious Learners Who Relish Real-World Challenges*. Carmarthen: Crown House Publishing Ltd.

OECD Directorate for Education and Skills (2018) *Framework for the Assessment of Creative Thinking in PISA 2021* (Second Draft). Paris: OECD.

Thomson, P., Hall, C., Jones, K. and Sefton-Green, J. (2012) *The Signature Pedagogies Project: Final Report*. London: Creativity, Culture and Education.

SECTION 1

TEACHING RELIGION AND WORLDVIEWS EDUCATION CREATIVELY: *AIMS AND PRINCIPLES*

INTRODUCTION

Creative RE, The 'Phunometre Scale'

Sally Elton-Chalcraft

Building on the first edition (Elton-Chalcraft 2015), this second edition of Teaching Religious Education Creatively includes 5 new chapters and 11 new contributors. The book provides a diverse and comprehensive guide to creative and effective RE under-pinned by current and established research for a wide ranging national and international audience of teachers, student teachers, teacher educators and all interested in teaching and learning.

This first chapter sets the scene for the whole volume by outlining what is meant by creative teaching and learning and how this can be put into practice in religious education. The book, and this chapter in particular, aims to answer the following four questions.

1. What is creative teaching and learning? (and the 'phunometre scale')
2. Why is it important to teach creatively and teach for creativity?
3. What is religious education and why is it important for children to engage in RE?
4. How can a teacher present non-biased RE creatively as a discrete subject and integrate it with other curriculum areas?

This first chapter introduces all four elements. Subsequent chapters expand on these top-ics, drawing on each author's wealth of experience and knowledge.

WHAT IS CREATIVE TEACHING AND LEARNING?

Creativity has been notoriously difficult to define. In some literature, it is defined as an abstract noun with particular characteristics as described in the NACCCE 1999 policy document (Table 1.1). In contrast, some authors define creative strategies actively as a verb for creative thinking (Buzan's 2014 mind mapping, de Bono's 2014 thinking hats, Cremin et al.'s 2012 possibility thinking). Creativity also has been discussed from differ-ent cultural perspectives (Craft et al. 2007), which is pertinent to the debate, because at the heart of religious education is a desire to learn about a variety of cultures.

DOI: 10.4324/9781003361480-2

▪ **Table 1.1** Definition of creativity from National Advisory Committee on Creative and Cultural Education (NACCCE 1999:29)

The policy document for creativity *All Our Futures* (NACCCE 1999:29), defines the four features of creativity as:

1.   Using imagination – generating something original, providing an alternative to the expected.
2.   Pursuing purposes – applying imagination to produce something (an idea, a performance, a product).
3.   Creativity involves originality
     - Individual, in relation to their own previous work.
     - Relative, in relation to their peer group.
     - Historic, uniquely original.
4.   Judging value – evaluating the imaginative activity as effective, useful, enjoyable, satisfying, valid, tenable.

School CCAF (Challenging, Creative and Fun) and School Hebs (Hard/Easy, Boring, Scary)

To gain an understanding of creative teaching and learning in practice, we could transport ourselves to two hypothetical schools in the UK where children are engaged in learning. Children experience a vibrant classroom environment with interactive displays and activities which encourage them to generate novel ideas or ways of working. Both the teacher and children are having fun but are also challenged. If you have read *Hooray for Diffendoofer Day* (Prelutsky and Smith 1998, but inspired by Dr Seuss) you may have some idea of what this exciting classroom looks like and what its mirror image in Dreary town is like too (which I call HEBS hard/easy, boring, scary). Both the teacher and children will look forward to coming to CCAF school most of the time. Things do not always run smoothly in our hypothetical classroom which is, after all, in the 'real' world, but there is usually an excited 'buzz' and any visitor will instantly know that learning is taking place.

From the very first moment the children enter the classroom, in school CCAF (challenging, creative and fun), the enthusiastic teacher engages them in creative learning, see Table 1.2. The learners at CCAF (challenging, creative and fun) school would possess characteristics which Claxton has defined as the 'magnificent eight' (Claxton 2007:123), listed in Table 1.3. So the teachers in CCAF school build their children's 'learning muscles' and 'learning stamina' (Claxton 2007) to achieve the magnificent eight characteristics of a powerful learner.

But Claxton (2007) warns the teacher against being overly stringent in 'building learning power'. Children are not to be seen as mini athletes who must be challenged almost to the breaking point. Elton-Chalcraft and Mills (2013) state that learning should be challenging and yet also must be fun. But it is a tall order for the primary teacher to plan and facilitate lessons which will allow children to be creative, use their imagination, be challenged and also have fun. However, these are not mutually exclusive. If children have a positive mindset towards learning, then they will be intrinsically motivated to

■ **Table 1.2** Characteristics of caricatured CCAF and HEBS schools

CAFF (Challenging Creative and Fun) School	HEBS (Too Hard/ Easy, Boring/ Scary) School
Children and teachers are challenged, have fun and are creative at school	Teachers and learners find school too hard or too easy, boring and/or scary
Children possess the magnificent eight qualities of a powerful learner (Claxton 2007- see table 1.3) – curious, imaginative, disciplined, reflective etc	Children are unmotivated to learn, get upset when they make mistakes or fail, are bullies or victims of bullying
Teachers enjoy the challenge of planning, teaching and assessing. They have positive relationships with their pupils and find their jobs tiring but rewarding	Teachers put minimum effort into planning, teaching and assessing. They dominate or are scared by their pupils. They are miserable, feel powerless, and only work to pay their bills

■ **Table 1.3** Guy Claxton's 'Magnificent 8 qualities of a powerful learner' (2007:123–126)

Magnificent 8 Qualities

1. Firstly a powerful learner is *curious*. They wonder about things, are open-minded and ask pertinent and productive questions.

2. Confident learners have *courage* to deal with uncertainty and complexity and admitting 'I don't know'. Mistakes are for learning from, not getting upset about.

3. Powerful learners are good at *exploration* and *investigation* – they are good at finding, making and capitalising on resources that will help them pursue their projects (tools, places, other people).

4. Powerful learning requires *experimentation* – they draft/make something, then evaluate and redraft/revise. They try different approaches, mess things up and make mistakes (if they are not too costly).

5. Powerful learners have *imagination* and draw on their own inner creativity. They make 'mental simulations' of tricky situations to smooth their own performances in their mind's eye. They know when and how to put themselves in another's shoes.

6. Creativity needs to be yoked to *reason* and *discipline* – powerful learners think carefully, rigorously, methodically. They analyse and evaluate as well as being imaginative. They spot holes in their own argument as well as other people's. Disciplined thinking enables knowledge and skill to guide learning.

7. Powerful learners have the virtue of *sociability*, making good use of collaboration. They are good at balancing sociability with solitariness – they are not afraid to go off by themselves when they need to think and digest.

8. Powerful learners are *reflective*; they step back and evaluate how the learning is going but avoid being too self critical.

(Claxton 2007:123–126)

■ **Table 1.4** Elton-Chalcraft and Mills (2013) 'phunometre scale' for measuring fun and challenge for both the learning environment and planned activities

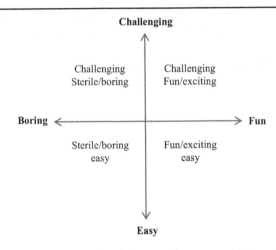

learn. The fun will spring from the satisfaction of struggling with a task but eventually making some progress.

Creative teaching and learning can be fun if both the teacher and children gain satisfaction from the challenge, if they know what it is like to feel exhilaration after a struggle. The children at CCAF (creative, challenging and fun) school enjoy the challenge of learning compared with their counterparts in HEBS (hard/easy, boring, scary) school, who are bored. While this is an exaggerated caricature, nevertheless, these two schools illustrate two opposing approaches to learning. Similarly children may display opposing characteristics as learners. Two characters in the film version of the Dr Seuss (1997) book *The Cat in the Hat* demonstrate this point. A sister's over-cautious disposition and fear of fun are contrasted with her brother's reckless risk taking and fun-loving disposition. By the end of the film, both children have moved from their polarised positions, realising that fun and risk taking (the characteristics of creativity) are necessary but in moderation. Their opposing characteristics were measured on a 'phunometre' (fun measurement) scale. Elton-Chalcraft and Mills (2013:2) adopt this fictitious 'phunometre' scale to evaluate teaching and learning contexts in the learning environment (for example interactive displays, working wall, mind mapping, use of stimulating resources) and planned activities (problem solving, open-ended investigation, creative thinking strategies). See Table 1.4.

WHY IS IT IMPORTANT TO TEACH CREATIVELY AND TEACH FOR CREATIVITY?

First, I argue that it is more fulfilling to work and learn in a school which exhibits creative and challenging learning and teaching. Second, I argue that teachers who teach creatively, and teach for creativity, move beyond a transmission model to a powerful and transformative model of teaching, thus the curriculum is more meaningful. In the third part of my argument, I suggest that a creative and transformative model of teaching and learning provides the children with resilience and learning power to prepare them for their future lives.

1. Better to Work and Learn in a Creative School

Our two schools, CCAF (creative, challenging and fun) and HEBS (hard/easy, boring, scary), may be caricatures; however, they show the extremes of two opposing philosophies. At school CCAF there are enthused, curious, resilient life-long learners working with motivated, hard-working and happy teachers dedicated to building the children's 'learning muscles' and 'learning stamina', thus avoiding 'learned helplessness' (Claxton 2007, 2008). In contrast, school HEBS is populated with bored and disaffected children frightened of failure with scared, demotivated and unhappy teachers. In reality most schools have elements of both these caricatures, but the aim would be to strive to be school CCAF. Thus, it is important to teach creatively and teach for creativity so that both the teachers and children feel fulfilled, enjoy the learning and experience a sense of achievement. Cullingford (2007) has argued that children need extrinsic rewards if the curriculum is sterile and boring, and behaviour management strategies are needed to keep children on task; whereas if children are given more ownership of their learning in an engaging and creative curriculum, they are more likely to be motivated to learn.

2. A Meaningful Curriculum

Educationalists such as Bruner (1996) and neuroscientists such as Heilmann (2005) and Claxton (1997) have all argued that children are more motivated by a creative curriculum which makes sense to them, includes problem solving and child-led investigation and develops their thinking skills. Neuroscience teaches us that knowledge makes more sense when it is contextualised (Heilmann 2005). Teachers who are skill and concept builders play a crucial role in making the curriculum meaningful as opposed to task managers and curriculum deliverers who merely transmit knowledge or keep children busy with tasks (Twiselton 2004). Task managers are described by Twiselton (2004) as teachers who view their role in terms of task completion, order and business with little reference to children making sense of their learning. Teachers who are curriculum deliverers also lack an understanding of a meaningful curriculum, seeing their role merely as delivering an externally decided set of skills and knowledge (Twiselton 2004). Skill and concept builders on the other hand see the 'bigger picture' and endeavour to design a meaningful curriculum which makes sense in terms of principles and concepts (Twiselton and Elton-Chalcraft 2024). Thus a creative and effective teacher is also a skill and concept builder (Twiselton 2004) who thinks carefully about what the children need to learn and why this knowledge and these skills are relevant. Such a teacher ensures the learning fits into the wider curriculum and she/he scaffolds the learner's experience. Teachers at CCAF school would be skill and concept builders designing and implementing a creative and challenging curriculum which is more meaningful for the learners.

▨ **Table 1.5** Poster in a school cited by Hymer and Gershon (2014:27) Fail = first attempt in learning

---

F irst
A ttempt
I n
L earning

---

3. Resilient Learners Prepared for an Uncertain Future

A third reason for teaching creatively and teaching for creativity is that such an approach prepares children more effectively for an uncertain future. Children attending CCAF school (see Table 1.2) would be better prepared to engage with what life throws at them in their future lives. This is particularly important in current times where pandemics, cost of living crises, political turbulence, protests and strikes have become the norm across many countries of the world. Also humanity is evolving at a fast pace with new technologies and new ways of thinking, working and living. To keep abreast of, and not be daunted by, such unprecedented change, the children from school CCAF might be better prepared to deal with the demands of an uncertain future than children from HEBS school, who may exhibit fear or anger towards situations where they feel unprepared or 'out of their depth'. Creative teaching and learning encourages children to learn from mistakes and to pick themselves up and move forward. Hymer and Gershon (2014) talk about the power of failure and making mistakes in order to progress; they cite a poster seen in one school they visited, see Table 1.5.

In CCAF school the children are encouraged to try out ideas, and their 'bounce-backability' allows them to have another go if their first attempt fails. In the next sections, I apply some of the principles of creativity discussed previously to show what characterises effective and creative RE.

WHAT IS RELIGIOUS EDUCATION AND WHY IS IT IMPORTANT FOR CHILDREN TO ENGAGE IN RELIGIOUS EDUCATION?

Before outlining the aims, principles and values underpinning RE, I begin this section by asking you to evaluate your own starting point.

1. Your Baggage

Before going any further it is important for the teacher to consider their own attitudes towards religion and RE. Religion and beliefs are notoriously contentious topics. So, reader, please consider the questions in Table 1.6. Your values and attitudes (your baggage) can have a positive or negative influence on your capacity to engage children in creative and effective RE. Before commencement of planning, the teacher of RE must ask themselves what 'baggage' they bring. Returning to our two schools described in Table 1.2, CCAF and HEBS, examples of good and bad RE planning are identified in Table 1.7.

■ **Table 1.6** Questions to ask oneself before planning any RE

YOUR BAGGAGE	What do you think about Religion? What influence did your upbringing have on the values you hold? What do you think the aims of RE ought to be?

■ **Table 1.7** Examples of how to plan good (or bad) RE

To Plan Creative and Effective RE (Akin to CAFF School- table 1:2):	To Plan Dangerous or Uninspiring RE (Akin to HEBS School – table 1:2):
Acknowledge your 'baggage'	Let your 'baggage' influence you
Understand aims and principles of RE (see below)	Misunderstand/ignore aims and principles of RE
Encourage children to *investigate* and *evaluate* a variety of belief systems. Support children in their realisation that sometimes belief systems contradict each other	*Indoctrinate* children into your belief system (eg Catholicism, atheism, Islam etc); or pretend that all belief systems are actually the same in essence
Plan RE which explores a range of belief systems through role play, re-enactments, artwork, lively discussion, visits, visitors, problem solving etc	Ask children to 'research' belief systems by copying from websites, printing out colourful pictures. Never discuss work with the children
Encourage a safe, open-minded environment for children to voice their opinions and challenge others respectfully. Try your best to manage controversial discussions helping children critically evaluate the validity of different views	Avoid controversial discussions. Or make sure you are always in control so children know there is a 'right' or 'wrong' viewpoint, ie the teacher's view is always 'right'
Provide opportunities for children to solve problems (eg how would you ensure a year one boy's leaving party would provide suitable food and party games for a Jewish girl, several vegetarian children, a diabetic child, a Muslim etc)	Ask children to colour in and label a photocopied resource sheet showing halal and Kosher food laws

2. Aims and Principles of RE

Once a teacher has acknowledged his/her baggage, see Table 1.6, the aims and principles of RE can be introduced, depending on your context. For example, in Britain RE holds a unique position as part of the 'basic' but not the national curriculum. In state schools the RE syllabus is currently determined by the local authority, Standing Advisory Council for Religious Education (SACRE). Many SACREs draw on the non-statutory guidance for RE suggested by the Commission for RE (CORE 2018) to write their Agreed Syllabus. In faith schools, a faith-based curriculum for RE is often drawn on. For example, Church of England and Catholic schools use their respective diocesan syllabi. There are some overlaps of aims and principles of RE in both state and faith schools, and in this volume we draw on the aims for RE as articulated in the CORE (2018), summarised in Chapter 2. In other parts of the world, RE is religious faith nurture, but as I explain in Chapter 12, there is a growing interest in non-religious belief systems as secular worldviews such as Humanism gain in popularity.

3. Values, Beliefs and RE

In this section, I investigate educational values and beliefs and show how RE can contribute to the debate. My argument is based on the following premises:

■ Teaching and learning in school is not value free.
■ Values and beliefs are communicated through school ethos.
■ RE provides an opportunity to evaluate, nurture, re-enforce or challenge values and beliefs.

Alexander and his team, in the acclaimed and influential *Cambridge Review*, asked the question 'what is primary education for' and deduced that it is 'fundamentally a moral pursuit' (Alexander 2010:174). More recently Biesta and Hannam (2021) have sought to remind RE teachers about the forgotten dimension of RE – namely that it is about 'religion' and also 'education', not sociology, anthropology, philosophy or theory of knowledge. Rather RE is a discipline which seeks to engage with religions and worldviews 'from the "inside"… as a lived meaningful reality' (2021:2). (For a useful summary of Hannam and Biesta's edited collection see Franken's (2021) book review.) So, RE is a valuable subject for learning how to evaluate a range of values and beliefs from an 'insider' perspective. I would argue it is vital for young people to understand differences and question why individuals, communities and societies behave in particular ways and why societies create, abide by or protest against certain traditions, laws and social norms. Here RE can play a major role in upskilling learners to hone their evaluative faculties. Values and beliefs are all around us – but sometimes hidden; teaching and learning in schools is not value free. Values and beliefs are communicated through the school ethos including the displays, curriculum content, body language and interactions and so on. In both faith-based and community (non-faith-based) schools, RE is an ideal place for teachers and children to explore different belief systems and values. For example in many schools there are 'codes of conduct' or 'school rules' and sometimes these are developed together by both children and adults working in the school. Thus everyone shares ownership of the 'rules' or 'ethos'. Examples might include 'overarching values' such as 'respecting everyone's right to education' and also specific rules such as 'don't run in the corridor'. During a topic on 'rules', children could examine the reasons why rules are important; they might investigate the Ten Commandments of Judaism and Christianity and compare this with the Eightfold Path of Buddhism, looking at similarities and differences. This investigation can then encompass their own school rules, ethos and values with the children learning 'about' different traditional belief systems and then learning 'from' these belief systems to reflect on how moral values relate to their own behaviour. While RE in a community school should not be religious instruction or faith nurture, even in a faith school RE should enable children to critically examine their own belief system in RE lessons. Acts of collective worship provide opportunities for faith nurture in faith schools, but we would argue that in both faith-based and community schools, RE should be education not indoctrination. In faith-based and community schools, beliefs and values may be communicated through the school ethos. RE provides a forum for open discussion about a range of values and different views of morality.

Within teaching itself there are values which are communicated via governmental directives. The UK government policy PREVENT (part of the government's anti-terrorism strategy called Contest) came into force in 2011, and 'extremism' is defined as 'vocal or active opposition to fundamental British values' (Elton-Chalcraft et al. 2017). On the face of it such a strategy would seem legitimate but, as Revell (2012) and Elton-Chalcraft et al. (2022) argue, such a policy has fuelled Islamophobia; in Chapter 11 Revell and Christopher discuss how Islam can be approached creatively and in an unbiased manner in the classroom. Chapters 3 (Elton-Chalcraft, Brown and Yates) and 12 (Elton-Chalcraft) both argue that RE has an important role to play in challenging racism, homophobia, sexism, anti-semetism and other forms of discrimination. Regulatory bodies (such as OfSTED in the UK) suggest that Religious and Worldviews Education (RE) should make a major contribution to the education of children and young people. At its best, it is intellectually challenging and personally enriching. It helps young people develop beliefs and values, and promotes the virtues of respect and empathy, which are important in our diverse society. It fosters civilised debate and reasoned argument, and helps pupils to understand the place of religion and belief in the modern world. Values permeate our lives, and when we have the space to do so, children and adults alike contemplate 'our place in the world', for example which friends to talk to, which hobbies to engage in, which food to eat etc. We act, sometimes unconsciously, according to a set of beliefs/ social conventions, or values, which are often determined by our upbringing.

Children, like adults, are usually very aware of injustices; but also children, like adults, delight when something inspires them. Primary school education can play a crucial role in how a child develops and how they begin to understand the world in which they live. RE, because of its nature to question and explore in a safe environment, can play a significant role in supporting a child's understanding of the varied nature of belief systems. RE can encourage children to respect but also critically evaluate their own and other belief systems in a non-biased fashion. So RE, in both faith-based and community schools, seeks to investigate and evaluate a range of beliefs and values, but RE sometimes should also allow children to nurture, re-enforce or challenge particular values and beliefs. While many teachers may desire to present non-biased RE, in practice they lack the confidence to achieve this. In some previous research, I found that while the majority of the student teachers in my sample were keen to teach for diversity, they also acknowledged lack of confidence and competence to do so (Twiselton and Elton-Chalcraft 2014). Teaching religious education creatively aims to provide the teacher with examples of effective and creative non-biased RE rooted in evidence from research.

HOW DO I TEACH NON-BIASED RE CREATIVELY, AS A DISCRETE SUBJECT AND INTEGRATE IT WITH OTHER CURRICULUM AREAS?

The previous sections outlined the aims and principles of effective RE, what should be learned and why. In this section I aim to explain how to make teaching and learning in

■ **Table 1.8** Characteristics of effective and creative enquiry in RE (adapted from OfSTED 2013)

Do	*Don't*
Involve the children, giving them ownership of learning – teachers and pupils discuss what the lesson will be about and where it will lead, making sure they can see the relevance and importance of the enquiry and how it relates to their own concerns. Children set up their own enquiry	**Communicate learning objectives mechanistically.** Pupils copy the objectives for the lesson into their books, taking up most of the lesson
Allow pupils to use their creativity and imagination – ensuring that experiential learning and opportunities to foster spiritual and creative development are built into the process of enquiry	**Not taking risks.** Teachers were unwilling to open up enquiry in case pupils asked challenging or controversial questions with which they felt ill-equipped to deal
Extending the enquiry – into more challenging areas of evaluation and reflection	**Focussing too much on the product of the enquiry rather than the process.** Teachers drew attention to the way in which the pupils presented what they had found out

RE creative, effective, non-biased and engaging for the learners and the teacher alike. The chapters in this volume provide insight into the characteristics of creative and effective RE. OfSTED's report highlights characteristics of effective enquiry which have been adapted in Table 1.8 into a series of dos and don'ts. Putting these dos and don'ts from Table 1.8 into practice entails emulating the CCAF (challenging, creative and fun) school rather than the HEBS (hard/easy, boring, scary) school approach and ethos (see Table 1.2). In RE children use their imagination; they know when and how to put themselves in another's shoes. This can be quite challenging for the RE teacher so an example is provided in Table 1.9 to illustrate how this might be managed.

Creatively Learning about Food in RE and Other Subjects

Teaching non-biased RE means encouraging children to see the familiar in an unfamiliar light and to make the unfamiliar more familiar. Using the topic of food as a way of achieving this in RE is suggested in Table 1.9.

Creative Integration of RE and Other Subjects

Taking the lesson ideas in Table 1.9, it is possible to link RE with other subjects using a webbed integration approach (see Table 1.10). Copping (2011:30) discusses Robin Fogarty's models of curriculum design, which include shared, threaded, integrated and webbed. The shared model is like viewing the curriculum through binoculars where two distinct subject areas are brought together into a single focus (Fogarty 1991:62), for example integrating two subjects emphasising their common skills and concepts. The threaded approach views the curriculum through a magnifying glass where the 'big ideas'

■ **Table 1.9** We are what we eat: Making the familiar unfamiliar and the unfamiliar familiar

We Are What We Eat – Food in RE

Working on their own, then in pairs and finally small groups, children investigate what they eat and why

- List your favourite three meals.
- List three foods you don't eat.
- Discuss in twos or threes why you chose the foods in a) and b).
- In groups of four or five compare what you and others eat and reasons why.
- In your group of four or five list reasons why people eat or don't eat certain foods.

Working as a class with teacher as scribe on white board

- List all the reasons why people eat or don't eat particular foods.
- Discuss reasons: medical (allergies), preferences (appearance texture, taste), religious, cultural, bad/good experiences or memories, availability, cost, political etc.
- Encourage the children to evaluate their own biases and preferences in a different light – (for example would they eat snake, octopus, seaweed, human?).
- Encourage children to put themselves into the shoes of another – why would other people not eat what they eat? (For example why do some people not eat meat or fish, or not eat dairy and meat dishes at the same meal?).

Working in groups utilising thinking skills to investigate food laws

- As tenacious researchers investigate religious food laws – in Islam (halal and haram), in Judaism (kosher separation of dairy and meat) etc.
- As skilled researchers children plan, design and implement an enquiry asking friends and family what they eat and why? Investigate religious/cultural/moral reasons behind choices. Decide the mode of presentation, a play, a poster, a powerpoint presentation, a quiz, an information leaflet, artwork, a podcast.

are enlarged and given more prominence than the content (Fogarty 1991:63). Fogarty (1991:63) likens the integrated approach to a kaleidoscope where subjects overlap and are not distinct. The webbed approach, adopted in Table 1.10, identifies a single theme; subject content, skills and concepts overlap in a relevant and meaningful way (Fogarty 1991:63; Copping 2011:33). In the lesson ideas in Table 1.9, the children are invited to investigate the idea behind 'we are what we eat' both from an RE perspective and linking with other curriculum subjects in a meaningful way using a webbed approach to integration. Throughout the cross-curricular topic, children are engaging in planning and designing investigations themselves, so they have ownership of their learning. They study new, interesting, contentious ideas making the familiar unfamiliar and the unfamiliar familiar. Before the commencement of this cross-curricular topic the children may have not questioned what they ate or why, but by the end of the topic children should have learned a great deal about the food we eat and the values and reasons underpinning choice. Throughout the topic they will be reflecting deeply, increasing their subject knowledge and skills in both RE and other subject areas.

Creative teaching and learning must be both challenging and fun (see Table 1.4) and some children may find some of the tasks challenging. For example when designing

■ **Table 1.10** Webbed integration (Fogarty 1991; Copping 2011) links RE with some curriculum areas

History: *How status defines what is eaten*: Investigate meals eaten in the period of history being studied eg Tudor England, looking at the differences between the diet of rich and poor people.

Food technology: *Making meals that we eat*: Design, prepare and cook a meal which is halal, or kosher or suitable for a vegetarian.

RE: *How belief defines what is eaten:* Investigate reasons for food choice – particularly looking at how belief affects action eg kosher (Judaism), halal and haraam (Islam)

We are what we eat

Geography: *How place defines what is eaten:* Investigate global and political trends – cost, availability and country of origin of food.

Science: *How knowledge of food groups and body requirements defines what is eaten*: Investigate food groups – what is current thinking about healthy eating? Investigate allergies and food related medical issues such as diabetes

Maths: *Gathering data about what we eat:* Design and produce a tally chart in Maths showing which are the most popular foods eaten by children's family and friends. This enquiry can be designed by the children in groups – a problem solving exercise

a questionnaire to collect data about family and friends' meal choices some children may make mistakes in their tally sheets, or they may be unhappy about their cooking or their PowerPoint presentations, see Table 1.10. So the teacher's role is to encourage 'bounce-backability' (Hymer and Gershon 2014). Creative teaching and learning requires children to be tenacious researchers, having the motivation to keep looking for that piece of information about kosher food, having the determination to get the texture of their halal burger right, re-doing their tally chart, working on their ICT skills to improve their podcast (Barber and Cooper 2012; Moss 2010) etc. Creative teaching and learning also requires providing 'incubation time' where children have time to ponder overnight their failed questionnaire design, cooking or podcast and return to school the next day with a better plan (FAIL = first attempt at learning; Table 1.5).

There are many RE books which focus on what to teach and appropriate approaches, most recently Mogra (2023). Some books focus on pedagogy and underlying principles of religious education suitable for master's-level enquiry, for example, Hannam (2019), Hannam and Biesta (2021), Chater (2020), Castelli and Chater (2018), and older, but still valuable books – such as Stern (2006), Jackson (1997), Erricker et al. (2011), Gates (2007) and Grimmitt (2000). There are many books and resources providing comprehensive introductions and creative RE with practical examples of good classroom practice, e.g. Mogra (2023), Webster (2010) and RE Today publications. This book draws on all these approaches and brings together the theory and practice in one volume aimed at the discerning student teacher and in-service teacher, as well as those studying at the master's level, wanting to learn more about innovative teaching and learning in RE. This book treads the fine balance between, on the one hand, educating the conscientious teacher about the 'accepted' canon of what constitutes a healthy RE curriculum and supporting children to become religiate (Gates 2007), appreciating and understanding the motivations behind belief systems and so on. On the other hand, this volume challenges the reader to understand religious education as both a transformatory and liberatory subject, thus ensuring children have the tools to be discerning towards religious and secular worldviews, to be challenged by and enjoy working out their own responses to puzzling questions and to consider how to take their place as pro-equality citizens.

In the UK there has been a suggested name change from religious education (RE) to Religion and Worldviews Education (RWE), or sometimes the phrase 'belief systems' is used. This book supports different naming of the subject, with the intention to celebrate diversity. Similarly, throughout the book you will notice that different chapter authors may interpret the aims and principles of RE/RWE in different ways. While this might seem at first confusing, we believe it celebrates diversity and acknowledges complexity, thus encouraging your professional autonomy.

Section 1 – Three Chapters which Unpack the Aims and Principles of RE/RWE

Chapter 1, by Sally Elton-Chalcraft, has set the scene by discussing the characteristics of creative teaching and learning, the 'phunometre scale' and the implications for RE/RWE.

In **Chapter 2**, new to the second edition, Ruth Flanagan and Linda Whitworth discuss policy and practice and how including worldviews can enrich RE lesson planning and assessing.

A new addition to the second edition, **Chapter 3**, considers the important role of RE in anti-discriminatory teaching and learning. Sally Elton-Chalcraft and two teachers Alexandra Brown and Jane Yates show how lessons can be underpinned by an informed understanding of discrimination and how to build classroom communities and teachers who can confidently promote equitable practice.

Section 2 – Seven Chapters Outlining a Variety of Approaches for Creative Teaching and Learning in RE/RWE

Chapter 4, by Georgia Prescott, discusses how P4C (philosophy for children) and the community of enquiry can be powerful approaches to engaging the learner in RE. She draws on classroom examples and practical activity ideas to illustrate good RE practice.

In **Chapter 5** Sally Elton-Chalcraft and Penny Hollander explain the TASC (thinking actively in a social context) model with examples of how the model has been used successfully in schools during RE lessons.

Fiona Moss and Katie Freeman, in **Chapter 6**, provide some key pointers for effective planning and assessment in RE. They discuss learning methods which are cross-referenced in other chapters in this volume.

Chapter 7 by Sally Elton-Chalcraft, Penny Hollander and Georgia Prescott considers what is meant by spirituality, with creative lesson ideas to support children's spiritual development in the classroom context.

In **Chapter 8,** a new chapter in the second edition, Linda Whitworth, Saima Saleh and Janet Orchard consider the learning opportunities which engage with religious art forms and artefacts, including examples of children's work. They explore music, drama, art and technology with RWE.

Chapter 9, new in the second edition, by Rebekah Ackroyd, Sally Elton-Chalcraft and Imran Kotwal, provides practical suggestions for using visits, visitors and persona dolls effectively in primary RE.

Another new addition – **Chapter 10** by Giles Freathy reveals how the *RE-searchers* approach can support effective and creative RWE and its assessment.

Section 3 – Two Chapters Considering the Relevance of RE/RWE in Education

In **Chapter 11** Kate Christopher and Lynn Revell examine how teachers can approach Islam and Islamophobia with their children in RE/RWE. They suggest strategies for developing skills and attitudes that challenge the way we think.

Chapter 12, by Sally Elton-Chalcraft, considers widening the scope of RE to include a range of contrasting belief systems such as minority denominations of Christianity and atheist belief systems such as Humanism. Creative lesson activities and examples of good and bad practice are provided.

I hope the chapters in this book will help to convince you (whatever your starting point) that RE/RWE, if engaged with creatively, can be an enlightening, transformative and liberating subject.

REFERENCES

Alexander, R. (2010) *Children, Their World Their Education: Final Report and Recommendations of the Cambridge Primary Review.* Abingdon: Routledge.

Barber, D. and Cooper, L. (2012) *Using New Web Tools in the Primary Classroom: A Practical Guide for Enhancing Teaching and Learning.* Abingdon: Routledge.

Biesta, G. and Hannam, P. (2021) *Religion and Education: The Forgotten Dimension of Religious Education* Leiden: Brill

de Bono, E. (2014) 'Six thinking hats'. Available at www.debonogroup.com/six_thinking_hats.php (accessed 18 April 2014).

Bruner, J. (1996) *The Culture of Education.* Cambridge, MA: Harvard University Press.

Buzan, T. (2014) 'Mind mapping'. Available at www.tonybuzan.com/about/mind-mapping (accessed 18 April 2014).

Castelli, M. and Chater, M. (eds.) (2018) *We Need to Talk about Religious Education: Manifesto for the Future of RE.* London: Jessica Kingsley.

Chater, M. (2020) *Reforming RE.* Melton: John Catt.

Claxton, G. (1997) *Hare Brain Tortoise Mind: Why Intelligence Increases When You Think Less.* London: Fourth Estate Ltd.

Claxton, G. (2007) 'Expanding young people's capacity to learn'. *British Journal of Educational Studies*, 55(2): 11534.

Claxton, G. (2008) *What's the Point of School*. Oxford: Oneworld Publications.

Copping, A. (2011) 'Curriculum approaches'. In Hansen, A. (ed.), *Primary Professional Studies*. Exeter: Learning Matters, pp. 23–43.

Commission on Religious Education. (2018) *Final Report: Religion and Worldviews: The Way Forwards. A National Plan*. London: Religious Education Council of England & Wales. Available at https://www.commissiononre.org.uk/wp-content/uploads/2018/09/Final -Report-of-the-Commission-on-RE.pdf.

Craft, A., Cremin, T. and Burnard, P. (2007) *Creative Learning 3–11 and How We Document It*. Stoke-on-Trent: Trentham Books Ltd.

Cremin, T., Chapell, K. and Craft, A. (2012) 'Reciprocity between narrative, questioning and imagination in the early and primary years: Examining the role of narrative in possibility thinking'. *Thinking Skills and Creativity*, 9: 135–51. Available at http:dx.doi .org/10.1016/). tsc.2012.11.003 (accessed 20 March 2014).

Cullingford, C. (2007) 'Creativity and pupil experience of school'. *Education 3-13*, 35(2): 133–42.

Elton-Chalcraft, S. and Mills, K. (2013) 'Measuring challenge, fun and sterility on a 'Phuno-metre' scale: Evaluating creative teaching and learning with children and their student teachers in the primary school'. *Education 3-13*, https://doi.org/10.1080/03004279.2013 .822904. Available at www.tandfonline.com/doi/abs/10.1080/03004279.2013.822904 (accessed 20 March 2014).

Elton-Chalcraft, S. (2015) *Teaching RE Creatively* 1st Ed. Abingdon: Routledge

Elton-Chalcraft, S., Lander, V., Revell, L., Warner, D. and Whitworth, L. (2017) 'To promote, or not to promote fundamental British values? Teachers' standards, diversity and teacher education.' *British Educational research journal*. 43(1) available at http://onlinelibrary .wiley.com/doi/10.1111/berj.2017.43.issue-1/issuetoc

Elton-Chalcraft, S, Revell, L. and Lander, V. (2022) 'Fundamental British values: Your responsibilities, to promote or not to promote? Ch 15'. In Cooper, H. and Elton-Chalcraft, S. (eds.), *Professional Studies in Primary Education* (4th ed.). London: Sage. https://us .sagepub.com/en-us/nam/professional-studies-in-primary-education/book273439.

Erriker, C., Lownded, J. and Bellchambers, E. (2011) *Primary Religious Education - A New Approach: Conceptual Enquiry in Primary RE*. Abingdon: Routledge.

Fogarty, R. (1991) 'Ten ways to integrate curriculum'. *Educational Leadership*, 49(2): 61–5.

Franken, L. (2021) 'Religion and education. The forgotten dimensions of religious education?'. *Religion & Education*, 48(4): 496–498. https://doi.org/10.1080/15507394.2021.2006540

Gates, B. (2007) *Transforming Religious Education: Beliefs and Values under Scrutiny*. London: Continuum.

Grimmitt, M. (ed.) (2000) *Pedagogies of RE*. Great Wakering: McCrimmon.

Hannam, P. (2019) *Religious Education and the Public Sphere* Abingdon: Routledge.

Hannam, P. and Biesta, G. (eds.) (2021) *Religion and Education - The Forgotten Dimensions of Religious Education?* Leiden: Koninklijke Brill.

Heilman, K. (2005) *Creativity and the Brain* New York: Psychology Press.

Hymer, B. and Gershon, M. (2014) *Growth Mindset Pocketbook* London: Teachers' Pocketbooks.

Jackson, R. (1997) *Religious Education: An Interpretive Approach*. London: Hodder and Stoughton.

McCreery, E., Palmer, S. and Voiels, V. (2008) *Teaching RE: Primary and Early Years, Achieving QTS*. Exeter: Learning Matters.

Mogra, I. (2023) *Religious Education 5–11 A Guide for Teachers* Abingdon: Routledge.

Moss, F. (ed.) (2010) *Opening up Creativity RE*. Derby: RE Today Publications.

NACCCE (National Advisory Group for Creative and Cultural Education) (1999) 'All our futures: Creativity, culture and education'. Available at www.cypni.org.uk/downloads/alloutfutures.pdf (accessed 20 February 2014).

OfSTED (2013) 'Realising the potential (130068)'. Available at www.ofsted.gov.uk/resources/130068

Prelutsky, J. and Smith, L. (1998) *Hooray for Diffendoofer Day*. London: Collins.

Revell, L. (2012) *Islam and Education*. Stoke-on-Trent: Trentham Books Ltd.

Seuss, Dr. (1997) *The Cat in the Hat*. London: Collins.

Stern, J. (2006) *Teaching Religious Education*. London: Continuum.

Twiselton, S. (2004) 'The role of teacher identities in learning to teach primary literacy'. *Education Review: Special Edition: Activity Theory*, 56(2): 8896.

Twiselton, S. and Elton-Chalcraft, S. (2024) in press 'Developing as a professional Unit 2.4'. In Cremin, T. and Burnett, C. (eds.) *Learning to Teach in the Primary School* (5th ed.). London: Routledge.

Webster, M. (2010) *Creative Approaches to Teaching Primary RE*. Harlow: Pearson.

POLICY, PRINCIPLES AND PRACTICE – FACILITATING CREATIVE TEACHING

Ruth Flanagan and Linda Whitworth

This chapter aims to:

- Interrogate what is meant by 'worldviews', including the historical debates around the term;
- Investigate how a subject including 'worldviews' might potentially improve the teaching of RE;
- Engage with policy changes and debates around religion and worldviews;
- Address concerns on breadth and depth of the curriculum; rather than 'adding more' content this approach aims to 'add more' understanding;
- Consider how a worldviews focus can potentially mitigate teachers' and pupils' unconscious bias;
- Suggest creative ways to introduce religion and worldviews in lesson planning;
- Provide examples of aspirational practice in religion and worldviews.

The chapter draws on current research into Religious Education/Religion and worldviews as well as on current teaching practice amongst teachers and pupils at both the primary and secondary phase.

AN INTRODUCTION TO RELIGIOUS EDUCATION IN THE UK, INCLUDING POLICY AND DEBATES AROUND 'RELIGION AND WORLDVIEWS'

A number of peculiarities exist around Religious Education (RE) in the UK, which has been a compulsory subject since the 1944 Education Act. This was confirmed in

DOI: 10.4324/9781003361480-3

England and Wales with the 1988 Education Act but RE is not found within the National Curriculum, neither the first edition in 1988 nor subsequent editions (2014). Instead, it is part of the Basic Curriculum, which consists of the National Curriculum, RE and sex education. A further peculiarity is that the UK has no united approach in setting out the curriculum for RE. In England and Wales, the curriculum is set by Standard Advisory Committees on Religious Education (SACREs) in local areas. Representatives from local councils, local faith leaders, teachers and teacher trainers serve on SACREs and write a locally agreed syllabus for all state schools in that area to follow. Each Standard Advisory Committee on RE (SACRE) produces a locally agreed syllabus which often sets out aims and rationale but there is no nationally agreed government directed aim or rationale. The aim was that the curriculum 'shall reflect the fact that religious traditions in Great Britain are in the main Christian whilst taking account of the teaching and practices of the other principal religions represented in Great Britain' (1996, section 375, 3). In Scotland, Religious Education is prescribed by the Scottish parliament. The Education (Scotland) Act 1980 provided for RE as a statutory core subject for all pupils attending primary and secondary education. In Northern Ireland the Education Department since 1989 has been tasked with setting out RE across the province. These curriculums vary on their aim and purpose for RE as well as their content.

The subject has undergone many changes since 1944, including changes of name from Religious Instruction (RI) to Religious Education (RE) and Religious Studies (RS) in part to distance the subject from any accusations of indoctrination. More recently in Scotland, the subject has changed its name to Religion and Moral Education (RME). It is a statutory core subject for all primary and secondary pupils under the provision of The Education (Scotland) Act of 1980. Nationally, the Commission of Religious Education (CORE) report recommended a further name change from Religious Education to Religion and Worldviews in 2018. Most recently the subject has changed its name in Wales to Religion, Values and Ethics as part of the New Curriculum for Wales, 2022. The name of the subject is not the only contentious area: the aims and purposes of the subject have also undergone great debate (CITE). Perhaps to some extent due to this lack of clarity, the subject is failing to realise its potential (Ofsted, 2013, 2021). As far back as 2004, Ofsted Inspectors identified weak subject knowledge and lack of confidence in teachers attempting to teach RE:

> Teachers' input too often lacks substance and depth' with 'insufficient explanation … Equally serious is teachers' lack of knowledge about the subject, its purpose, aims and most appropriate pedagogies.
>
> (Wintersgill, 2004, 1)

In primary education this is a particular problem. In the NATRE, 2022 primary survey, over a fifth of primary respondents in the UK said they had had no ITE training and over half said training was between 0–6 hours (NATRE, 2022). Lack of time for a focussed introduction to the subject can lead to weak subject knowledge and a lack of confidence. Yet there is evidence of excellence in RE lessons, with the work of organisations like the National Association of Teachers of RE (NATRE) and Lead Teach Learn RE (LTLRE). Much research and work has been undertaken to see how this excellent practice could be replicated in more classrooms.

THE COMMISSION ON RELIGIOUS EDUCATION

In 2016, the Council of Religious Education in England and Wales commissioned a report to assess the state of RE and to produce recommendations for improvement. The report was published in 2018 and proposed 11 recommendations, including changing the name of the subject to 'Religion and worldviews'. Briefly summarised, these recommendations include:

1. Changing the name to 'Religion and worldviews'.
2. Providing a National Entitlement.
3. Setting up a national body to set programmes of study.
4. Removing the requirement for SACREs.
5. Examining GCSE, A levels and technical courses in light of the National Entitlement.
6. Setting baseline study on ITE courses e.g. 12 hours for Primary ITE.
7. Establishing government funding for CPD.
8. Local advisory networks established in place of SACREs.
9. Ofsted to assess provision of the National Entitlement.
10. Call for DfE to consider impact of RE with exclusion from Ebacc.
11. Call for DfE to review the parental right to withdraw.

(see report for fuller details, CoRE, 2018)

The report has caused much debate but has provided opportunity for rethinking the nature and intention of Religious Education and its value in the curriculum. Therefore, through-out this book you will notice different chapter authors interpret the aims and principles of RE in different ways. While this might seem at first confusing, we believe it celebrates diversity and acknowledges complexity, thus encouraging professional autonomy (as outlined in Chapter 1).

WHAT IS MEANT BY 'WORLDVIEWS'?

The CORE (2018) report recommended changing the name of RE to 'Religion and worldviews' in England and delineates between 'personal' worldviews and 'institutional' worldviews (2018, 4). Institutional worldviews refer to worldviews which have a recognised or agreed on body of beliefs and values that are codified and often embedded in institutions. The report cites 'Humanism, Secularism and Atheism' as examples (2018, 26). Writing prior to the CORE report, Van der Kooij et al. (2013) preferred the term 'organised', as 'institutional' can hold negative connotations. This change has had a mixed response from some who are concerned that this will add more content into an already overburdened RE curriculum, and others who fear that this will dilute religion out of RE. However, others see this approach as instrumental in improving the teaching of religion(s) and non-religious worldviews (Cooling, 2020).

Part of the challenge stems from the term 'worldview', which is employed across subject disciplines and has a variety of definitions. For example, in psychology, Freud (1933) defines worldviews as static and rigid whereas Jung (1942) defines them as elastic and fluid. In theology, the term is often attributed to a religion implying a fixed body of knowledge, like a Christian worldview or an Islamic worldview. However, as RE teachers, we know that there is not a fixed rigid body of knowledge in any religion. For teachers to teach worldviews, a clear explanation of the different definitions about worldviews will enable them to understand the variety of views on this change and clarify what is actually expected of them and what a worldviews approach might entail in the classroom. An examination of the history of the term 'worldviews' might assist in demonstrating the differing definitions and how this might assist in improving RE.

A HISTORY OF THE TERM

The term *Weltanschauung*, translated worldviews, was first employed by Kant (1790) in his *Critique of Reason*. However, he provided no definition of the term. Nineteenth century philosophers debated the term and recent debates around worldviews in RE actually reflect their original discussions. These centre around the content, character and construction of worldviews alongside the issue of choice.

Content

What does a worldview actually contain? There are a range of suggestions in the literature including an explanation of the world (Samovar and Porter, 2004), a vision of the future (Hedlund de Witt, 2013), values and answers to ethical questions (Valk, 2009), a view of what knowledge is and a view of how to live effectively (Walsh and Middleton, 1984; Koltko-Rivera, 2004). Politics, religion, values and societal norms are all impacted by, as well as being aspects of, individuals' worldviews. If this all-encompassing definition of worldviews is adopted, then religions are not synonymous with 'worldviews' but rather may be an aspect of an individual's personal worldview. This is where personal worldviews can be examined in the classroom. As an introduction to the subject, teachers could examine with pupils what personal worldviews are – using the activities mentioned in the next section of the chapter.

Character

It has been suggested that worldviews are a static body of knowledge (Freud, 1933), such as an 'institutional' or organised worldview. However, when attempting to describe these in more detail, challenges arise. Every RE teacher knows the inappropriateness of stating 'the Islamic worldview' or 'the Christian worldview' as in reality there are different views usually relating to differences in interpretation of scripture (Duderija, 2007; Walters, 1985). An alternative suggestion is that worldviews could have fluid, dynamic and evolving dimensions, as proposed by Valk and Toscun, 2016, and originally by Dilthey, 1907. As a teacher adopting this perspective, you would support learners to understand the variety of practices in each religion. For example, infant baptism in a Church of England church, adult baptism in a Baptist church, etc.

Construction

The discussion around construction originates with the question of whether individuals make a conscious decision to solve 'the riddle of life' (Dilthey, 1907), or whether this process is simply part of an individual's life experience (Hegel, 1807). Hegel proposed that an evolutionary socio-constructed process forms worldviews. This aspect helps learners to understand how worldviews evolve: how each individual has values, beliefs and behaviours which have been informed and learn through informal (community, family norms, media) or formal methods (through schooling or institutional expectations).

Choice

Lastly, there is the question of choice. Do we as individuals choose a worldview or are we embodied through life experience in a worldview? Additionally, Hands' (2012) assertion that having a worldview is optional reflects Kierkegaard's (1843) suggestion that not all have a worldview or life view as he described it. However, other scholars suggest that there is no optionality, rather everyone 'inhabits' (Cooling, 2020) or embodies a worldview. Embodying a worldview portrays the interconnectedness between an individual's behaviour, values and beliefs – their worldview lived out.

With each of these aspects, we have presented the binary debates but perhaps a combination may occur with an individual absorbing some social norms and values formally, through education and institutions, and informally through peers, families, community and social media. Additionally, there may be other aspects of an individual's worldviews that they choose explicitly and consciously to adopt.

HOW MIGHT ADDING 'WORLDVIEWS' IMPROVE RE?

A variety of metaphors exist to define worldviews: glasses or lenses, a map of the mind, a guide, a big picture, a frame of reference, an overarching philosophy. Yet as Sire (2004) points out, worldview definitions are worldview dependent! This range of definitions for the term 'worldviews' can be confusing, but we want to seek out which is the most useful one to adopt to improve the subject of RE. The aim of the CORE report (2018) was to seek out ways to improve the subject of RE in England and Wales. We propose that employing the term worldviews as an individual's embodied frame of reference evolving from their life experience, may provide a useful tool for improving the teaching of RE. We also recognise that organised or institutional worldviews are both the content and lenses of study in RE.

Lenses are often employed as a simple metaphor to assist pupils to understand individuals' worldviews. This is helpful but needs caution as a lens can be easily removed whereas an individual's worldview cannot – as these are assumptions, values and norms that are held consciously and unconsciously. The unconscious aspect may be particularly powerful as well as difficult to identify. Frames of reference as suggested by Aerts et al. (2007), reflecting Hegel's (1807) conceptual frameworks, provide a useful metaphor. Everything that an individual experiences enables them to know about the world and informs a 'frame of reference' through which to understand the world:

> A world view is a system of co-ordinates or a *frame of reference* in which everything presented to us by our diverse experiences can be placed. It is a symbolic system of representation that allows us to integrate everything we *know about the world* and *ourselves* into a global picture, one that illuminates reality as it is presented to us within a certain culture.
>
> (Aerts et al., 2007: 7 – Italics our emphasis)

This process demonstrates the embodied nature of worldviews. Another helpful metaphor to illustrate the nuanced and intricate nature of worldviews may be smart tech eyewear. This has become increasingly popular through fictional books and films, such as the *Mission Impossible* franchise, which employ Smart Wear glasses with their augmented reality experience. These resemble sunglasses but contain the capability to perform real time cross-referencing against central databases to provide information on individuals, corporations or situations that the wearer finds themselves in. In a similar way, worldviews provide individuals with information about the situations they are in – people they meet, places they go, norms of practice, value of events/interactions/individuals etc... Information is provided from a data base – what the individual has read, or been taught through informal (community, family norms, media), or formal means (through schooling) or has experienced themselves. These databases are constantly updated with new information received through education or life experience. These experiences or information can then alter the individual's worldview to a greater or lesser degree.

This provides an effective picture between the greater interconnectedness of worldviews and their constantly evolving dynamic. The limitation of this metaphor lies in the fact that while these glasses may be removed, individuals cannot so easily detach their worldviews. Even so, the metaphor is useful for teachers and learners to be made aware of the influences that are constantly impacting their lives and, therefore, their worldview. A more accurate metaphor may be of an internal database such as the robot in the *Terminator* films. In parts of the first film, the audience glimpses the world through the robot's red eyes with all the information appearing from its database as and when he needs it.

HOW DO WORLDVIEWS RELATE TO RELIGIONS?

There are various suggestions about how worldviews and religions relate. For some they are two very separate entities.

For others they overlap in some areas.

And for others, religions are a subsection of an individual's worldview.

In order to capture the ongoing process of an individual's worldview formation, we suggest the following diagram – where the boundaries are incomplete, evolving and adapting as the individual encounters new experiences. Religion may play a large role in the individual's worldview, which dominates in some areas of their lives and in others to a lesser extent – hence the graded section in Figure 2.4. This diagram relates to personal

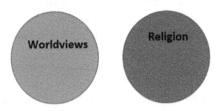

▪ **Figure 2.1** Worldviews and religions as two separate entities (Figures 2.1, 2.2 and 2.3 are based on a model presented by Anstice, 2021 Strictly RE).

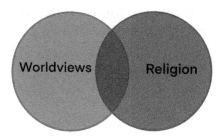

■ **Figure 2.2** Worldviews and religion with overlapping elements.

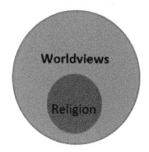

■ **Figure 2.3** Worldviews encompassing religion.

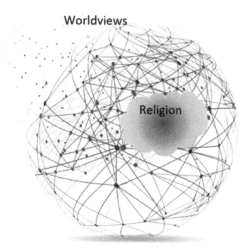

■ **Figure 2.4** Evolving personal worldviews encompassing religious elements (Author's own).

worldviews. An individual may have a religious affiliation and therefore religion is a part of their personal worldview. This may impact some areas more strongly than others – hence the shading is stronger in some places than others. The actual worldview is not fully formed as it continues to evolve as an individual experiences life and their views may/may not change in response.

How Employing 'Worldviews' may Improve the Teaching of RE or 'Religion and Worldviews'/the Benefits of a Worldviews Approach

A number of potential benefits in employing the concept of worldviews have been identified in current research and literature. Confusion over the definition of the term has led some to reject the usefulness of 'worldviews' within RE. For example, the Welsh consultation document for RE does not employ the term, preferring instead 'Religion, Values and Ethics' (2020). Yet to dismiss the term entirely may miss potential benefits which have been identified:

- To provide a link for the growing number of 'nones' in England (Woodhead, 2016) making RE relevant to all (Jones, 2013);
- To counter the challenge of religious illiteracy (Prothero, 2007; Valk, 2016);
- To aid meaningful interaction between differing worldviews (Mulder and Berg's, 2019, hermeneutical communicative model);
- To enhance global citizenship (Miedema and Bertram-Troost, 2015);
- To challenge bigotry and intolerance (Barnes, 2015);
- To assist integration into a multicultural society (Miller and Mckenna, 2011);
- To prevent exclusivist teaching (Miedema, 2014);
- To recognise the value laden-ness of all teaching (Miedema, 2014, 94);
- And to focus more on views that sit well with the teachers' own.

(Flanagan, 2020)

'Nones' refers to people with no faith allegiance. They may find religion 'alien' or 'exotic' and therefore a challenge to relate to and study. Employing the concept of 'worldview' as a frame of reference which everyone possesses may build a bridge between their own values, norms and beliefs, and the study of those who have a religious element to their worldviews. From our own experience of training teachers, enabling them to start by identifying and examining the origin and evolution of their own worldviews has enabled them to relate to the subject of RE, and, where necessary, provide a bridge for those teachers and pupils who have no religious affiliation or engagement.

Teachers develop understanding and empathy as religions are no longer seen as exotic or 'alien' but a response to shared life experience. This provides them with an approach to new subject knowledge. The teacher's confidence is raised through knowing what to examine in religions and non-religious worldviews. Therefore, rather than merely examining superficial differences with their learners such as food and clothing, they address key questions of each faith.

ADDRESSING CONCERNS ON DEPTH AND BREADTH OF CURRICULUM

As we previously mentioned, there are critics of the CORE (2018) report's recommendations. It is important to engage with criticism to enable the teacher to have a sound understanding and strong personal rationale for why they teach in a certain way. Additionally, often addressing criticism prevents unnecessary mistakes from being made. Concerns around dilution of the curriculum and overburdening teachers and pupils stems from one interpretation of worldviews. As teachers, you can use the criticism to hone your teaching – ensuring that what you teach is not diluted but that you maintain depth rather than breadth.

Worldviews can be perceived as an **extra topic** with a body of knowledge of facts, dates, core beliefs and values, key individuals and institutions etc. for pupils to learn. This extra topic would add to an already overly burdened curriculum and may be yet another topic which the pupils cannot relate to. Rather than assisting RE to reach its potential (Ofsted, 2013), this would add more barriers.

For example, Damian Hinds (2018, Secretary of State for Education) expressed stakeholders' 'concerns that making statutory the inclusion of "worldviews" risks diluting the teaching of RE'. Including humanism and other non-religious worldviews in RE led Barnes (2015) to caution that this may lead to potential lack of depth. However, the CORE report does not specify a long list of 'institutional' or organised worldviews to study.

Furthermore, Smalley queried the usefulness of the name change and called for greater academic debate over which worldviews were deemed **worthy of study** (2018). This criticism ties in with the definition of worldviews and was a useful call to clarify the term and prevent misunderstanding. If worldviews are seen as discrete bodies of knowledge to be studied, this raises the challenge over which should be chosen to be studied and by whom. Does humanism, paganism, secularism, veganism, communism, national socialism or hedonism, for example, deserve a place in our syllabus for 'Religion and worldviews'? This challenge does not negate the usefulness of worldviews but rather demonstrates a need for clarity over defining the term. Cooling (2020) whilst acknowledging the 'messiness of the term' stresses the usefulness of it for improving the teaching of RE. Rather than a list of extra subject material to include, worldviews may be seen as a paradigmatic tool to introduce students and teachers who may have no faith allegiance to religions (Flanagan, 2020). Or to assist those with faith allegiance to understand those who do not.

Viewing worldviews as a **paradigmatic tool** sounds complex but is in reality simple and relates back to 'personal' worldviews. All individuals have worldviews – a way that they see the world, which they hold subconsciously and consciously (Sire, 1988). Identifying and examining the origins of their own worldviews can help teachers and pupils to develop a greater understanding of those who have different worldviews to their own. The study of religion(s) and non-religious worldviews becomes the study of fellow human beings and their worldviews – a search, which all have in common to understand and make meaning in and of the world, whether or not that contains a religious or spiritual aspect. Worldviews, in this sense, become a paradigm – a model for human understanding (Flanagan, 2020).

In the following section we provide examples of how this can be enacted in the classroom.

CREATIVE WAYS TO TEACH A 'WORLDVIEWS APPROACH'

This book contains many ways to teach religion and worldviews creatively. This chapter is concerned with the starting point for teachers and pupils alike. Identification of the existence of, origin and evolution of individual's worldviews is crucial if religion and worldviews is to avoid superficiality. The following activities have been tried and tested with student teachers, primary and secondary school pupils and with practising teachers.

One of the key challenges with the term worldviews is that values, norms and beliefs are consciously and subconsciously held (Sire, 2004). Identifying the subconscious aspects is a challenge, but one in which RE is actually ideally suited. Mezirow's work (1996, 2000) on transformational learning provides guidance on this. Transformational learning

> holds that our acquired frames of reference and the beliefs and values that they endorse may be transformed through critical reflection on one's assumptions and the resulting interpretations validated through discourse.
>
> (1996, 237)

Critical reflection is essential in teacher education and various strategies are suggested such as writing self-reflections. For example, Kanitz (2005) and Kyles and Olafson (2008) employed written reflection to identify aspects of teachers' worldviews. Yet there is a danger that reflection without understanding can merely reinforce bias or misunderstandings rather than unearth or excavate an individuals' worldviews, particularly when aspects of their individual worldviews may be buried deep in their subconscious. However, Mezirow argued that 'disorientating dilemmas' might assist. These involve the impact of conflict or challenge:

> When the meaning of what is communicated to us is problematic or contested, we explore the meanings--assumptions, implications, action consequences--made by others. We engage in a dialectical process of discourse to share the experiences of others across differences. The more diverse the differences, the broader and more potentially valuable the experience brought to bear.
>
> (1996, 237)

RE/RW provides many opportunities to experience this phenomenon as teachers and pupils investigate values, beliefs and norms that might be in conflict with their own. Examples of this include studying 'truth' claims that clash with the teacher's or pupil's own worldview, views on the role of women, sexuality, prescribing social status etc. When teaching in rural India, I met practising Hindus for whom the caste system was inextricably linked to their religious beliefs. However, Hindu families in the UK may delineate clearly between the caste system as a social entity and their own religious beliefs (as found in a survey of Hindu parents by Insight UK, 2021). Yet without guidance for teachers, this clash can lead to a rejection of some of the more contested elements of religions and non-religious worldviews. The potential danger is that RE can become a watered-down version of the most palatable versions of the religion(s) or non-religious worldviews which adhere to the individuals' personal worldviews (Flanagan, 2019), or focus on the 'brighter' rather than the 'darker' side of religion(s) (Kueh, 2017). We therefore employ opportunities to experience 'disorientating dilemmas' at the same time as purposefully addressing the presence of and impact of personal worldviews. The concept of worldviews assists with understanding the extensive range of beliefs, values and behaviours that may exist within any one religion.

■ **Figure 2.5** Burka vs bikini, Evans (2011).

Images and Videos

Images and videos are used to 'disorientate and to create disorientating dilemmas'. These are purposefully chosen as they may 'shock' or conflict with the individual's personal worldviews to enable them to actually identify elements of these. Images such as optical illusions can be employed to demonstrate seeing in different ways, but the most effective are images that actively challenge/disorientate. For example, Malcolm Evans created an excellent cartoon which he has given us permission to reprint.

This image, Figure 2.5, enables us to see an alternative perspective and to consider how another individual might perceive our choices, actions, values and behaviour. Out of all the images that we employ, this one creates the most debate. Some applaud the challenge to consider why we choose to wear certain clothes, others hate the idea that their choice of clothing might be informed by society rather than simply free choice, etc. Yet within the discussion, fruitful moments can occur where individuals stop and consider their individual worldviews which may well differ significantly from others in the group or those represented in the images (see Chapter 11 for a further discussion).

Concentric Circles

This activity enables individuals to consider the origins of their worldviews. Individuals are given a range of questions of moral dilemmas suitable to their age group: 5–11, 11–18, student teachers or in-service teachers. These include questions such as: Is it ever OK

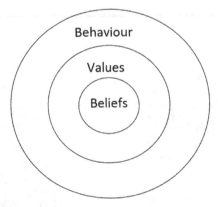

■ **Figure 2.6** Concentric circles to trace the belief and values that may underpin behaviour.

to lie? Do you buy fair trade products? These are then discussed in groups before being mapped onto concentric circles to display the interconnection between our beliefs, behaviour and values. Participants choose one answer and complete that as their behaviour. For example, 'Yes, I lie sometimes' on the behaviour section. Then they attempt to complete the value and belief which informs that behaviour.

An extension to this is to consider where these beliefs originated – family, friends, school, social media, community etc. This enables the individuals to begin to see how their personal worldviews have evolved over time and who and what have been influential in their development.

Worldview Questions

In this activity, in Figure 2.7, individuals can be given time to consider a range of worldview questions. These originate from Valk's work on worldviews and he refers to them as 'ultimate questions'. One primary school teacher has renamed this the 'ponder page', as pupils ponder the questions to see if they can identify aspects of their worldviews. It is important to note that they may have never considered some of these and may have no answer, but the process of consideration is what will assist them as they come to study RE/RW.

In the classroom these activities, Figures 2.5, 2.6 and 2.7, can help pupils move on to see how different religions and non-religious worldviews might answer such questions, thus providing a link between themselves and the subject they are due to study. It is important to note that not every religion or non-religious worldview would consider these. Such questions relate more closely to the three monotheistic religions: Islam, Judaism and Christianity. However, the fact that some religions and non-religious worldviews do not ask or answer these specific questions provides another way of comparing them and understanding that not all religions nor non-religious worldviews are the same. This helps preserve the distinctiveness of each whilst acknowledging the shared elements of worldviews. (A note on the use of non-religious worldviews is commonly used in the literature).

What is the purpose of life?   How do I discern what is right/wrong?

Do I have any responsibilities or obligations?

Is there a greater force/being?

How can I right any wrong?   Is there an after life?

■ **Figure 2.7** Ultimate questions sheet.

The ultimate questions activity, Figure 2.7, can be extended by then placing photos of religious followers in the centre of the page and trying to discover answers for these individuals. It is important not to reinforce stereotypes or promote misconceptions in the photographs that are employed. For example, Christianity is not a white, British, middle class religion that was only exported to the world through colonialism. Indeed, the Church in Ethiopia and Egypt predate the church in the UK by some 500 years. Evidence for the establishment of the Ethiopian Orthodox Church exists from around 300 years before Augustine's mission to Britain, and the Egyptian Coptic Church was founded by the Apostle Mark some 500 years earlier. As teachers, we have wonderful opportunities to provide our pupils with facts to enable them to challenge stereotypes, misconceptions and myths.

In the search for different religions' or non-religious worldviews' possible answers to these ultimate questions, learners may realise that for many followers within the same faith, questions may be answered differently. This enables them to see that there is no singular 'Hindu worldview' or 'Muslim worldview' or 'Christian worldview'. Rather there are a range of embodied worldviews that individuals personify, who may or may not adhere to a faith. The ultimate questions activity, Figure 2.7, provides them with a point of similarity in which they can understand where others may answer questions differently from them but yet these may be valid and authentic answers for that individual. Therefore, the teaching of religions and non-religious worldviews becomes less an 'exotic' subject about which individuals may lack understanding but more an understanding that, for some, religions answer their ultimate questions and form part of their worldviews. Religions and non-religious worldviews can be seen as a shared human response to life's questions and experiences.

OFSTED AND DISCIPLINARY KNOWLEDGE

In the UK, Ofsted inspects schools on behalf of the government. During the Covid pandemic (2020–22) Ofsted inspectors produced research reviews on their subjects whilst they were unable to inspect schools. The Ofsted Research Review series for RE (2021) is probably one of the best subject reviews written during this time. The author, Dr Richard Kueh, has a thorough understanding of the subject, current research and ongoing academic debate. Whilst technically relevant only to the UK, the report is interesting for a wider audience due to Kueh's delineation of knowledge: substantive knowledge, ways of knowing/disciplinary knowledge and personal knowledge. Substantive knowledge refers to the content of the subject. Ways of knowing or disciplinary knowledge to a variety of approaches or lens that can be employed to teach the subject: e.g. sociology, history, theology, philosophy. Personal knowledge refers to pupils' understanding of their own point of view or perspective in values, beliefs and norms.

Each of these three aspects of knowledge are impacted by personal worldviews. For example, with substantive knowledge, who decides which content is necessary or valuable? At the start of the chapter, we provided information on how the syllabus for RE is constructed in different ways throughout the UK and who the authority figures are who decide what is the subject of RE/RW. As a teacher, it would be worth finding out which voices are most dominant in the writing of your local syllabus. Ways of knowing or disciplinary knowledge may be impacted in that schools may focus on one discipline or way of knowing rather than another. There is a risk that a particular school might teach RE through a purely historical lens (which we do not think was Kueh's intention) – therefore not covering theological, sociological or philosophical dimensions of religion(s). This would be like studying football by studying the history of Manchester United but never watching a current match. Personal knowledge fits with the worldviews approach in enabling the pupils to identify and understand their own worldviews. Furthermore, this equips them to relate to others who may have a religious element to their worldviews.

CONCLUSION

This albeit brief introduction to RE in the UK has hopefully enabled you to understand the history and peculiarities of the subject in the UK. Teaching RE creates challenges for teachers who may have little subject knowledge and no specific faith allegiance. Employing a worldviews approach to teaching religious education can assist teachers and pupils in having a greater depth of understanding of religion(s) and non-religious worldviews. It provides a starting point to understand the self and in turn others. This can raise teachers' confidence, as they know what subject knowledge they need to search for and what role this plays within a religious person's life. There are many creative ways to teach about worldviews and religion and we hope that these ideas have inspired you as you begin to plan with this approach.

USEFUL WEBLINKS

https://www.natre.org.uk
https://ltlre.org
Homepage - Culham St Gabriel's (cstg.org.uk)

Home - RE:ONLINE (reonline.org.uk)

Culham St Gabriel's Trust Moodle (cstg.org.uk) short courses for CPD

For more information on RE in Scotland see Curriculum for Excellence: Experiences and outcomes (education.gov.scot)

For more information on RE in Northern Ireland see Religious education core syllabus | Department of Education (education-ni.gov.uk)

REFERENCES

Aerts, D., Apostel, L., De Moor, B., Hellemans, S., Maex, E., Van Belle, H., & Van der Veken, J. (2007). *Worldviews. From fragmentation to integration. Internet edition of original 1994.* VUB Press. Retrieved from http://www.vub.ac.be/CLEA/pub/books/worldviews .pdf.

Apostel, L., & Van der Veken, J. (1991). *Wereldbeelden,* DNB/Pelckmans. Translated with some additions in (Aerts et al. 1994/2007).

Barnes, L. P. (2015). Humanism, non-religious worldviews and the future of religious education. *Journal of Beliefs and Values, 36*(1), 79–91. https://doi.org/10.1080/13617672 .2015.1013816.

Commission on Religious Education. (2018). *Final Report: Religion and worldviews: the way forwards. A national plan.* London: Religious Education Council of England & Wales. Retrieved from https://www.commissiononre.org.uk/wp-content/uploads/2018/09/ Final-Report-of-the-Commission-on-RE.pdf.

Cooling, T. (2020). Worldview in religious education: Autobiographical reflections on The Commission on Religious Education in England final report. *British Journal of Religious Education.* https://doi.org/10.1080/01416200.2020.1764497.

Dilthey. (1907). The types of world views and their Unfoldment within the metaphysical systems. In W. Kluback & M. Weinbaum (Eds.), *Dilthey's Philosophy of existence: Introduction to Weltanschauungslehre* (pp. 171–248). Westport, CT: Greenwood Press, 1978, 1957.

Duderija, A. (2007). Islamic groups and their worldviews and identities: Neo-traditional Salafis and progressive Muslims. *Arab Law Quarterly, 21*(3), 341–363.

Education Act. (1996 Section 375 (3)) / School Standards and Framework Act (1998, Schedule 19, para.5).

Flanagan, R. (2019). Implementing a Ricoeurian lens to examine the impact of individuals' worldviews on subject content knowledge in RE in England: A theoretical proposition. *British Journal of Religious Education.* https://doi.org/10.1080/01416200.2019.1674779.?

Flanagan, R. (2020). Worldviews: Overarching concept, discrete body of knowledge or paradigmatic tool?. *Journal of Religious Education, 68,* 331–344. https://doi.org/10.1007 /s40839-020-00113-7.

Freud, S. (1933). *Lecture XXXV: The question of a weltanschauung 1933* (published 1957) (Vol. 22). London: The Hogarth Press.

Hands, M. (2012). What's in a worldview? On Trevor cooling's doing god in education. *Oxford Review of Education, 38*(5), 527–537.

Hedlund-de Witt, A. (2013). Worldviews and their significance for the global sustainable development debate. *Environmental Ethics, 35*(2), 133–162.

Hegel, G. W. F. (1807). *The phenomenology of the spirit* (A. V. Miller, Trans. and Intro. A. Findlay). Oxford: Oxford University Press, 1977.

Hinds, D. (2018). Letter to the very reverend Dr John Hall. Retrieved from https://www.religio useducationcouncil.org.uk/wp-content/uploads/2018/12/Letter-to-The-Very-Reverend -Doctor-John-Hall-from-Rt-Hon-Damian-Hinds-MP...-1.jpg.

Insight UK. (2021). *A report on the state of Hinduism in religious education in schools in the UK* Hinduism in R.E. – INSIGHT UK. https://insightuk.org/wp-content/uploads/2021 /01/Hinduism-in-RE_Project-report.pdf

Jones, A. (2013). The Irony of religious education? It needs to include atheists and humanists. *The Guardian.* Available at The irony of religious education? It needs to include atheists and humanists | Teacher Network | The Guardian.

Jung, C. G. (1942). Psychotherapy and a philosophy of life. In R. Hull (Ed.), *The practice of psychotherapy: Essays on the psychology of the transference and other subjects* (pp. 76–83, 2nd edition). Bollingen series vol 20. New York: Pantheon Books 1966.

Kant, I. (1790). *Critique of Judgement* (P. Guyer, Ed. and Trans.). University of Pennsylvania.

Kanitz, L. (2005). Improving Christian worldview pedagogy: Going beyond mere Christianity. *Christian Higher Education, 4*(2), 99–108. https://doi.org/10.1080/15363750590923101.

Kierkegaard, S. (1843). *Either/Or, edited and translated with introduction and notes by Hong, H. and Hong, E. (1987) 2 volumes.* Princeton: Princeton University Press.

Koltko-Rivera, M. E. (2004). The psychology of worldviews. *Review of General Psychology, 8*(1), 3–58. https://doi.org/10.1037/1089-2680.8.1.3

Kueh, R. (2017). Religious Education and the 'knowledge problem'. In M. Castelli & M. Chater (Eds.), *We need to talk about religious education* (pp. 53–70). London: Jessica Kingsley.

Kyles, C., & Olafson, L. (2008). Uncovering Preservice teachers' beliefs about diversity through reflective writing, *Urban Education, 43*(5), 500–518.

Mezirow, J. (1996). Contemporary paradigms of learning. *Adult Education Quarterly, 46*(3), 158–172.

Mezirow, J. (2000). Learning to think like an adult. In J. Mezirow and Associates (Eds.), *Learning as transformation* (pp. 3–33). San Francisco: Jossey- Bass.

Miedema, S. (2014). From religious education to worldview education and beyond: The strength of a transformative pedagogical paradigm. *Journal for the Study of Religion, 27*(1), 82–103.

Miedema, S., & Bertram-Troost, G. (2015). The challenges of global citizenship for worldview education. The perspective of social sustainability. *Journal of Teacher Education for Sustainability, 17*(2), 44–52.

Miller, J., & McKenna, U. (2011). Religion and Religious Education: comparing and contrasting pupils' and teachers views in an English school. *British Journal of Religious Education, 33*(2), 173–187.

Mulder, A., & van den Berg, B. (2019). Learning for Life: A Hermeneutical Communicative Model for Worldview Education in Light of White Normativity. *Religious Education, 114*(3), 287–302.

NATRE. (2022). An analysis of the provision for RE in primary school – autumn term 2022. Retrieved from https://www.natre.org.uk/uploads/Free%20Resources/NATRE %20Primary%20Survey%202022%20final%20(002).pdf

Ofsted. (2013). Religious education: Realising the potential. Retrieved from www.ofsted.gov .uk/resources/130068.

Ofsted. (2021). *Research review series: Religious education.* Research review series: Religious education. GOV.UK. Retrieved from www.gov.uk.

Prothero, S. (2007). *Religious illiteracy: What every American needs to know – and Doesn't.* New York: Harper One.

Samovar, L., & Porter, R. (2004). *Communications between cultures.* Boston, MA: Wadsworth/ Thomson Learning.

Sire, J. (1988). *The universe next door.* Westmont, Illinois: Intervarsity Press.

Sire, J. (2004). *Naming the elephant. Worldview as a concept.* Westmont, Illinois: IVP.

Smalley, P. (2018). *Response to the commission on religious education's final report, religion and worldviews: The way forward.* National Association of the Standing Advisory Councils on Religious Education. Retrieved from https://nasacre.org.uk/file/nasacre/1 -166-response-to-core.pdf.

Valk, J. (2009). Knowing self and others: Worldview study at Renaissance college. *Journal of Adult Theological Education, 6*(1), 69–80.

Valk, J., & Tosun, A. (2016). Enhancing religious education through worldview exploration. *Discourse and Communication for Sustainable Education, 7*(2), 105–117.

Van der Kooij, J., de Ruyter, D., & Midema, S. (2013). Worldview': The meaning of the concept and the impact on religious education. *Religious Education, 108*(2), 201–228.

Walsh, B. and Middleton, R. (1984) *The Transforming Vision.* Downes Grove, Illinois: Intervarsity.

Wintersgill, B. (2004). Managing more effectively the contribution of Non-specialist teachers. Retrieved from www.shapworkingparty.org.uk/journals/articles_0506/Wintersgill.rtf

Woodhead, L. (2016). The rise of 'no religion'in Britain: The emergence of a new cultural majority. *Journal of the British Academy, 4*(1): 245–261.

Wolters, A. (1985). *Creation regained: Biblical basis for a reformational worldview.* Michigan: Eerdmans.

CHALLENGING DISCRIMINATION AND PREJUDICE THROUGH CREATIVE AND INCLUSIVE RE

CHAPTER 3

Sally Elton-Chalcraft,
Alexandra Brown
and Jane Yates

This chapter is organised in three sections. First we ask you to consider your own mind-set towards anti-discriminatory practice and the following two sections are case studies where Jane Yates and Alexandra Brown exemplify aspects of their pedagogy and practice, relating this to their identities and journeys as teachers.

The chapter aims to help you:

▪ Interrogate your own mindset.
▪ Understand terms such as intersectionality, anti-racism, white allyship, white saviourism, unconscious bias, bystander and change maker.
▪ Learn how to plan lessons which promote anti-racism, gender equality, raise awareness of LGBTQ+ issues and challenge antisemitic and other discriminatory attitudes.

In order to teach for diversity, Elton-Chalcraft (2020) suggests that teachers could begin with an interrogation of our mindset, opening our eyes to the reality of inequality including racism, Islamophobia, homophobia, anti-semitism, prejudice against women, transgender or other groups. Next we can draw on wide ranging resources (including this chapter and references listed) to upskill ourselves in order to gain an informed understanding of how and why our views are shaped by the dominant culture. Finally we need to draw on our learning in order to work collaboratively to challenge any form of discrimination or prejudice, carefully considering how we plan and execute our lessons. Sometimes we may disagree with each other about the best way to do this.

DOI: 10.4324/9781003361480-4

Our chapter is certainly not claiming to have all the answers – the three of us are continuing to learn and develop our own practice. But we hope that the argument we present and the examples we provide will give you an idea of how to progress on your journey as a teacher who is willing to challenge discrimination and prejudice.

UK policies promoted 'community cohesion' and 'preventing radicalisation', yet both policies have more recently been viewed as problematic (Ratcliffe, 2012; Elton-Chalcraft et al., 2017). This chapter problematises the term 'community cohesion' as a complex concept and suggests teachers talk about building community rather than community cohesion. Ideas are further developed in Chapter 11 Islamophobia and Chapter 12 Widening the Scope of RE. Whilst we concentrate on anti-racism in this chapter, we acknowledge the need to eradicate superficial lenses which refer to one intersection e.g. religion/race. We believe intersectionality to be complex – including gender, race/ethnicity, class/prosperity, LGBTQ+ and so on, as well as religion and worldviews. Our two case studies provoke the reader to consider their own biases and identity, in order to be honest about the impact of our own mindset, experiences and values on our teaching of religion and worldviews.

MINDSET INTERROGATION – AN ANTI-RACIST MINDSET EXAMPLE

In Table 3.1, we encourage the reader to plot attitudes you and teachers at your school might hold concerning multicultural/anti-racist practice. We encourage teachers to be critical multiculturalists, which means, for RE, choosing a variety of different religions and belief systems to be explored (see Chapter 12; Warner and Elton-Chalcraft (2022). For example a critical multiculturalist teacher would use BCE (before the Common Era) and CE (Common Era) in their lessons to avoid the Christian-centred BC (before Christ) and AD (Anno Domini in the year of our Lord). However, we realise that we are all at different starting points and also at times we may slip into one of the other categories. In the two case studies in this chapter, two very different individuals share their own stories of how they approach RE and demonstrate how they endeavour to adopt a critical multiculturalist stance in their practice or how they build on this typology.

CASE STUDY 1 JANE YATES

How My Anti-Racist Practice in RE Has Evolved, and Examples from Practice

I am a trained primary teacher with much experience as a primary RE subject lead, and also with RE class teaching in a secondary school. I am an advanced trainer for SAPERE, the national charity for Philosophy for Children, Communities & Colleges (P4C).

Following many years as the Chair of my local SACRE, I am now their Professional RE Adviser and provide CPD for RE and P4C. I am the North West RE Hub Lead and completed the Culham St Gabriel's RE Leadership Scholarship Programme Stage 2 in 2022–23.

I volunteer and work as a facilitator for Anti-Racist Cumbria. Philosophically, I align with intersectional feminism.

■ **Table 3.1** Diversity attitudinal scale (adapted from Warner and Elton-Chalcraft, 2022; Elton-Chalcraft, 2009: 82)

1 Mono culturalists	are 'tokenist'. They attempt to address diversity issues but, deep down, they believe in the superiority of Western (white) patriarchal (male dominated), heterosexual, mainstream Protestant culture. *This is a starting place for many teachers, but this stance is superficial – there is no pro-active commitment to diversity*
2 Colour-blind/kind, tolerant pluralists	are dedicated towards working to 'one race', 'one culture' etc. They attempt to gloss over differences in an attempt to make everyone equal and the 'same' ('they' are the 'same' as 'us' – they just happen to be a different colour, gender/sexual orientation/belief system). *Some teachers think this is 'equality in action' but actually they are adopting a 'colour-blind' stance, denying that diversity exists, tolerating or 'othering' those who are different*
3 Dominant (colonial) multiculturalists	think diversity is exotic and interesting, but inferior, to their own culture. There is cultural 'tourism' where 'they' (as opposed to 'us') live in an exotic parallel world. For example, Hanukkah is the Jewish Christmas. *These teachers attempt to celebrate diversity, but they use their 'own' cultural language to describe the 'other' (inferior) culture. There is white saviourism, Islamophobia, faux anti-sexism and anti-semistism, but little genuine equality*
4 Inverted multiculturalists	are extreme in promoting the minority culture, to the extent that the dominant culture is seen as 'bad' and the marginalised as 'good'. *This stance is the opposite of the dominant multiculturalist – here the teacher elevates the 'other' culture and demotes the dominant culture. There is militant white allyship with a denial of the BBR voice, not genuine equality*
5 Critical pro-active multiculturalists	believe in acknowledging differences and dismantling inequality with the promotion of an individual's consciousness as a social being. They promote an awareness (self-reflection) of how and opinions and roles are shaped by dominant perspectives. *This teacher appreciates that there are differences within, as well as between, cultures and there is open discussion of the causes of white supremacy and how to challenge racism and discrimination. Safe spaces provide opportunities for discriminated groups to share their pain and communities work together to pro-actively fight inequality*

My special interest is leading collaborative and research-informed projects. Most recently this includes: The Cumbria Virtual Voices in Religious Education (VVRE) Project (CDEC, 2023); and the SAPERE (2023) Thinking Together in Science and RE Project. https://www.sapere.org.uk/why-sapere-p4c/thinking-together-in-science-and-re/ Before you start reading this case study,

■ Spend no more than five minutes quickly recalling the names of at least ten people that come to mind when you hear the question: *Who are some religious leaders?*
■ If you can write more than ten, please do.

After completing your list, notice who you wrote down first and any patterns e.g. gender, religion, skin colour, disability, sexuality, age, ancient or contemporary.

■ Does your list show a bias towards a certain grouping?
■ Or a bias towards an intersection of two or three groups? E.g. ancient white male or female young Muslim.
■ What do these patterns tell you about your own Religious Education you've encountered?
■ How do these patterns connect to your upbringing and personal worldview?
■ What are your assumptions for the criteria of a 'religious leader'?
■ Why might it be important to do this kind of activity with young people?

Arguably you could say that, on the surface, this activity is a simple recall activity, providing the teacher with a summative assessment of the pupils' knowledge of religious leaders. In this case study, I want to explore the idea that recall activities can also ascertain a deeper kind of knowledge – a knowledge that exists as assumptions and bias. This kind of knowledge can be powerful as it can inform values and attitudes, for both pupils and teachers. It is why I think that disrupting this kind of recall activity is so important as part of an anti-racist approach to education in religion and worldviews.

Recall Activity

I have carried out a variation of this recall activity with every class I have taught for the past five years. It never fails to challenge my assumptions of the impact of my teaching on the children in front of me. I originally got the idea from Darren Chetty's chapter in the book: *The Good Immigrant* (Chetty, 2017). In his chapter, Chetty invites the teacher-reader to ask their pupils to write down their favourite twenty-five book characters. Despite Chetty teaching in multiracial, multicultural and multifaith classes in the East End of London with a good collection of multicultural picture books on offer, he found his children did not draw on their own experiences to write characters of colour into their *own* story writing. This opened up conversations where one child made a statement which became the title for Chetty's (2017) chapter: "You can't say that! Stories have to be about white people."

On reading the chapter for the first time, I immediately rose to the challenge of Darren's invitation with my own class of 9–11 year olds. As English and RE subject lead at a small, rural monocultural Cumbrian primary school, I had taken pride in making sure the books in school included characters that were diverse and inclusive. I naively assumed this would show up in the favourite book characters of my class. It was a tough lesson for me as their teacher as child after child shared their personal list of mostly *non-disabled white boy* characters.

The most valuable part of this recall activity was using the 'class reveal' as a talking point. This put the children in the role of human or social scientists, fitting well with a disciplinary approach to an education in religion and worldviews. As my pupils analysed their class lists as 'data', they considered the grouping patterns, but then questioned why their lists were so limited. Given more reflection time, they were collectively able to recall a more diverse and inclusive list of characters. But most importantly, the activity became memorable and changed the way they approached future recall activities listing people.

There is much useful reflection to be made as teachers and with pupils about what we recall – the ability to remember – especially when we have to respond rapidly. Arguably, recalling a list of people goes beyond simply remembering people as facts as it draws on wider personal experiences and so is more complex and multifaceted. Psychologist Gordon Bowers suggests that memories are constructed during the recall process but are prone to manipulation and errors which can lead to memory bias (Bowers, 2000). Memory bias is a cognitive bias that either impairs or enhances the recall of a memory by altering the content of what we remember. Cognitive or memory bias might be confused with the idea of 'unconscious bias' which is often referred to in anti-racist education training and approaches. However, they are different in that cognitive bias relates to thinking and unconscious bias relates to perceptions.

Availability Bias; Thinking Harder

In this example of a recall activity, the list represents memory of people that come readily to mind. This can sometimes be called 'availability bias' and is not always representative of personal experience (Le Cunff, 2022). For example, if someone recalls one person, this may influence a whole chain of similar people in the recall process. One way of disrupting availability bias would be to explicitly ask pupils to 'think harder' to come up with a diverse and inclusive list in the first place, with additional thinking time. Arguably, availability bias could be compared to an internet search – the information is there, but some examples come further down the search engine pages than others. Each person's cognitive internet search engine can be influenced by their personal algorithm. In my view, the downside of regular recall activities is that unless they are being used to strengthen retrieval, they don't really get pupils to 'think harder'.

I have found this kind of recall activity valuable as an assessment activity at the start of a new unit of work. Not only to build on previous experience, but also to bring forth any assumptions and bias the pupils might have. Before starting a unit of work on religious leaders with a different class of 9–11 year olds, I was once again surprised to find that most religious leaders the pupils listed were *dead white males*. However, with prompting to make suggestions on a more diverse and inclusive list, this did raise examples such as Martin Luther King, Nelson Mandela, Malala Yousafsai and Ghandi. It led to further discussion on the concept of leadership in a general sense and questioning who decides if someone is a leader. We explored the concept of leadership relating to the pupils themselves and how they were or could be inspired to become leaders. I have always found that teaching and learning that involves being led by the pupil's curiosities to be valuable, building in time for responsive opportunities into medium term planning.

Scientists Can't Be Religious, Can They

Another example of this kind of recall activity was with a new class of 11–12 year olds in a secondary school. Linking with a unit of work on science and religion, I had asked the pupils to quickly recall a list of scientists. The class 'data' showed that most examples were availability biased towards *dead white men*. All except one pupil revealed a general but curious assumption that scientists were not religious. In comparison with Chetty's findings about his own class around book characters, this gave a similar cry from the class of: 'Scientists can't be religious, can they?' However, when one pupil told the class his mum was a scientist *and* religious, this was a real talking point and prompted much enthusiasm to carry out independent research.

From their independent research, the pupils were surprised to find out that many of the scientists they had listed were religious but that in most cases there was complexity. For example, although the renowned physicist and mathematician Albert Einstein was born to a Jewish family and raised as a Jew, he attended a Catholic school. Their research suggested that Albert Einstein said a lot about God, but he claimed he was agnostic. Assuming that the founder of evolution Charles Darwin was an atheist, the pupils were surprised to find that he had identified as a Christian.

The pupils found many examples of more diverse and inclusive scientists from historical examples such as Charles Drew who invented the blood bank, to more contemporary names such as space scientist Dr Maggie Aderin-Pocock and atmospheric physicist Dr Mark Richards. With the power of the internet, this was an easy research task for the pupils. They questioned why some of these names are less famous and seemingly 'hidden' from their curriculum learning. The most striking realisation was that although the pupils knew that Edward Jenner invented the first vaccine for smallpox, they were surprised to discover that inoculation was already common across Europe, Asia and Africa. In particular, they were drawn to the account of Cotton Mather, an American churchman who was told about inoculation by his enslaved worker, Onesimus, who had been inoculated as a child in Africa.

Decolonising the Curriculum

In his powerful TEDTalk on decolonising the curriculum, science teacher and educator Pran Patel describes decolonising the curriculum as exposing children to the 'richness of knowledge' from a global curriculum. He makes a call for knowledge to be deconstructed and reconstructed. Pran poignantly introduces listeners to Indian scientist and Nobel Prize winner Sir Chandrasekhara Venkata Raman who discovered why the sea is blue, otherwise known as the Raman Effect. Pran shares how easy it is to find this hidden knowledge and these hidden figures (Patel, 2019) and this certainly chimes with the ease experienced by my pupils in their independent research.

In other academic writing by Chetty, he suggests that "gate-keeping takes place in the selection of starting points" (Chetty, 2014). In this work, Chetty is referring specifically to Philosophy for Children (P4C) practitioners, but I think it has application when planning starting points for an education in religion and worldviews. There are many possibilities for starting points where pupils are introduced to 'people' in an education in religion and worldviews. These might include fictional or real characters in religious or non-religious stories and texts; people in non-fiction books; historical or contemporary figures of importance; and non-religious or religious class visitors in class or on visits. This is not only relevant to the more obvious schemes of work such as 'religious leaders' but is important across all planning. Is there ever an RE scheme of work that does not include people?

Undertaking this kind of recall activity and personal background reading on the many layers to anti-racist education has helped me to see cognitive bias in my own curriculum planning. I realise that decolonising the curriculum *requires* my awareness and understanding of issues around race (historical and on-going) and colonial experiences and power relations. Decolonisation is a process that involves my long-term commitment of effort and reflection. It requires me to be more creative with my planning and I know I will develop an enhanced personal worldview as a result. Like my pupils, I need to carry out my own research to make sure that I am including examples of people that might ordinarily be hidden from the curriculum. I should not rely on my personal knowledge which may be subject to availability bias.

Teachers have a powerful responsibility in what they choose to include or exclude in their planning. The reality is the assumptions and bias that pupils bring often comes from previous teaching and learning. There is a danger this will negatively impact on pupils' values and attitudes.

> *As a teacher you are in a position of power. It is the school system which is the starting point for how children learn to view the world and accept knowledge; and you have the power to impact change to create a more inclusive and diverse society.*
> (Pran Patel, 2022)

Unconcious Bias Training – Helpful or Counter Productive

The term 'unconscious bias' is an unfair prejudice in favour of/or against one thing, person or group compared with another. It can manifest in many ways, such as how we judge and evaluate others, or how we act towards members of different groups. Unconscious bias training involves identifying the biases people have about race, gender, religion, class and even which football team people support. There is much debate in anti-racist education circles about the value of unconscious bias training in isolation, suggesting that it allows blame to lay solely at the door of things that can't be controlled and to blame individuals rather than looking at systems and processes (Anti-Racist Cumbria, 2021). Unconscious bias training is not a means to an end. As an RE teacher, it is important for me to *be aware* of personal bias and sensitivities, especially when covering more topical or controversial topics. Often bias and sensitivity will manifest itself as an emotional response that may lead a teacher to shut down more challenging conversations or not provide spaces that are safe for discriminated pupils. Not only do I have power as a teacher in an RE classroom, but I have a responsibility to make sure no Black, Brown or racialised pupil is harmed.

Aspiring to Be a Critical Multiculturalist

When I consider myself in relation to the diversity attitudinal scale on Table 3.1, I certainly *aspire* to be a critical multiculturalist at all times. However, I recognise my positionality in the RE classroom as a white, middle class, cisgender, heterosexual, anti-racist, philosophical, humanist, non-religious female. I also recognise this means there is always the potential for me to unconsciously slip into superficial RE practice aligning with 1–4 on the diversity attitude chart. When I reflect back on my early teaching career, I know I mostly provided learning experiences with an attitude that was tokenistic, colour-blind, white saviourist (especially around global charity activities) and elevated marginalised cultures. This isn't an excuse that it was early in my career: I wish I had done more reading back then about anti-racism and intersectionality. As a white teacher, being a critical multiculturalist is not something I can perfect, rather I need to *keep myself in check* at all times. For example, I recognise I have a tendency to stray back into being an inverted multiculturalist because of my personal interest in inequality of marginalised groups. In my view, for me to become a true critical multiculturalist, it means going beyond my own RE practice in the classroom. It is how I am pro-active with other white teachers, and ultimately my white family and white friends.

CASE STUDY 2 ALEXANDRA BROWN

My Identity, Experiences and Examples of Authentic Anti-racist Practice

I am a secondary school Philosophy, Ethics and Religious Studies teacher. As well as this, I am an academic, visiting lecturer, writer and poet whose work focusses on Christian theologies of liberation (namely Black Liberation Theology, Womanism and Asian Feminist Theology), Islam within the Black American experience and decolonising issues of social justice pertaining to gender, race, class, disability and sexual identity within the England and Wales RE curriculum. Theologically and philosophically, I align with Black Liberation Theology, Womanism and Afro-Pessimism. Additionally, I engage in advisory and consultancy work within primary and secondary schools and HE institutions.

In keeping with Warner and Elton-Chalcraft's table, (Table 3.1) my pedagogy most aligns with that of the critical multiculturalist, though I prefer to identify as described in the preceding paragraph. So I find the table helps me think about my practice but I would not use the label 'critical multiculturalist' to describe my identity.

My Impact On the School Context

Within my section of this chapter, I will be drawing on my time and experiences in a school I previously worked in. The school is a co-ed independent school in Surrey. The demographic of the school is white, British, middle class and male, of which, the majority identify as atheists. This is reflected in the staff and student body. Additionally, religious illiteracy in the school is very high and as such, there is little knowledge or even real awareness of anything outside of a white Western euro-patriarchal understanding of Christianity. I also believe it relevant to note that I was the only Black teacher at the school at that time.

My short time at the school saw me do the following,

▓ Led on five whole school CPDs on decolonising knowledge (with a strong focus on anti-racism).
▓ Delivered the school's first Black History Month assembly.
▓ Launched an Afro Caribbean Society.
▓ Launched a 'Safe spaces' for LGBTQ+ students.
▓ Created the ground-breaking unit 'Black Religion and Protest' which has been embedded within the year eight curriculum, which consists of double lessons on the following topics:
1. What is whiteness?
2. What is Black Protest?

3. What is Black Liberation Theology?
4. Who is Jesus the Liberator?
5. What is the global impact of Black Liberation Theology (focus on Asian Feminist Theology)?
6. C21 century conversations about race in the Black community.

Whilst many would consider my mere presence, work and outspokenness, in the school as essential to the cultural shift that needs to occur in such an environment, others have experienced me as deeply problematic to the point of being extreme. Others believe I am someone that must be curtailed, to the point of being silenced.
They mistook my righteous anger and 'unapologetic and unrepentant truth telling' (Riley, 2023: 90) as hatred and an inability to 'get over the past'.

Sadly, the attitude that was displayed by many of my colleagues was that of mono-culturalist and colour-blind/kind, tolerant pluralists (Table 3.1). Both were simultaneously present as they deeply struggled to reckon with their colonial heritage. Subsequently, the logic that in many ways defined the school, was imbued in whiteness.

By whiteness, I am referring to white (Anglo Saxon/European) cultural practices and beliefs, norms, traditions, languages, physical attributes/standards of beauty etc as normal, universal and the standard by which all others must be judged.

Whiteness is a way of being, doing and thinking.

When one has internalised whiteness, one comes to understand 'white culture, history, intellectual scholarship, institutions etc' are inherently superior and the standard that others must aspire to white folks and Western-Eurocentric institutions as the eternal teacher, that knows everything, and needs to learn nothing (Jennings, 2020). Consequently, rendering everything and everyone outside of this tradition perpetual learners. This typically benefits cis-gendered, able-bodied/minded, neurotypical middle class, heterosexual white men. The colonial logic of whiteness dictates that the further away you are from this archetype, the more you are rendered 'the other', 'inferior' and thus susceptible to institutional and systemic marginalisation and violence.

I must preface everything that I write and say beyond this point with the following.

It costs to do this work.
It truly costs to do this work.
Physically, intellectually, emotionally, socially, spiritually and in ways that words cannot attest to – this work costs.

My section of this chapter seeks to provide an anti-racist critical analysis on previous reflections made on 'community building' and the role of RE within this transformative process. I answer the three questions below in the following sections to give you, the reader, an insight into what I consider authentic anti-racist RE work.

A. What does it mean to embed 'anti-racism' within community building work?
B. What are some practical examples of community building work?
C. How can using African folklore contribute to community building within RE?

■ **Figure 3.1** Kindness without action is meaningless.

What Does It Mean to Embed 'Anti-racism' Within Community Building Work

Refer to Figure 3.1. What is your response to 'kindness without action is meaningless'? Do your own experiences, upbringing and identity influence your response?

There is a common misconception that occurs within conversations not just about anti-racism, but also within issues surrounding anti-sexism/misogyny, homophobia etc. Anti-racism work can be met with typical responses such as:

■ *'Surely the answer [to racism] is that we need to teach students how to be kind'.*
■ *In some folks minds, supposed issues surrounding race, gender, class etc can be remedied with politeness, manners and respect.*

I will provide a personal example to demonstrate the woeful inadequacies and indeed harm of such responses. Students often come to me and voice their concerns and grievances about experiences of racism, sexism, homophobia, transphobia etc that they witness and endure. They are not solely coming to me so that I will meet their disgruntlement and indeed pain with sympathy, or even empathy. In short, they are not coming to me with the sole purpose of receiving kindness.
They have their friends and family for that.

They do not explicitly need me for that.

When such students would bypass their form tutors, HOYS, members of SLT and walk up two flights of stairs to come and speak to me, yes of course, they desire to be met with compassion, but more to the point, they are coming with an expectation.

Sometimes it would be explicitly, or implicitly stated, but none-the-less, there was an expectation that I would advocate for them.

What does advocacy look like? Why is kindness is not enough?

Advocacy requires political literacy and engagement. Subsequently, it requires literacy of the law, school policy, rules, regulations etc.

Kindness does not advocate.
Kindness does not question, call out, disrupt, dismantle or eradicate systems of violence, or harmful/violent ideologies, or discriminatory beliefs and practices.
At its best, kindness listens and acts as a mild anaesthetic.
Kindness permits acts of violence to continue on two conditions.
1. It goes unheard.
2. It goes unseen.

Consequently, not drawing attention to itself permits the harmful status quo to remain invisible and thus intact.

When students and colleagues perpetuate racism and other systems of discriminatory violence, we must not seek to remind them of the tenants of kindness.
How would you feel if someone said that to you?

Do you think that was a nice/appropriate thing to say?

Instead, we must seek to support them in identifying the harmful logic behind their words and actions. I would go as far as to verbally articulate how they understand their own humanity in relation to and independent of the group they have harmed. For example, preferable responses might be

■   'Do you believe that you are in some way superior to "X" because you identify as "Y"?'
■   'Do you believe that "X" has inferior attributes/characteristics'?

We may be surprised and indeed shocked by what we learn, but it is through this level of honesty and openness that we can do away with superficial conversations that only have the capacity to address the symptoms but never the cause.

The next section offers suggestions to structurally embed anti-racism on a whole school level.

Practical Examples of Community Building Work – Whole School

As a Black queer differently abled-bodied woman, my identity intersects along multiple minoritised and marginalised groups. In the most enriching and humbling of ways, I have come to learn that, being in community with those who look like me/identify as I identify, is paramount for not only my growth and flourishing, but I would go as far as to say it is a key component for my existence and mental wellbeing. Sexual and gender identity does not align with cis-gendered heterosexual normativity. Furthermore, my queerness also informs my politics; consequently it is more than just a label/letter in an acronym.

We are after all, relational beings.

There are two key facets of anti-racist community building which I think every primary school teacher must have at the forefront of their mind, and deeply embedded within their pedagogy.

■ Anti-racism requires that we build our own sub-communities whilst simultaneously reshaping the ones we currently exist in.

■ The lived experience of our BBR siblings (an acronym for 'Black, Brown and other racialised' folks. This is a term I have adopted as BAME and POC further entrenches the colonial and racist idea that white is the normative). Alternatively, one could also use the term 'The Global Majority'.

■ Hold and share similar stories, pain and wounds, as a result of structures within the school, education system and wider society. As such, they can speak to, understand and can help to sooth each other's aches in ways their white counterparts simply cannot. Additionally, they wish to speak and commune with those who share their experiences, independent of the white gaze.

I will now offer four whole school approaches to embedding anti-racism on a cultural and structural level.

1. Creating A Safe Space for BBR Groups (Independently and Co-existing) – One Exclusively for Black/Black Mixed and Another for BBR Colleagues

In the school I previously taught in, as well as being the only Black teacher, I was one of three Black members of staff (within a staff body of over 150). Furthermore, Black students were also in the minority. Owing to the lack of racial, ethnic and cultural diversity, my championing of Black History Month (BHM) was met with one of the following responses.

a) It is irrelevant to my subject (STEM in particular).

b) Why should there be a focus on Black people? What about other groups, what about white people?

c) It is something I know is important, but I lack the knowledge and confidence to proceed.

d) BHM is regressive. Racism rarely happens, we must talk about love, kindness and common values. We should not see colour.

All of these rebuttals and responses, whether intentional or not, add to the alienation and emotional and intellectual labour of racialised teachers. Black teachers are affected in particular (as they in most instances are the ones spearheading EDI initiatives). The alienation and additional labour presents in the following ways.

■ Social isolation (strained relationships with colleagues).

■ Feeling as though one cannot bring their 'full selves' into their school community.

- Disproportionately leading on BHM and other race related agendas because their white counterparts refuse to engage/do not have the confidence to participate and lead.
- Much of this work goes unpaid as it is not on the TLR and as such, is not under the title of a leadership position. This in many ways impacts the level of reinforcement it receives from SLT. Subsequently, effective dissemination to the HODs and classroom teachers can be varied.

For a BBR teacher there is a fine line between

- Going above and beyond.
- Free labour.
- Exploitation.

Whilst schools must do more to ensure that they do not fall into the second and normalise the latter, BBR teachers must seek to impose boundaries rather than constantly trying to find a balance in the mountainous workload they do.

Consequently, this labour requires a safe space for BBR teachers to offload, support each other, come up with strategies to embed anti-racism into their school without the 'white gaze'/white members of staff undermining their very lived experienced. To do this work in schools such as my previous one, I would suggest that periods of separation are absolutely necessary.

There must be periods of relief within the working week. Without this, one's school environment could easily become a prison without relief (Gordon, 2021).

I think white teachers who wish to, should engage in anti-racist work, but their support (in both theory and in practice) must support and champion the creation of safe spaces for BBR teachers. White teachers need to understand that when the door closes so that the conversation can begin, they must be on the other side of the door.

Figure 3.2 shows the images of the grounding principles of the 'safe space' I created for BBR members of staff.

There is a difference between a safe space and a learning space; we must know and respect the difference.

The Aesthetics Of the School – 'Institutional Body Language'

The institutional body language (Dadzie, 2000) of a school reveals to the school community and visitors the values, mission and ethos of the school. The visual representation through media such as artwork, posters etc is key. This can be affirming to the BBR students, because they firstly see themselves in places of prominence in their learning environment. Secondly, it sends a clear message to all students (of all racial backgrounds) that racialised bodies have a right to be represented, which then critiques notions of racial hierarchies.

Schools, like every other working community space, must have visual depictions of what anti-racism looks like and what anti-racism demands of us. On that note, we must make a clear distinction between anti-racism and diversity and inclusion, within a racial context.

Diversity and inclusion along the lines of race is typically seen in images such as Figure 3.3.

Grounding principles for our safe space

1. This is a safe and welcoming space for all who attend, by being respectful, inclusive, considerate and understanding

2. If someone is here, it is because they identify as Black, Brown, or belong to other racialised groups. As such they are welcome

3. Be aware that everyone here is experiencing oppression, marginalisation and discrimination in some form or another. Be aware of your privilege and think about how your words, opinions and actions influences and who they might harm or exclude (EG/LGBTQIA+ folks, economically underprivileged, non-normative bodies, neurodivergent (dyslexia, autism, dyspraxia etc), disabled bodies, people with mental health conditions)

4. Be aware of the group dynamics. This is a space for everyone to feel welcome and can discuss and contribute to the discussion equally and freely, if they want to. No one should be made to speak if they do not wish

Themes for weekly topics

1. Our mental health and well being
2. Support/ lack thereof by department, wider school and SLT
3. BHM
4. Supporting our BBR students/ forging positive collaborative relationships with parents/ carers
5. Embedding anti-racism within the curriculum / whole school
6. Checking in our mental health and wellbeing
7. How can our white colleagues 'show up' in effective, positive and meaningful ways?

Safe space for Black Brown and Racialised staff

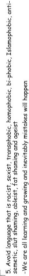

5. Avoid language that is racist, sexist, transphobic, homophobic, bi-phobic, Islamophobic, anti-semetic, slut shaming, ableist, fat shaming and ageist
- We are all learning and growing and inevitably mistakes will happen
- When this happens, please correct said person from a place of love and respect. Think about how you would wish to be treated if you were in the same position
- Anger is a valid response, but we are all humans

6. Be careful of using gendered pronouns (she/he/they). Do not assume pronouns Its best to ask

7. Use trigger warnings if you are going to talk about potentially difficult issues. Before you start, make it clear

8. Respect confidentiality- No recordings, photos. If you wish to take notes, write something down, be transparent and ask for permission (preserve folk's anonymity and only use for personal use)
- Generally speaking, what happens in this room stays in the room, but, if you are also concerned about your/ another person wellbeing, please go and speak to safeguarding or a trusted member of SLT

9. Call in rather than call out. If you would like to speak, please raise your hand

■ **Figure 3.2** Themes for discussion and ground rules for safe spaces for BBR staff.

▪ **Figure 3.3** Poster 'We are all different in our own ways.'

Images of this nature, including the ubiquitous 'welcome posters in a variety of languages', do admittedly undermine notions of racial superiority. However, these resources fail to address the impact of racism that is currently present within the school community and could be viewed as tokenistic (see Table 3.1 at the beginning of this chapter). Furthermore, the poster in Figure 3.3 fails to speak directly to those who experience racism, but more to the point, it presents a utopian notion that if we are 'loving' towards each other, then we won't need to speak about race, because 'we do not see colour because we are all one'. This relates to the 'colour-blind pluralists' in Table 3.1. It is this positionality that we must unlearn and de-link ourselves from, as it allows for racism to become an abstract theoretical concept that has no material life or consequences. In other words, it does not provoke introspection nor does it stimulate conversations that lead to transformative change.

Instead, anti-racism posters should be affirming as they would speak directly to those who experience racism. See an example in Figure 3.4. This 'Black is beautiful' poster (Figure 3.4) would also invoke critical engagement as it would directly confront racism. This popular and much loved statement within the Black community directly challenges the notion that Black skin and beauty is ugly/inferior to white European standards of beauty. Furthermore, the inclusion of Pan-African colours (the political endeavour to create a sense of unity amongst Africans on the continent and in the diaspora. The red represents the blood that was shed during slavery, yellow represents the sun, gold represents the abundance of natural minerals and the green represents the richness of the land and vegetation), further acknowledges and celebrates the boldness of Black beauty in the midst of a society that struggles to understand, let alone respect, their mere humanity.

■ **Figure 3.4** Black is beautiful anti-racist poster.

■ **Figure 3.5** Poster – If you're tired of hearing about racism, imagine how exhausting it is smiling whilst living through it.

Anti-racist visual depictions, such as Figure 3.5, seek to centre those who have and continue to be negatively impacted by racism, whilst calling out the ironic reasons as to why this is still prevalent. This image wonderfully demonstrates how the holistic impact of racism (mental, social etc) is often minimised when comparing it to white colleagues' annoyance, or 'fatigue' at mere discussions of racism.

The centring of BBR teachers' voices, lived experiences and thoughts are key. The answers and the solutions will come from them and collectively we must endeavour to create and establish it. See the critical multiculturalist and pro-active anti-racist stances in Table 3.1.

1. **Parental Collaboration/Advisory Group**

Teachers must seek to cultivate 'solution based discussion groups' with members of the school community. This very much requires the active participation of parents/carers. Their voices are key for the following reasons:

▨   Teachers are not the sole holders and authority of knowledge. Anti-racism requires acknowledgement that BBR bodies create, hold and transmit knowledge that is as applicable, powerful and as transformative as the knowledge that children typically learn from white male thinkers in textbooks (hooks, 2015).

▨   A community minded school means that every part of the body must be included and the body of the school extends beyond the confines of the wall and includes the parents/ carers. Sadly, many of them would have also experienced racism within their own schooling experience. Consequently, they may have retrospectively thought about how best certain lessons could have been delivered and difficult topics addressed. The insight they could provide could be invaluable.

▨   Parents offer pragmatic support in the following ways:

▨   Providing teachers with the appropriate language/terminology.

▨   Having direct access to certain communities and religious spaces etc and as such, they could help facilitate trips and guest speakers (also see Chapter 9).

▨   Could offer their time and come and speak to the students. E.g. Show and Tell. A parent could bring in religious/cultural items and tell stories of their significance. The teacher could then create learning resources and plan a lesson around this.

Teachers are very much overworked and under-resourced. Whilst time is rarely on their side, it is important to know that the responsibility of embedding anti-racism in schools is not solely for the teacher to carry. Schools must allow and support such meaningful dialogue to occur and teachers must utilise help and support when it is offered and available. This should not become an opportunity for parents who are uncomfortable with talking about race to derail, undermine and take away from such progressive and necessary conversations. A space for parents to voice concerns must be given, but this would not be the forum for that.

Community Building Through African Folklore

Within this section I explore how my lesson on African folklore can enable RE to become a community building subject in the following four sections:

1. Context and reasoning behind the creation of the lesson.
2. A breakdown of the lesson 'African Folklore: Stories, Truth and Knowledge'.
3. A gallery of students' folklore.
4. Anti-racism community building – Closing thoughts.

2. **Context and Reasoning Behind the Creation of the Lesson**

During Black History Month, I thought it was a great opportunity to decolonise sites of knowledge whilst simultaneously centring a traditional African epistemology (It is necessary to note that within this context, I am referring to folklores within West Africa, namely Ghana and Nigeria).

Typically, Western euro-patriarchal thought presents knowledge as truth that is created within the academy, that can only be accessed by 'gatekeepers of knowledge'. Furthermore, such knowledge is then disseminated into places of formal education such as schools and universities and can then only be accessed through books, journal articles etc.

However, in wanting to decolonise sites of knowledge, I began to explain to my students that within many articulations of African Philosophy, there is no hierarchy of knowledge (regardless of gender and age etc) and that knowledge can be found, created and transmitted anywhere. I then reiterated that the knowledge transmitted from teachers and found in books are only some of a vast array of ways. They are not the only way.

After premising the conversation with this, I drew my students' attention to question 1 (see Figure 3.6). I had taught this lesson to five different classes and every class struggled to initially conceive of the idea that knowledge (truth, wisdom, etc) still held value and was worthy of being shared despite it not being in a book or coming from 'an adult who had an authority of knowledge'. After unpacking and dismantling this deeply entrenched misconception, the students offered the following answers:

- ▨ The playground.
- ▨ Life.
- ▨ Friendship groups.
- ▨ Sports teams.
- ▨ Experiencing grief.
- ▨ My imagination.
- ▨ TV.
- ▨ My parents' bedroom. After the initial roar of laughter which came from both myself and the other students in the class, I eagerly asked my student to explain what he meant. The student's answer was incredibly profound. He said that often, when he is seeking the comfort and advice of his parents, they are often in their bedroom talking and discussing important family matters.

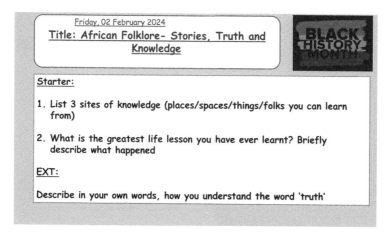

■ **Figure 3.6** African folklore lesson during Black History Month.

His contribution was a necessary reminder that you can hold two sites of knowledge, which can intertwine and enrich one another. They are not inherently separate entities. For my student, his parents' bedroom was a site that offered calmness, a discussion forum and a place where guidance is offered in abundance. Upon reflection, it is no wonder he experienced it as such. I think it interesting that perhaps on some level, my student thought that having difficult conversations with his parents in this carefully constructed environment is perhaps a place he feels safe and a place in which his parents would respond to him in a calm, empathetic and measured way.

Whilst it is essential to remember that knowledge created, transmitted and disseminated is not born in abstraction (Salami, 2022), we must remember that the location, time, setting etc is something that must also be taken into account as this too interplays with said knowledge (Figure 3.7).

I then provided the students with a sound definition of folklore. I made a point of reiterating that folklores are not inherently African, but because it was BHM, our focus would be folklores from the African continent.

I mentioned to students that the passing of knowledge from one generation to another was something that was deemed as a cultural and social practice, to the point of being a moral obligation and duty.

When I asked all five classes to name any folklores within their own culture, no students could name any (though I suspected that for some, it was that they did know, but they did not feel comfortable sharing). Whilst the demographic of the school is overwhelmingly white British, I thought it strange that there was no understanding of stories, myths, fables etc that they had been taught as children. When I asked students if they had heard of stories such as 'Little Red Riding Hood' and 'Goldilocks and The Three Bears,' there was a sense of 'Augh... I understand'. And it was at that point that they felt they could relate to the lesson.

I found it interesting that when I worded it as a 'childhood story' and divorced it from any cultural connotations, there was an increased sense of comfortability and familiarity. This was not the first time I noted how many white British students struggle to identify 'cultural practices'.

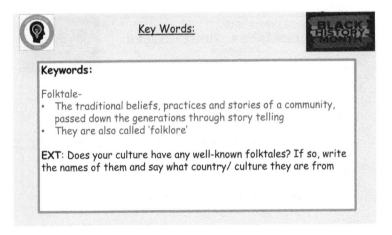

Figure 3.7 Lesson plan key words.

Important Information!

- Within many African, Caribbean and countries around the world where there is a large black population, folktales are an integral part of their culture and sense of identity.

- Folktales have been effective ways to teach the younger generations important life lessons and community values.

- They have also been an effective way to preserve their culture and history (this became even more important during slavery and colonialism)

- We are going to listen to two very famous African folktales 'Anansi the Spider goes to lunch'
- Anansi (pronounced: An-an-si) is often described as a cheeky, mischief maker, and a wise, lovable creature who often finds himself in unfortunate situations, but often learns valuable life lessons from them.

- The Anansi stories originated from Ghana within the ethnic group called 'The Akan'. During slavery, enslaved Africans taken from Ghana to Jamaica in the 1600s held onto the Anansi stories and it became embedded within Jamaican culture

■ **Figure 3.8** Lesson plan important information.

I think that, had I not made that explicit link to such examples, they would have felt like outsiders looking into another culture and world of which they could not relate to and thus access.

Though one student did reference Greek mythology, which I thought was an impressive answer. However, this did not strictly speak to his own cultural background (Figure 3.8).

It was this section that allowed for me to detail the historical significance of African folklore. After asking three students to read the information above, I began to speak about the impact of slavery and colonialism. I began by saying that although a frequent response to slavery is 'it happened ages ago we need to move on', the following needed to be acknowledged. Consequently, I orally transmitted the following to all of my classes,

> The project of British colonialism (which was only made possible because of slavery) included the ripping of a people from their homes and essentially saw them trafficked to a land that was not their own. Slavery also involved the stripping and subsequent loss of language, religion, history, culture and name. Enslaved Africans

were stripped of their names and given the names of their enslavers. As I am sure you all know, I'm half Ghanaian half Jamaican. Both sides of my ancestry were greatly impacted by slavery. I have the surname 'Brown' because my biological father is Jamaican, and I was given his surname. He has this surname because his ancestors were enslaved Africans. Slavery and colonialism may have happened 'long ago', but the consequences of them still remain in the most brutal and painful of ways.

A way that enslaved Africans on the continent, those trafficked to the Caribbean and the Americas etc tried to hold onto their history and culture was through sharing their folklores. Because of course they were not allowed to read and write, and when formal education was allowed, it was done with the intention to indoctrinate and justify, as opposed to remedy and recover what had been lost. As a result, enslaved Africans kept their traditions alive and folklore was used to retain and share what had always been sacred to them.

The lesson then saw me provide the following context to the folklores we would then explore (Figures 3.9 and 3.10).

Detailed answers (from higher attaining students) are given in (Figures 3.11, 3.12, 3.13, 3.14 and 3.15).

I was particularly proud of this, because this student responded to the invitation of centring their cultural background, and they disrupted one of the many enduring legacies of British colonialism. Many students' folklore, perhaps unintentionally, boldly declared the following 'English is a language like any other language, it is not a measure of intelligence' (Figures 3.16, 3.17 and 3.18).

The folklores on poverty in particular did not explicitly have anything to do with race or even culture. It is important to note that race will not be at the forefront of every culture's intra-communal conversation. For example, in countries such as Ghana where the overwhelming number of inhabitants are Black, race is not at the forefront of their political thought/identity. Rather, their ethnic group, Ghanian and African identity is of far greater significance. It is important to acknowledge different cultural depictions on their own terms, whilst trying to understand the social issue from which it was born.

- We are going to listen to two very famous African folktales 'Anansi the Spider goes to lunch'
- Anansi (pronounced: An-an-si) is often described as a cheeky, mischief maker, and a wise, lovable creature who often finds himself in unfortunate situations, but often learns valuable life lessons from them.

- The Anansi stories originated from Ghana within the ethnic group called 'The Akan'. During slavery, enslaved Africans taken from Ghana to Jamaica in the 1600s held onto the Anansi stories and it became embedded within Jamaican culture

■ **Figure 3.9** Anansi story.

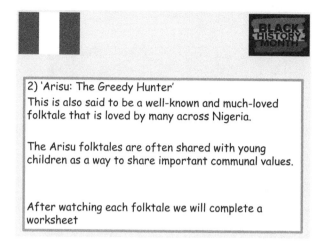

2) 'Arisu: The Greedy Hunter'
This is also said to be a well-known and much-loved folktale that is loved by many across Nigeria.

The Arisu folktales are often shared with young children as a way to share important communal values.

After watching each folktale we will complete a worksheet

■ **Figure 3.10** Arisu the greedy hunter.

It dawned upon me when I was in Ghana during the Christmas break of 2022 that my 'Blackness' did not have the same level of prominence as it does when I am in Britain. To be Black in Ghana is to be part of the majority. Consequently, what took more of a central role within my identity was my difficulty in understanding my 'Africanness', in light of my complexities that I am of Ghanian and Jamaican heritage and that I am British born.

How Can An Anti-racist RE Curriculum Lends Itself To Community Building

Whilst the ultimate goal of community would be to follow each other to a place that does not require any leaders, this can only occur when we question who is it that we constantly follow and in what direction. It also requires an acknowledgement that some directions are seen as superior and others as unwanted background noises. To quote Leah Lakshmi Piepzna-Samarasinha (queer, disabled writer, educator and disability/transformative justice worker of Burgher/Tamil Sri Lankan and Irish/Roma descent), 'I will [only enter into communities] where I am needed and understood as a leader, not just someone for people to grudgingly provide services for' (Piepzna-Samarasinha, 2021: 76).

Neither should anti-racist community building come under the banner of being a favour or tokenistic. We must ask ourselves why accountability and equity have become bitter and bloody words in our mouths.

Neither is anti-racist community building about likability. Such a community minded school should adhere to the 'radical' notion that folks need to see themselves authentically reflected in every structure of their learning community. Consequently, reparative justice, unlearning and decolonising is an essential part of this process.

Furthermore, through a crip theory lens, we are required to consider the offering that can be cultivated when we apply a racialised disability lens (Piepzna-Samarasinha, 2021). Part of the decolonial work within the curriculum is to question the lens and framework we deem as 'traditional', universal and the standard by which all others must seek to achieve and thus are accountable to. In an attempt to further decolonise the 'able-bodied'

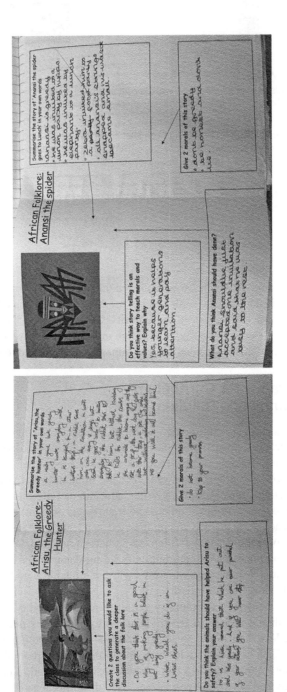

▨ **Figure 3.11** Examples of students' work.

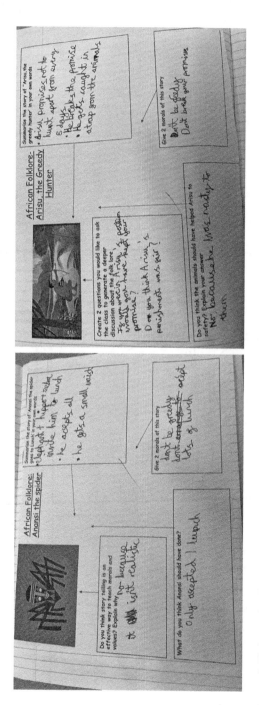

■ **Figure 3.12** Less-detailed answers (from lower attaining students).

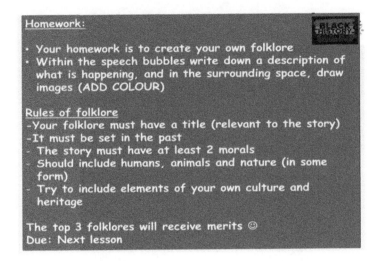

■ **Figure 3.13** Students were then given the following instructions for their homework.

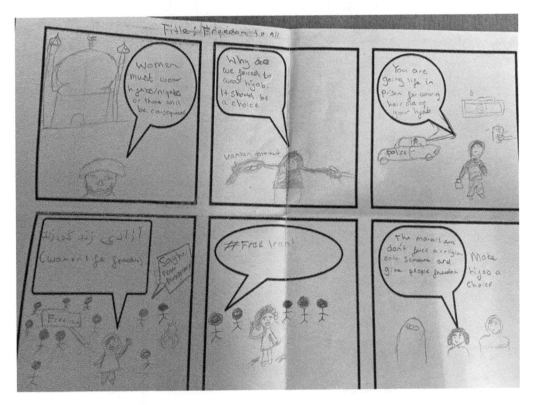

■ **Figure 3.14** Women and the hijab within Iran – images of pupil's own folklores.

■ **Figure 3.15** Culture, health and natural remedies.

■ **Figure 3.16** A folklore about greediness and food – written in Welsh.

■ **Figure 3.17** Those in poverty and the needy.

positionality on what it means to build community, I wish to engage with 'crip lens' to allow us to reimagine justice, though centring the differently able-bodied.

Through crip theory, we further understand that disabled bodies, similar to BBR bodies, are not

> liabilities, something that is [innately limiting] and brings pity or something that should be nobly transcended. On the contrary their cultures, history, experiences stories and wisdom of [racialised] bodies act as 'assets that teach us things that are relevant to ourselves, our [school]community and the whole damn planet.
>
> (Piepzna-Samarasinha, 2021: 75)

Anti-racism community building schools must be predicated on the following:

1. It is centred on the epistemology and lived experience of it BBR community members.
2. White school community members must acknowledge and understand that 'anti-racism' and 'race' (more broadly speaking) is not exclusively a 'Black concern'. The mere failure to even concede this is in itself is a manifestation of whiteness. The idea that

■ **Figure 3.18** Wealth and self-image.

white is the normative becomes even more entrenched when those who inhabit white bodies fail to see and understand themselves in relation to race. Consequently, it is only a 'problem for the coloured people' (Roediger et al., 2022: XIX).

This in itself is one of the greatest barriers for racial justice.

    a. Do not 'do the work' because you have been forced to.

    b. Do not endeavour to be a 'white ally'. This plays into the white saviour complex and the 'good white person narrative (The 'good white person' does not push for structural change. Rather they take pride and comfort in knowing they are not like the 'other' white people).

    c. 'Do the anti-racist work' because as a human you understand that the colour of your skin affords you privilege and a level of ease which harms BBR folk both on an interpersonal and structural level. Not doing this anti-racist work harms white folks because it infects the white body with delusions of grandeur and an over-inflated sense of one's self-worth and historical contribution.

3. An anti-racist RE must be birthed and cultivated within a holistic understanding that 'your liberation is bound in my liberation, [as such we must] work together' (Watson, 2012: 1).

SUMMARY

This chapter firstly outlined that teachers need to consider their mindset before engaging in RE. We presented in Table 3.1 a set of stances, positive and negative, which all teachers hold to varying degrees. Acknowledging our own stance and becoming informed, 'doing our homework', is fundamental before engaging in planning. The two case studies from highly skilled teachers provide authentic voices and reveal how these two teachers feel about the subject of RE and their pedagogy, as well as giving practical teaching and learning examples.

We hope you will engage in this transformative practice – it is important work.

REFERENCES

Anti-Racist Cumbria. (2021) *Why we don't do unconscious bias training Anti-Racist Cumbria website* why we don't do unconscious bias training. Cumbria: Anti Racist Cumbria (not sure how to reference a website article!).

Bower, G.H. (2000) A brief history of memory research. In E. Tulving & F.I.M. Craik (Eds.), *The Oxford handbook of memory* (pp. 3–32). Oxford: Oxford University Press.

CDEC (2023) Cumbria Virtual Voices in Religious Education (VVRE) Project (CDEC 2023). https://www.cdec.org.uk/what-we-offer/projects/cumbria-virtual-voices-in-religious-education/.

Chetty, D. (2014, January–June) The elephant in the room: Picture books, philosophy for children and racism. *Childhood and Philosophy Rio de Janerio*, 10(19), 11–31.

Chetty, D, (2017) *You can't say that say! Stories have to be about white people! Chapter in the good immigrant* (N. Shukla, Ed.). London: Unbound Publishers.

Dadzie, S. (2000) *Toolkit for tackling Racism Stoke-on-Trent*. Trentham Books Ltd.

Elton-Chalcraft, S. (2009) *It's not just Black and White, Miss: Children's awareness of race* Stoke-on-Trent. Trentham Books

Elton-Chalcraft, S. (2020) Student teachers' diverse knowledge and experiences of religion – Implications for culturally responsive teaching. *Journal of Higher Education Theory and Practice*, 20(6). https://articlegateway.com/index.php/JHETP/article/view/3130.

Elton-Chalcraft, S., Lander V., Revell, L., Warner, D. and Whitworth, L. (2017, February) To promote, or not to promote fundamental British values? Teachers' standards, diversity and teacher education. *British Educational Research Journal*, 43(1). http://onlinelibrary.wiley.com/doi/10.1111/berj.2017.43.issue-1/issuetoc.

Freire, P. (1972) *Pedagogy of the oppressed*. Harmondsworth, Middlesex: Penguin Education.

Gordon, L.R. (2021) *Freedom, justice, and decolonization*. New York: Routledge, Taylor & Francis Group.

hooks, bell (2015) *Yearning: Race, gender, and cultural politics*. New York: Routledge, Taylor & Francis Group.

Jennings, W.J. (2020) *After whiteness: An education in belonging*. London: Wm. B. Eerdmans Publishing Company.

Le Cunff, A. L. (2022) *Memory bias: How selective recall can impact your memories ness labs*. London: Sage.

Patel, P. (2019) *Decolonise the curriculum TEDX Norwich*. Norwich: TEDX.

Patel, P. (2022) *Anti racist educator*. Corwin. London: Corwen.

Patel, P. (2023) *Decolonise the curriculum the Teacherist website* Home. The Teacherist.

Piepzna-Samarasinha, L.L. (2021) *Care work dreaming disability justice.* Vancouver, BC: Arsenal Pulp Press.

Ratcliffe, P. (2012) 'Community cohesion' : Reflections on a flawed paradigm. *Critical Social Policy*, 32(2), pp. 262–281.

Riley, A.C. (2023) *This here flesh: Spirituality, liberation, and the stories that make us.* New York: Convergent.

Roediger, D.R., Gopal, P. and Cleaver, K. (2022) *The wages of whiteness: Race and the making of the American working class.* London: Verso.

Salami, M. (2022) *Sensuous knowledge: A black feminist approach for everyone.* London: Zed Books.

SAPERE (2023) Thinking together in science and RE project. https://www.sapere.org.uk/why-sapere-p4c/thinking-together-in-science-and-re/.

Warner, D. and Elton-Chalcraft, S. (2022) Teaching for Race Culture and Ethnicity Awareness and Understanding Ch 14 In Cooper, H. and Elton-Chalcraft, S. (Eds) *Professional Studies in Primary Education* 4th edition London: Sage https://us.sagepub.com/en-us/nam/professional-studies-in-primary-education/book273439

Watson, L. (2012) The origin of "our liberty is bound together". *Invisible Children.* https://invisiblechildren.com/blog/2012/04/04/the-origin-of-our-liberty-is-bound-together/ (Accessed: March 22, 2023).

WEB RESOURCES

After Religious Education

Available at https//:www.afterre.org (Accessed May 14, 2023).

Racism and discomfort in the community of philosophical enquiry: Darren Chetty in conversation with Joanna Haynes | BERA

Religious Communities: Religion, Community, and Society | Encyclopedia.com

CDEC (2023) Cumbria Virtual Voices in Religious Education (VVRE) Project (CDEC 2023) https://www.cdec.org.uk/what-we-offer/projects/cumbria-virtual-voices-in-religious-education/

Community cohesion | GOV.WALES

NASUWT | Community Cohesion

Religious Education and Community Cohesion – RE:ONLINE (reonline.org.uk)

SAPERE (2023) Thinking Together in Science and RE Project https://www.sapere.org.uk/why-sapere-p4c/thinking-together-in-science-and-re/

National Association of Teachers of Religious Education (NATRE) – Anti Racist resources Primary Classroom Resources (natre.org.uk)

SECTION 2

CREATIVE APPROACHES IN RELIGIOUS EDUCATION/ RELIGION AND WORLDVIEWS EDUCATION

CREATIVE THINKING AND DIALOGUE

P4C AND THE COMMUNITY OF ENQUIRY

Georgia Prescott

the thought of a child may be a priceless gift to a parent or teacher with ears to hear.

Gareth Matthews (1994 p. 15)

This chapter aims to help you

- Understand what constitutes creative thinking and dialogue in RE
- Learn about P4C (Philosophy for Children) and the Community of Enquiry with practical lesson ideas
- Consider different types of thinking
- Learn how to record and assess creative thinking and dialogue

Religious education (RE) creates a perfect opportunity for children to think and talk creatively and philosophically because it is concerned with exploring differing views of the world and our place as humans within it. Religions and worldviews concern themselves with philosophical and contestable questions and issues and people have their own interpretations of the world. Religious texts, stories and teachings introduce, question and explore these ideas and concepts. RE therefore can engage children in investigating and evaluating a range of views and in exploring their own ideas and beliefs, whatever their standpoint.

This chapter will explore reasons to include opportunities for creative thinking and dialogue in your RE lessons, as well as some practical strategies for doing so. Although the focus is primarily on younger pupils (3-11 years), many of the approaches are equally suited to or adaptable for older pupils (11-18 years).

CREATIVE THINKING AND DIALOGUE IN RE

Whilst developing children's substantive subject knowledge (Ofsted 2021, CORE 2018) of a range of religious beliefs and practices is crucial to increasing religious literacy, creative

DOI: 10.4324/9781003361480-6

RE must involve more than just imparting the 'facts' about religion to children and hoping that they might engage with them.

In inspecting RE lessons, OfSTED (2013) commented, 'While pupils had a range of basic factual information about religions, their deeper understanding of the world of religion and belief was weak' (p8). Low-level tasks such as filling in worksheets after being given some information, writing/retelling stories in their own words and cutting and pasting activities really only require skills such as remembering or sequencing, and they do not engage children with the concepts and ideas behind the information or texts. '*Pupils rarely developed their skills of enquiry into religion: to ask more pertinent and challenging questions; to gather, interpret and analyse information; and to draw conclusions and evaluate issues using good reasoning*' (ibid. p. 9).

Real learning has to come from getting children to engage at a deeper level with the concepts within the subject matter (CORE 2018; Erriker, Lowndes & Bellchambers 2011) and apply it to their own experiences and beliefs. This should involve opportunities and space for children to think, both collectively and individually (Fisher 2013; Hymer & Sutcliffe 2012; Nottingham 2013).

One of the key methods for children to develop their thinking is through dialogue, in a setting where they feel safe enough to express themselves openly through the mutual exchange of ideas. Despite the downplaying of speaking and listening by some governments in the past, its importance is still acknowledged within the English National Curriculum (DfE 2013); and few educators would deny the central importance and benefits of dialogue in the classroom as a key to real learning (Littleton & Mercer 2013; Fisher 2009, 2013; Alexander 2009).

One of the key statutory requirements of the 'Spoken Language' strand in the 2013 English National Curriculum (DfE 2013) includes this: 'use spoken language to develop understanding through speculating, hypothesising, imagining and exploring ideas' (DfE 2013 p. 17). It is this type of spoken language that has particular relevance to the use of dialogue in RE.

So, what does creative thinking and dialogue look like, and how does it differ from other types of classroom talk? Ken Robinson (2011 p. 151) talks about creativity as 'the process of having original ideas that have value' and says 'creativity involves putting your imagination to work' (ibid. p. 143). Creative thinking in RE involves giving children the space and chance to think about beliefs and ideas about the world and our place in it. They can do this as individuals, but it is much more effective as a group engaged in dialogue. Through collaborative dialogue, children can be introduced to a range of ideas and worldviews and can build on these together. This helps them to struggle collectively with complex concepts and possibly to create new ideas as a result. Butler and Edwards (in Nottingham 2010 p. 185) called this struggle the 'pit', which they see as an essential part of the process of learning. This concept is developed further by Nottingham (2010 p. 188, 2013 p. 86). Fisher (2009 p. 8) sees the value in 'playful and divergent ideas' and 'challenging them [children] to be creative and to think in new ways'.

For creative thinking and dialogue to be really effective, it needs time, and teachers should not be afraid of giving value to this type of learning. RE should not require written responses for everything that we do. We need to recognise, plan for and value the quality learning and engagement that can take place through dialogue. 'Creative dialogue cannot be left to chance, it must be valued, encouraged and expected - and seen as essential to good teaching and learning (Fisher 2013 p. 41).

There are many methods through which children can become engaged in creative dialogue in the classroom. This chapter will explore some of these in terms of how they might be applied to RE.

P4C AND THE COMMUNITY OF ENQUIRY

Creative thinking and dialogue in RE can take place through the development of a Community of Enquiry. This is where the community enquires together as a group, as discussed earlier. Philosophy for Children (P4C) is now a well-established approach to learning in the classroom which involves children working in a Community of Enquiry. Much has already been written about P4C (Cam 1995, 2006; Fisher 2009, 2013; Haynes 2002; Hymer & Sutcliffe 2012; Nottingham 2013; Stanley 2004). P4C was originally developed by Matthew Lipman (1993) and later Ann Margaret Sharp (Splitter & Sharp 1995) in the 1960s and continues to be developed in the UK under the direction of the Society for the Advancement of Philosophical Enquiry and Reflection in Education (SAPERE; www. sapere.org.uk/) and DialogueWorks (https://dialogueworks.co.uk/).

P4C involves children in reflecting on and enquiring into philosophical ideas, and because the philosophy of religion is a major school of philosophy, RE is a natural context in which to use P4C. P4C follows a set process, which can be used as outlined in this chapter, but also some of the techniques and approaches within P4C can be usefully applied as shorter activities to use within a RE lesson. Furthermore, P4C needs to be distinguished from circle time. The two can often be confused because both require children to sit in a circle. The distinction is that P4C requires children to talk and think together as a group, a process facilitated by sitting in a circle. The full process goes as follows:

- **Starter activity** – a community-builder type of activity which helps the group come together and work as a community
- **Thought-provoking stimulus** – e.g. a story/photo/picture/object/music/ poem
- **Initial thoughts and question raising** – children identify concepts/ideas and raise (hopefully open-ended, philosophical) questions
- **Question airing** – questions are shared with the group and sorted
- **Question choosing** – a democratic process whereby questions are voted for and the most popular is chosen by the group
- **Enquiry** – the group have an enquiry around their chosen question which is facilitated rather than led by the teacher
- **Final thoughts** – children have a chance to reflect and air some of their final thoughts, tracking possible changes in their thinking through the enquiry
- **Review** – students are given a chance to review the process and their involvement in it

DialogueWorks has consolidated these processes to form four key stages. (For extended details about the process see Buckley 2012a, 2012b; Hymer & Sutcliffe 2012; Nottingham 2013 and https://dialogueworks.co.uk/.)

This can be quite a lengthy process, and undoubtedly the more children are used to it, the better at it they get. There is value in sometimes running a full enquiry process and other times doing some elements of it or running it over two sessions.

STIMULI FOR P4C IN RE

In RE there are many things which can be used as a stimulus for an enquiry. These could include religious stories or teachings, proverbs, photographs depicting religions, religious artworks, music and religious artefacts. It is useful if the stimulus is in some way interesting, challenging or even controversial, to encourage the raising of questions. By using the P4C approach you are ensuring that the children engage with the material in their own way, and you are not setting the agenda. Sometimes a teacher will say about RE, 'I'll tell them the story and then tell them what it means.' By doing this, they are imposing their own interpretation of what the story means, rather than enabling children to work out what it might mean to them or to question the puzzling or interesting aspects of it to them. This involves a change in perception of the teacher, not always as fact/information giver, (which is a crucial part of their role too) but as learning facilitator and sometimes co-enquirer.

We might also be encouraged to use a full range of stories and writings, particularly from Christianity, rather than going back to the same stories time and time again. How many times during their primary years do children hear the story of the Good Samaritan or Noah's ark from the Bible? Is there is any progression in the way they engage with the story and its messages? Using proverbs from the book of Proverbs from the Bible, for example, makes for interesting discussion. There are many of these types of 'wise' sayings within different religious traditions. There are also interesting stories that are less well-used that children can and should be introduced to. Religious and secular artworks, in both 2D and 3D, are often thought-provoking or even controversial, and give an artist's interpretation of an aspect of religion. These can be interesting stimuli for P4C enquiry. Internet search engines make access to these relatively easy, and postcards or copies can be accessed from a range of sources and depict Jesus from a range of cultural perspectives. RE Today produces several picture packs which contain a variety of religious artworks and images from different cultures (www.retoday.org.uk).

In Table 4.1 is a list of questions classes have asked and the one they have chosen to enquire into in response to a range of stimuli. In most cases I have not included all the questions asked; instead I provide a sample of some of the more philosophical ones. This illustrates the type of thinking children can do in order to create questions from a range of stimuli in RE. Several observations can be made about the questions. Younger children tend to ask questions that are more rooted in the stimulus. This is a natural part of their developing the ability to ask philosophical questions, which tend to be more removed from the original stimulus. A skilled facilitator can use their chosen question to encourage the group to develop their discussion so it does begin to get into the more philosophical issues within their question. The Year 5/6 group was very experienced at P4C, so their questions tended to be more philosophical in nature. Philip Cam (2006 p32-36) has used a 'question quadrant' to help distinguish between different types of questions that children may ask, which is a useful reference point for facilitators. With ages 7-11 years, it can also be used with children to help them sort the questions themselves that they have asked. In doing this, they begin to develop an understanding of the types of questions that they need to be asking.

Another observation is that many of the questions may not be specifically religious in nature. Again, this is not a problem, as the children are really engaging in issues and concepts rooted in the stimulus. Through this, their engagement with the stories or other stimuli is far greater than listening to a teacher read a story and rewriting it in their own words. Hopefully, therefore, their learning will be more inclusive of all children regardless of their faith or non-faith background, and their engagement will be far deeper.

DEVELOPING THINKING THROUGH EXPLORATION OF CONCEPTS

In effect, through different approaches, RE can encourage children to explore and develop their thinking around various key concepts. These concepts can fall into different categories as outlined by Erriker, Lowndes & Bellchambers (2011 ch.4) and are used as a basis for conceptual enquiry at the centre of the Hampshire Locally Agreed Syllabus for RE.

They identify such concepts as universal concepts common to all such as 'love' or 'forgiveness' ('category A'), universal religious concepts common to all or many faiths such as 'prayer' or 'god' ('category B'), and finally specific religious concepts which are exclusive to one faith such as 'Sewa' in Sikhism or 'Incarnation' in Christianity ('category C'). Enquiry into these can be encouraged through careful selection of a stimulus for P4C that might yield questions about a concept or that might lead into discussion around one. The photo in Figure 4.1 shows children's work from St Mary's CE Primary School, Kirkby Lonsdale, in Cumbria after they had begun to enquire into the universal religious concept of worship and before looking at worship in Christianity specifically.

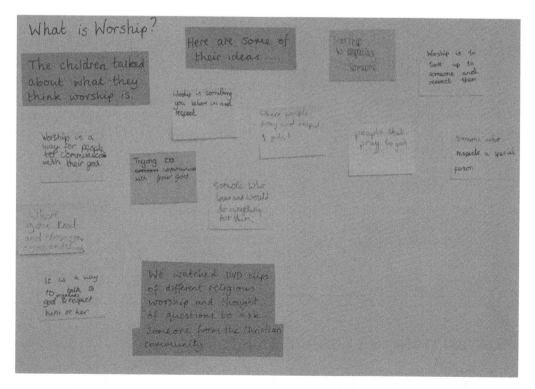

■ **Figure 4.1** Enquiring into the concept of worship (Photo David Angell) ** This belongs with the photo.

■ **Table 4.1** Examples of questions raised and chosen by children

Year Group	Stimulus	Questions Asked	Chosen Question
Y5/6	The Short and Incredibly Happy Life of Riley – Colin Thompson and Amy Lissiat (Secular story – links well to Buddhist teachings)	■ Why do humans always want more? ■ Is a rat's life better than a human's? ■ Was Riley happy all his life or was he sad sometimes?	Why do humans always want more?
Y5/6	Images of Jesus from different cultural perspectives	■ Why can't we have one image of Jesus in the world? ■ Why do people have different opinions of Jesus? ■ Does Jesus like everyone? ■ How do we know what Jesus looks like if we haven't seen him?	How do we know what Jesus looks like if we haven't seen him?
Y5/6	The Bowl of Milk and the Jasmine Flower – story from Sikhism	■ Why do people have hatred in them? ■ What is rudeness? ■ Why are people rude? ■ Why are people jealous about other people? ■ Why are people selfish?	Why are people rude?
Y5/6	Music – John Zorn – 'Ghetto Life' (music depicting Kristallnacht in the Holocaust)	■ Can music tell a story? ■ What is this music trying to tell us? (The children didn't know the context of the music before they heard it.)	Can music tell a story?
Y5/6	Music – Queen – 'Heaven for Everyone'	■ Could the earth be heaven for everyone? ■ Do people want heaven if they don't believe in God? ■ What is heaven?	What is heaven?
Y2	The Man and His Goat (story from Hinduism from the Panchatantra)	■ Why did a plan that sounded so silly work? ■ How did the man end up believing the thieves? ■ How did the thieves get away with it?	Why did a plan that sounded so silly work?

SHORTER THINKING EXERCISES

We can also do shorter P4C-style activities that help children enquire into concepts in RE. Vivianne Baumfield (2002) and Philip Cam (2006) have each introduced different thinking tools to help children develop their skills in enquiry and dialogue. Philip Cam (2006) introduced the skill of making distinctions and connections. Some examples for RE might include the following:

What is the distinction between:

■ *Prayer and worship?*
■ *Love and devotion?*
■ *A church and a cathedral?*

What is the connection between:

■ *A mosque and a synagogue?*
■ *Sewa and Zakat?*
■ *Baptism and Bar Mitzvah?*

Doing these kinds of exercises helps children to use higher order thinking skills to explore religious concepts, practices and features more deeply. Vivianne Baumfield (2002) also introduced the 'Odd One Out' exercises (Figure 4.2), again designed to help children think about religious objects or features in more depth.
Which is the odd one out?
    The answer could be:

■ The cross because it is a symbol.
■ The mosque because it is not linked to Christianity.
■ The cross because you can hold it in your hand.

Can you think of one?
The great thing about this is it can encourage divergent thinking if you keep asking for different answers or reasons. It is also very difficult to be 'wrong'. All ideas are acceptable as long as the argument or reason given is sound. These kinds of activities use two Thinking Moves (Dialogue Works 2023) of 'Connect' and 'Divide'. Thinking Moves is an A-Z of Metacognition for children devised by Roger Sutcliffe, that usefully defines many different types of thinking, such as connecting and dividing. Many of these moves are required or used in a Community of Enquiry approach.

■ **Figure 4.2** Odd one out.

All of these activities involve children in developing their thinking skills and involve them in RE in different ways, which is preferable to them just regurgitating information. Many of these can be developed to be interactive by creating sets of laminated cards that can be re-used for different exercises. Internet search engines can give you access to a wealth of such images.

Thinking by sorting

Children can be asked to sort a larger group of images into sub-groups and think of a heading for the groups. This way they are thinking in order to make connections and distinctions. They could be asked to choose ten images from the group that represent Christianity for example. If we select our images carefully we can use this type of activity to challenge children's stereotypes of a faith by including images from different cultures. This is explored in more depth in chapter 12. Another good activity is created by sorting statements, some of which are more controversial or difficult to sort than others. If you create the statements carefully to ensure they are at an appropriate level, this can even be done with children as young as four or five years old. For an example of this, see Table 4.2.

TYPES OF THINKING THE FOUR CS OF P4C

Four types of thinking are identified as being developed through P4C when it is used to its best effect in the classroom. They could also be developed through some of the activities described earlier. These four types of thinking are caring, collaborative, creative and critical. The most effective way to explore these types of thinking is by illustrating them through a class enquiry. Development in these areas is much more likely to occur with sustained and regular use of P4C and thinking skills activities in a class and throughout a school. Table 4.3 shows edited extracts from a P4C enquiry with a class of aged 9-11 pupils, which was conducted as part of a research project. This class had done P4C throughout their primary years and were an experienced group. The quality of their thinking and interactions reflects their level of experience. The enquiry stimulus, as shown in Table 4.1, was the song track, 'Heaven for Everyone' by Queen. Pseudonyms have been used for the children's names. The question chosen by the group was 'What is heaven?'

Caring thinking demonstrates care about the subject and each other and involves showing respect for people and views. All the children in this enquiry showed caring thinking. They were all very involved in the discussion; even those who did not contribute were listening and following with interest. The children respected one another's ideas and built upon them. They show examples of disagreeing respectfully (Blaylock 2007 p. 4) throughout because no one puts down another contribution. For example, Gloria shows that she respects but disagrees with Kate's first point, and puts forward her own ideas instead.

Collaborative thinking involves listening to and building on each other's ideas, but not necessarily agreeing with each other. Peter, Gloria, George and Kate all show they are building on previous contributions and develop ideas introduced earlier in the discussion. George can be seen developing his thinking in response to other ideas through his three contributions. As a group they develop their collective thinking and challenge each other to consider different ideas about heaven.

■ **Table 4.2** Activity 'charity or not charity'

Charity or Not Charity?

Give out about 10–15 cards to each child/pair to discuss and decide whether to put under the heading 'charity' or 'not charity'. They have to decide where to put it and give a reason why – thus developing their skills of decision-making, reasoning and justification.

Charity	Not charity

Getting a neighbour's shopping in snowy weather

Buying a copy of *The Big Issue*

Giving your aunty a lift to hospital

Helping out at a homeless shelter

Paying a direct debit to a cancer charity

Having some statements in the group that are unclear or more difficult to decide helps promote confusion (the 'pit of learning'; Edwards in Nottingham 2010, 2013) and dialogue about what actually constitutes charity. In this example we could extend this activity by replacing 'charity' with 'generosity' and see if we might change any statements, or get children to rank the statements from most to least charitable or generous by ordering them in a line or in a 'diamond ranking' (Nottingham 2013 p63) This activity could then link to work about Sewa in Sikhism or Zakat in Islam.

Adapted from Cam (2006 p79)

■ **Table 4.3** Extract from discussion with children 'what is heaven?'

Teacher:	So you're thinking of heaven as being like a place?
George 1:	Well, yes, I think of it as a new world; a world which is basically the same but there's no death, disease sadness or anything of that – it's just endless happiness. I think that for some people who aren't Christians, they don't believe in God. Well, I think you don't have to believe in God to have a heaven.
Leo 1:	I think there's two types of heaven: people think that when they die they go up to heaven and then people can say that heaven is like . . . people can say they're in heaven because they've got something they really enjoy doing or they have something that they really, really like.
Teacher:	There's two ways of using that word isn't there? People talk about being in heaven here in this life, and they also think about heaven as an afterlife thing. That's a useful distinction isn't it?
Kate 1:	Well, not all people's heavens are like happiness. They are but it's sort of heaven just the way you like it really to someone. It's whatever someone likes, it probably will be there. And, and it doesn't always have to be good because you if you feel like in a bad mood, sometimes you just want everything else to be in a bad mood – it's just not everything has to be happy there – but everything's just the way you like it.
Teacher:	What you're saying is people would have an individual idea of what heaven looks or feels like. . . . That's an interesting new idea isn't it – related to feelings.
Peter 1:	Well, when I first heard the word heaven it seemed to remind me it was something happy for you. So you can make it how you want it to be and others can make it how they want it for them.
Gloria 1:	If you, say if you don't feel happy in a place you wouldn't really call that place heaven in a way. Heaven is for people somewhere where they can feel good and not so worried or anything. It doesn't make them feel bad.
George 2:	When Kate said that you could be in a bad mood and that place would be unhappy. What I think of heaven is once you're in heaven there is nothing that can make you in a bad mood. But then when I've just stopped and thinking it over there is kind of theory where you might be looking down on one of your descendants – and they might be in jail quite a lot or something and that might be you looking down on them and thinking wow that's really sad.
Teacher:	You mean looking down on someone who is still alive?
George 3:	Yep. So it's kind of hard to say whether you can be sad in heaven. After thinking that, I think perhaps you could be sad in heaven if something like that happened. But literally in the place heaven I don't think there is anything that can upset you, but if you look down on earth, not literally, but you know what I mean.
Teacher:	Yes – so what you're saying is that you don't think there are things in heaven that will make you sad, but there may be things – connections on earth that might make you sad.
Kate 2:	I know in heaven if you were sad and if you wanted everyone else to be sad that would happen. Sometimes when I'm a bit moody and someone comes along and she's really cheerful, I get really annoyed. So sometimes you wanted people to be annoyed because that would make you feel happy. Everything would go the way that you wanted it to be even if you're unhappy. Like if you were sad and everyone else was sad that's the way that you want it and that's the way it would happen.

Creative thinking is introducing new ideas/new ways of thinking about things. George (1), Leo (1) and Kate (1) all introduce new ideas, and it is the thinking introduced by Kate (1), considering whether there is anything unpleasant in heaven, that challenges the other children and forms the basis of most of the subsequent discussion. She considers whether you can be unhappy in heaven, because sometimes she actually enjoys being grumpy. Others either reject or accept this idea and use it to develop their thinking.

Critical thinking involves clarifying, challenging and evaluating ideas. We can see in George's second and third contributions that he is really thinking about the ideas introduced by Kate and evaluating them. Many of the children are trying to make sense of these ideas and assimilate them into their own previous perceptions. Peter and Gloria are also evaluating and challenging Kate's ideas. Peter and George consider Kate's idea and seem to agree with it in some form, whereas Gloria rejects it.

'A vital feature of philosophy is its interest in rearranging, shifting, displacing and reframing ideas and beliefs' (Haynes 2002 p. 42). Through P4C, as illustrated in the previous enquiry extract, we can see children doing just this. Wittgenstein (2009) observed that all categories and concepts can be broken down under interrogation because words are tools not essences. P4C is seeking to do just this by pulling apart what we mean when we use words to label concepts. These are often words that we take for granted and don't take the time or opportunity to work out what they might mean. The four Cs of thinking are explored in more depth in many P4C sources. Consider Fisher (2009, 2013); Nottingham (2013); Cam (1995, 2006); Haynes (2002) and Hymer & Sutcliffe (2012).

RECORDING CREATIVE THINKING AND DIALOGUE

As mentioned earlier, RE is a subject that should not always require children to write something every session, and that is one of the things children often enjoy about it. The challenge for the teacher, though, is when and how to record the children's attainment and progress through creative thinking and dialogue. After a wonderful discussion like the one in Table 4.3, it can be a really demotivating experience for children to have to go away and 'write about the discussion'. There are a number of strategies for managing this process of keeping a record of children's enquiries and development of thinking skills.

Here are a few suggestions:

- **Teacher's field notes** the teacher keeps a reflective diary and records the enquiry and any notable features in terms of key contributors; progress made by particular individuals; someone who is unusually quiet or involved.
- **A record sheet** which looks for particular thinking and speaking and listening skills, such as giving a reason; making decisions; agreeing or disagreeing; following on from a previous point. This can be recorded by an observer of the discussion such as a teaching assistant.
- **A class record/scrapbook** where a class record is kept of children's thinking on Post-it notes and with sample pieces of work. Children can be free to add to this through the week if they think of extra ideas.
- **A child's reflective diary** children can complete this in a variety of ways as and when they deem it necessary. They could record thoughts in thought bubbles, or on Post-its, or by drawing or creating thought maps.

■ **Use of a digital recorder** allows discussions to be recorded and analysed at a later time if needed.

■ A **question/thinking wall display** which allows children to add thoughts/ questions through the week.

Examples of a scrap book are presented in Figures 4.3, 4.4, 4.5 and 4.6. These photos show some of the work of children in St Mary's CE Primary School in Kirkby Lonsdale, Cumbria and demonstrate how a scrapbook for RE can effectively keep a class record of the children's talking, thinking and learning. (Thanks to Emily Morris, RE subject leader at St Mary's School, for allowing us to share the children's work.) Figure 4.3 shows a record of the children's thoughts about the concept of love. Figure 4.4 shows the children's work after thinking about things they feel strongly enough to stand up for. The following photos (Figures 4.5 and 4.6) show the children reflecting their ideas about the concept of conflict through artwork in the style of artist Keith Haring. This work followed exploration of Keith Haring's artwork and a lot of discussion around the concept of conflict.

THE POWER OF P4C

P4C and the other thinking strategies that encourage collaborative and creative thinking and dialogue in the classroom have many benefits, both visible and hidden. P4C often enables unexpected children to flourish, as it does not necessarily equate to ability in

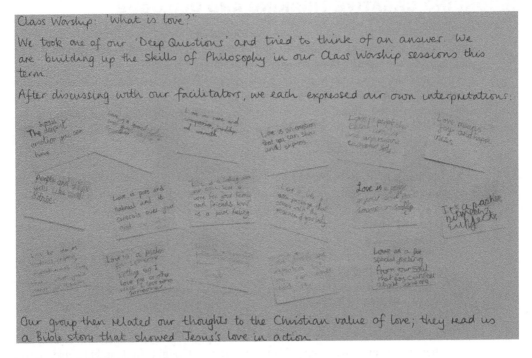

■ **Figure 4.3** What is love.

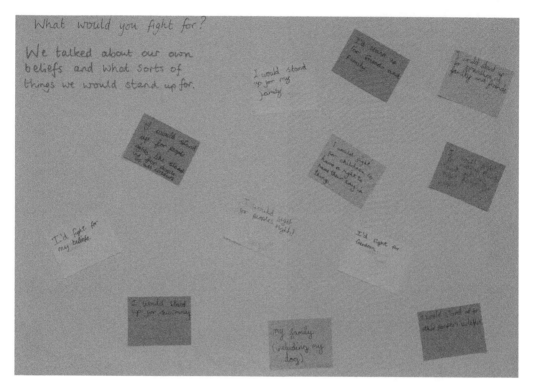

■ **Figure 4.4** What would you fight for.

other areas, particularly literacy. It can challenge labels such as 'more able' or 'less able', which supports the arguments of Dweck (2000, 2006) against labelling children in such ways and advocates development of 'growth mindsets'. Hymer & Gershon (2014) and Nottingham (2013) explore this theory in more depth and give many more practical ideas for doing this in the classroom that could be used in RE. Because P4C is not dependent upon reading and writing skills, it allows all children to participate on an equal footing, which can be an unusual and empowering experience for many children (Prescott 2017). The value of having your voice heard or your question chosen by the group can be very transformative, particularly if this does not often happen in other areas of the curriculum (see the section of chapter 7 entitled 'Igniting a spark'.) Creative thinking and dialogue in RE also offers important opportunities for spiritual, moral, social and cultural development (see chapter 7). It allows children to develop in all these areas because it involves them in thinking for themselves in order to express their ideas. In order to operate effectively as a group, they have to develop the skills to think and listen and talk together. In RE they are often thinking about the transcendental, and so opportunities for the different dimensions of spirituality to be developed are offered. Cultural development can be offered by introducing children to music, writing and artwork from a range of cultures to show diversity within and between religions.

■ **Figure 4.5** 'Conflict' pictures in the style of Keith Haring (Photo David Angell).

CONCLUSION

In this chapter we have considered the benefits of creative thinking and dialogue in RE, as well as practical ways of making this happen in the classroom. It remains to be said that one essential requirement of the teacher in all of this is that they are willing to reflect and think for themselves about some of the questions the children will be considering. We must model this ourselves and see ourselves as co-enquirers alongside the children. If we are obviously interested in ideas and new thoughts, we will encourage them to begin to play around with ideas and begin to develop their own arguments in support of their ideas. This links to DialogueWorks' notion of the 'philosophical teacher' (https://dialogueworks .co.uk/).

■ **Figure 4.6** More 'conflict' pictures in the style of Keith Haring (Photo David Angell).

In P4C enquiries we also have to let go of control somewhat in order for the process to give them real voice. It is important that the children choose the question they like, even if the teacher does not think it is the most interesting one. This can be difficult to do sometimes, but it is a necessary part of giving them voice, both collectively and individually.

Finally, we need to be genuinely interested in what children think and what they have to say. We need to respect their ideas and their emerging understanding of concepts. Children can surprise us with the level of their thinking, and this can happen from Early Years upwards. We need to both hear this and respect it. To return to where we started, the question to ask yourself is this: do you have the 'ears to hear'? (Matthews 1994 p. 15).

REFERENCES

Alexander, R. (2009): Children, Their World, Their Education: Final Report and Recommendations of the Cambridge Primary Review . Abingdon: Routledge.

Baumfield, V. (2002): Thinking Through Religious Education. Cambridge: Chris Kington Publishing.

Blaylock, L. (2007): Inclusive RE. Birmingham: RE Today services.

Buckley, J. (2012a): Pocket P4C: Getting Started with Philosophy for Children. Chelmsford: One Slice Books Ltd.

Buckley, J. (2012b): Thinkers' Games: Making Thinking Physical. Chelmsford: One Slice Books Ltd.

Cam, P. (1995): Thinking Together: Philosophical Inquiry for the Classroom. Alexandria, NSW: Hale and Iremonger.

Cam, P. (2006): 20 Thinking Tools: Collaborative Inquiry for the Classroom. Camberwell, Victoria: Australian Council for Educational Research Press.

Commission on Religious Education (2018) Final Report: Religion and Worldviews; The Way Forward. A National Plan for RE. London: Commission on Religious Education.

Department for Education (DfE) (2013): The New National Curriculum for England. London: Department for Education.

Dialogue Works (2023) teaching and learning available at https://dialogueworks.co.uk/ accessed on 15.4.23

Dweck, C. (2000): Self-Theories: Their Role in Motivation, Personality and Development. Hove: Psychology Press.

Dweck, C. (2006): Mindset: How You Can Fulfil Your Potential. London: Constable and Robinson.

Erriker, C., Lowndes, J. & Bellchambers, E. (2011): Primary Religious Education - A New Approach: Conceptual Enquiry in Primary RE. Abingdon: Routledge.

Fisher, R. (2009): Creative Dialogue. Abingdon: Routledge.

Fisher, R. (2013): Teaching Thinking (4th edition). London: Bloomsbury.

Haynes, J. (2002): Children as Philosophers: Learning Through Enquiry and Dialogue in the Primary Classroom. Abingdon: Routledge/Falmer.

Hymer, B. & Gershon, M. (2014): Growth Mindset Pocketbook. Alresford: Teachers' Pocketbooks.

Hymer, B. & Sutcliffe, R. (2012): P4CPocketbook. Alresford: Teachers' Pocketbooks.

Lipman, M. (1993): Thinking Children and Education. Dubuque, IA: Kendall Hunt Publishing.

Littleton, K. & Mercer, N. (2013): Interthinking: Putting Talk to Work. Abingdon: Routledge.

Matthews, G. (1994): The Philosophy of Childhood. London: Harvard University Press.

Nottingham, J. (2010): Challenging Learning. Berwick upon Tweed: JN Publishing.

Nottingham, J. (2013): Encouraging Learning: How You Can Help Children Learn. Abingdon: Routledge.

OfSTED (2013): Religious Education: Realising the Potential. Manchester: OfSTED.

OfSTED (2021): Research Review Series: Religious Education. Manchester: OfSTED.

Prescott, G. (2017): Challenging Assumptions and Making Progress in Anderson, B (Ed.) Philosophy for Children: Theory and Praxis in Teacher Education. Abingdon: Routledge.

Robinson, K. (2011): Out of Our Minds: Learning to Be Creative. Chichester: Capstone Publishing Ltd.

Splitter, L. & Sharp, A. (1995): Teaching for Better Thinking. Camberwell, Victoria: Australian Council for Educational Research Press.

Stanley, S. (2004): But Why? Developing Philosophical Thinking in the Classroom. Stafford: Network Educational Press Ltd.

Wittgenstein, L. (2009): Philosophical Investigations. Hacker, P. & Schulte, J. (eds). Chichester: Wiley-Blackwell.

CREATIVE SKILLS AND STRATEGIES

CHAPTER 5

The TASC Model

Sally Elton-Chalcraft and Penny Hollander

Within religious education (RE) as well as other curriculum areas, the capacity for creative and critical thinking is essential for effective life-long learning. Enquiry and reflection are vital components regardless of age or ability.

This chapter aims to

- Explain the TASC model and how it can be used in RE
- Use the TASC model to explore a Hindu concept of Brahman
- Present other practical lesson ideas drawing on the TASC model

The Ofsted report Realising the Potential on RE provision in schools emphasises that the most effective RE placed enquiry at its heart and from the outset engaged pupils in their learning (Ofsted 2013, 5). There are many different ways to develop an enquiring and questioning approach to the RE curriculum but this chapter will focus on one particular model, **Thinking Actively in a Social Context**, commonly abbreviated to **TASC**. This model can be used widely across many curriculum areas, ages and contexts. It is well suited to RE in that the whole process promotes active thinking, questioning and reflection which is the bedrock of good RE in the classroom. These vital skills help children to learn about Religions and Worldviews in a variety of contexts and so this chapter in particular is relevant for both British and international audiences. The TASC model is not exclusive to Religion and Worldviews education, (Alhusaini 2018), it can be utilised in any curriculum area in any educational context worldwide. The TASC model encourages:

- Asking questions
- Investigation
- Drawing conclusions
- Evaluation
- Reflection
- Expression

DOI: 10.4324/9781003361480-7

This chapter will outline the different elements within the TASC process as a generic tool for promoting effective learning across a wide range of curriculum and also how it can be adapted for use within RE. An example of how it has been used within one primary RE classroom for the first time is also included, with both teacher and pupil evaluations of its usefulness for learning within an RE topic on Hinduism. Cross-curricular links are woven into their work. There are further suggestions for other ways of incorporating TASC into other RE topic areas.

THE TASC MODEL

The inspiration for this approach to learning was inspired by Belle Wallace, who has written extensively about it both from a general educational perspective and also for specific subjects and for different age phases (Wallace 2001, 2009, 2015). The TASC website, www. tascwheel.com, shows how it has developed within schools of all ages and contexts, nationally and internationally, and contains many practical examples of where it has been successfully implemented. TASC is not only a practical tool but also has a strong theoretical basis drawn from the work of Vygotsky (1978) and Sternberg (1985). Wallace incorporates Vygotsky's emphasis on the importance of language in the development of higher psychological processes, using existing knowledge or 'hooks' to extend learning and create new networks of understanding (Wallace 2001, 7). For Vygotsky, learning can be developed by providing educational support for the gap between what has already been mastered and further achievement. This zone of proximal development (ZPD) is an integral part of the TASC process. Sternberg's view of intelligence and effective learning processes for all learners by using a range of thinking skills and strategies to reflect, consolidate and transfer (i.e. key processes of metacognition) are also key to the TASC model (Wallace 2001, 8). TASC runs alongside Bloom's taxonomy of learning (1956) which is commonly regarded as foundational within educational thinking (Figure 5.1). It was revised by Anderson, Krathwohl et al. (2001) to reflect a more active form of thinking and slight re-ordering. Figure 5.2 then, perhaps, is more accurate in teachers' application in creating an effective climate for learning within their classrooms. To understand the principles of TASC, Wallace (2009, 2015) uses the imagery of a wheel to explain the ongoing cycle of learning (see Figure 5.3).

TASC as an acronym is explained in the following way:

Thinking – We are all capable of thinking, and improving our thinking! Thinking makes us human, capable and caring

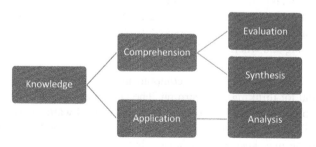

■ **Figure 5.1** Bloom's taxonomy of learning.

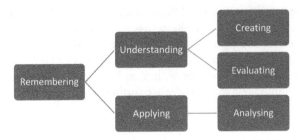

■ **Figure 5.2** Anderson, Krathwohl et al.'s revision of Bloom's taxonomy.

■ **Figure 5.3** A wheel of learning.

Actively – We all need to be active and do our own thinking – no one can do our thinking *to* us! We need to be involved and interested and to do our thinking for ourselves – with appropriate guidance, of course

Social – We learn best when we can talk and work with others. We do a lot of learning when we share activities, testing out our ideas, listening to alternative ways of doing the task and often copying 'better' ideas

Context – The context needs to be relevant to our background and stage of development. We all learn when we understand not only what we are learning but also why we are learning and where it will lead us

The TASC wheel has different components or stages in the thinking process. Each step is essential for thinking and learning. The wheel provides visual imagery for stages in the whole process in that it can travel forwards or backwards or stop at particular points, so that children of differing abilities may move at the pace that is best suited to their learning. Some may keep moving forwards through the stages, others may need to retrace their steps, whilst there may be those who can only go so far and then need to stop. The structure is important, and at each stage children are encouraged to reflect, question and consolidate their own learning. There is for many the temptation to skip a stage or two, e.g. from the 'generating ideas' stage to 'let's do it' without the 'best idea' segment. This needs to be resisted because too many ideas, insufficiently considered or refined in terms of whether they are possible to achieve within the constraints of the classroom, may result in both frustration and failure to complete the task. Thus, effective learning will not be achieved (except that it might be a useful lesson to bear in mind for future tasks). The last stage, 'learn from experience', is equally vital in that it crystallises learning and allows children to take what they have learned in this context, apply it to other areas of work and reflect on what they might change on another occasion.

THE TASC PROCESS

As a process, TASC takes both time and independent thinking by the children. At each stage, they are asked to reflect on the following questions to ensure that their thinking is clear, focussed and may involve risk taking which will add to their learning from experience (see Table 5.1).

Wallace (2001) points out that the TASC process can be introduced to children in a number of ways, including whole school projects, as a means of reporting back from what has been learned from a visit and problem-solving activities. As children become accustomed to this way of working, they become increasingly effective and independent learners. However, by definition a process takes time.

Developing children's problem-solving and thinking skills initially takes time, but once children are familiar with the skills and with using them, they learn more efficiently and we save time.

(Wallace 2001, 12)

THE TASC MODEL AND RE

To see how the TASC model provides a good vehicle for learning in RE, it is first necessary to consider the purposes and challenges of RE in the curriculum, outlined more comprehensively in Chapter 2. At its best, good RE makes a significant contribution to children's education by challenging them to think about the meaning and purpose of life, beliefs about God, the 'big' questions of life, what it means to be human and issues of right and wrong. They need to learn about different religious and other worldviews as well as explore their own viewpoints, reflecting and expressing ideas and insights about the impact of different faiths and worldviews (see Religious Education Council 2013, 10). Alongside knowledge and understanding of Religion and Worldviews and what they can learn from it, children's progress in RE also requires the use and application of a range of general educational skills in each key stage. We have drawn on skills outlined by Rivett and Blaylock (2006, 545) in their handbook for teachers of RE which incorporate both critical and creative thinking skills to:

■ **Investigate** – use books or websites to select information and highlight what is relevant, collect information from churches, other places of worship, charities etc.

■ **Table 5.1** Using the TASC process (Wallace 2015)

Gather and Organise	What information do I have? How much do I understand? Have I done anything like this before? What questions can I ask?
Identify	What are my goals… What am I trying to do? What do I need to complete the task? What are the obstacles to completing the task?
Generate	Where can I find more information? Which resources will help me the most? How many ways are there to complete the task? What do other people think of my ideas?
Decide	Which idea/s would be the most effective and why? How will I plan what I am going to do? *(What will I need and how will I go about completing the task?)* How will I know if what I am doing is effective/working?
Implement	Is everything going to plan? *(Do I need to adapt or change my plan?)* Have I got everything I need to complete the task? How well am I doing?
Evaluate	What have I managed to do? Did everything go according to plan? Did I work well on my own/or as part of a group? Am I ready to share my ideas/work with others?
Communicate	Who will I be presenting my ideas/work to? How could I best present my work/ideas to others? *(What would I need to prepare and in what way?)* Have I included all of the information that I need to?
Learn from Experience	*Looking at the whole task from start to finish:* What do I feel worked particularly well and why? How could I improve aspects of my work if completing similar tasks in the future?

Watch and listen to visual/audio sources about different religious stories, beliefs and practices

■ **Interpret** – talk about meaning in artefacts, pictures, paintings, symbols and respond to questions about them, e.g. what do you think it is? What is going on? Read prayers and meditations, then talk about what they show about a person's beliefs and feelings

■ **Reflect** – provide opportunities for pupils to describe how actions and atmosphere in different religious situations make them feel. Ask them to explore the thoughts and feelings associated with different religious music. Can they write a prayer or poem that a Christian, Jewish or Muslim child might use? Provide a 'wall of wisdom' for pupils to record their insights

■ **Empathise** – use role play or freeze frames to capture essential religious ideas or themes. Use hot seating to see another person's perspective in relation to a religious story

■ **Analyse** – what are the key beliefs, religious vocabulary associated with a particular aspect in a religion. Identify similarities and differences between religious faiths/ worldviews and practices and practices within and between faiths studied

■ **Synthesise** – notice similarities between stories and practices from religions and talk about the prayers, texts and places of worship, drawing conclusions about similarities

■ **Express** – use creative approaches, e.g. drama, role play, dance, mime, music to illustrate a religious story or teaching. Make a collage, diagram, video, presentation, (written or oral) to show your understanding of the meaning of the particular teaching or practice

■ **Apply** – write a story which shows the meaning behind a faith story or religious teaching in a different or modern context. Design your own symbols which illustrate what a particular religion believes and teaches. Think about the response of a religious leader such as Jesus, Guru Nanak, Buddha to a particular dilemma

■ **Evaluate** – what are the most important statements for a Christian, Jew, Muslim, Hindu, Buddhist in relation to different life issues and contribute your own response

While some regulatory bodies (for example Ofsted) might emphasise that the need for enquiry is a central element of the learning process in RE, and stress the importance of enquiry-based learning in RE to raise standards and expectations, their surveys show insufficient evidence from schools visited that this has been successfully addressed (Ofsted 2013). So when there is a perceived need for more independent learning, cross-curricular links and challenging tasks, the TASC model provides a solution. Webster (2010, 989) cites an example of how one student teacher adapted the TASC wheel to inform medium-term planning for an RE unit of work on sacred spaces. Sacred spaces for Year 2 pupils, within a topic on 'People Who Help Us':

Gather:
Who helps you
Who helps in religion
Identify:
What is your sacred space
How do you feel
Generate:
Visit a church
How does it help people
Decide:
What do you think a special space is for
Implement:
Visit a Gurdwara

Create questions
Evaluate:
What do we know about sacred spaces and how people help
Communicate:
What is your own special place
Create one
Learn from experience:
What have you learned about how people use a sacred space
How does it help people? How might a special place help you
Further examples are presented in the section below

WORKING THROUGH THE TASC WHEEL IN EXPLORING HINDU BELIEFS ABOUT THE CONCEPT OF GOD

The following example is taken from RE lessons within a small village church school. The teacher involved and the Key Stage 2 children (Years 5 and 6) had never used the approach before. The teacher was keen to use the TASC wheel to develop children's independence in learning and also develop their reflective and evaluative skills within RE. She also wanted to challenge the children to use skills they had developed through literacy, drama and IT. After the experience of using the TASC approach in RE for the first time, she evaluated the process and shared what she had learned from experience for both herself and the children. She was particularly pleased with how it helped her to evaluate individual children's progression in their learning and how she could encourage them to develop their learning further (see Table 5.2).

■ **Table 5.2** A teacher's view of TASC: Baking a cake

A teacher's view of TASC: Baking a cake

At first glance, the TASC wheel looked rather complicated to use until more research provided a wealth of information, including case studies, which I found very helpful, giving me an insight of ways to use the wheel with the class.

I used the example of baking a cake in order to explain the way the wheel works, e.g. we cannot start baking (*implement*) until we know which cake we are baking and what ingredients we need (*gather/identify/generate/decide*); we cannot taste the cake to see if it has turned out right (*evaluate/communicate/learn from experience*) until we have baked it.

The children seemed to understand this analogy and therefore found it useful when they came to use the wheel, knowing the logical steps they needed to take to complete the overall learning objective, but also realising that they could (and often needed to) refer back around the wheel. The majority of children understood that they should always look back to the success criteria so they didn't migrate off topic.

I will definitely use the wheel again, as it can sometimes take too long to refresh learning of a topic before moving on. I found it a helpful tool for me to assess the progression of children's learning from week to week and also their own reflections of their learning.

I will definitely use the wheel again... I found it a helpful tool for me to assess the progression of children's learning from week to week and also their own reflections of their learning.

Gather and Organise	Identify
Hindu beliefs about God – Brahman	**What do Hindus believe about God?**
Hindu traditions are diverse	*What do we need to do*
Many Hindu traditions believe there are three main deities: **Brahma, Vishnu and Shiva**	Find out what the following tell us about Hindu beliefs in God:
The lotus flower represents cleanliness	■ The Trimurti
When a Hindu dies they come back as something else – **reincarnation**	■ Stories about Brahma, Vishnu and Shiva
	■ Stories about Brahman and Creation

The RE lessons for this class were on a one-hour-per-week basis. The children worked in small groups to plan a presentation on Hindu beliefs about God. As this was their first use of the TASC approach, the teacher decided it would be helpful to all the children to get used to the idea of using the TASC wheel to complete the first two sections, gather and organise and identify, as whole class activities (see Table 5.3).

The outcomes from these two parts of the wheel were added to a master copy for each group to use and to give weekly reminders about what had already been done. Ideas and information were generated through a mix of teacher-led activities and independent research from books and the internet. Success criteria were also included on the wheel to ensure that the children remained focussed on what they were trying to achieve throughout the topic. Appropriate teacher intervention also ensured that pupils stayed on task. The progression through each stage of the TASC wheel addressed the issue raised by Ofsted (2013, 10) about the need for pupils to process their findings through evaluation and reflection. As part of this whole class work, children in their small groups researched Hindu beliefs about God from both the internet and materials from *RE IDEAS: GOD* (Moss 2013, 1924). In particular they looked at stories about Brahma, Vishnu and Shiva and thought about the questions that were posed, e.g. what does this story have to say about God? Why do you think this story is popular today? Each group then produced a freeze frame of a key moment in their chosen story, thus linking RE with work done in drama. The intention was to help them to gain a deeper understanding of the story and what it had to say about God from a Hindu perspective, as well as to make links between Hindu teachings and their own ideas of God or their beliefs about the meaning of life. This fulfils Level 4 requirements in RE (the expected level of attainment for the majority of children at the end of Key Stage 2). The other segments of the wheel, including the content of the presentation and how it would be presented, were done independently by each small group. The teacher acted as a facilitator and ensured that all children kept on task.

Generate ideas: Pupils used a mixture of sources to gain information and also to generate ideas for the focus of their presentation. Ideas from information sourced from books in the school library, the internet and specific resources given by the teacher were discussed by each group as well as ideas about possible ways to present the information.

Decide: Each group decided independently which God/s they would use as a focus for the presentation. All groups decided to focus on only one God as this followed on from their earlier freeze frame work. This seemed the safest option given that this was a new way of working.

Implement: The use of PowerPoint was the universal choice for the presentations with a mixture of images and written material. Most groups divided out the different roles of researchers, preparing the words to say, finding images and incorporating them into the PowerPoint presentation. Adaptations were made as they went along in order to ensure the presentation had sufficient detail but was clear enough to present to others in the class

Evaluate and communicate: Children in each group were both pleased with what they were doing but also quite self-critical (e.g. see Figure 5.4).

Learn from experience: Children commented on their experiences of using the TASC approach from both an RE perspective and a more general thinking skills perspective.

The general consensus was that it was a good way to gain a deeper understanding of the place and purposes of different gods and goddesses in Hinduism and the signifi-cance of the symbols identified with each of them. They were more confident in using the religious vocabulary associated with some aspects of Hinduism. The structured stages

▨ **Figure 5.4** Pupils reflections about the TASC process.

of TASC helped to clarify their thinking, even though some children found it confusing at first and were anxious to create the presentation at the outset! They acknowledged that this approach requires practice and on another occasion could use alternative means of presentation, e.g the use of posters to illustrate what they were saying. Listening to the ideas of others in the group was another suggested idea of improving what they did another time.

There were other comments related to general learning principles (see Figure 5.5). As one pupil explained:

If I were to use it (TASC) in future with my homework on my own, I think it would help by reminding me what different aspects I need to add to my work. I think I will get more done if I use the TASC wheel.

Although not stated explicitly, there is perhaps the idea that more thinking through the different stages of the TASC process produces for this pupil more effective learning.

Not all comments were expressed as positively but as the teacher explained:

The majority of children thought that although at first the TASC wheel looked complicated to use, the more they used it, the easier it became to understand how it was a helpful tool to aid their learning and progression.

Other points made included:

■ The enjoyment of collaborating and working together to develop ideas; everyone felt involved in the process.
■ Virtual stimulus of the TASC wheel to refer back to in order to refresh their memory and keep focussed.

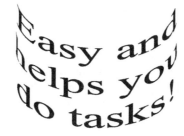

■ **Figure 5.5** Pupils first reactions to learning through TASC.

FURTHER IDEAS FOR USING TASC WITHIN THE CONTEXT OF RE

The TASC website (www.tascwheel.com) provides a multitude of ideas for using the process with children of all ages and multiple abilities within different curriculum areas. Although religious education is not specifically mentioned, ideas can be easily adapted to fit in with the RE curriculum and include cross-curricular links, particularly with art, music, drama, literacy, design technology and food technology:

▨ Following a visit to a place of worship, consider the most important features within a place of worship and how they are relevant for believers. Design your own place of worship, giving an explanation of what is important to include and the reasons for your choices

▨ Create a dance that describes a religious celebration and its significance for believers

▨ Create music that can be used to tell a sacred story. Choose sounds and rhythms that match the mood of the story. Can you explain what the story is teaching believers? How does this relate to your own experience

▨ Write a poem that describes a concept that is important within Christianity and what you can learn from this, e.g. creation, salvation, forgiveness, heaven

▨ Investigate what it means to belong to a community within Buddhism. How can you demonstrate that through art and drama

▨ (Possible starting point: REtoday 2012 *Opening up Community*)

▨ Design an Easter egg box which reflects the key elements of the Easter story

▨ Plan and prepare for a religious celebration meal. Get the food ready. Design the invitations, decide about music and other activities you will include (e.g. Shabbat from Judaism)

▨ Create an interactive display which shows how and why a religious leader you have been studying is an inspiration to believers

The list is not extensive or exclusive but rather provides a few suggestions as to how TASC may be flexibly applied within an RE unit of work.

SUMMARY AND CONCLUSIONS

TASC is a tool that can be used in a wide range of effective learning experiences. It has a strong theoretical basis from two important theories about how children best learn and it underpins the practice. It is a generic model which is not confined to particular curriculum areas. Rather it helps to develop many skills that are necessary for effective learning. It can be used in a cross-curricular way, without losing sight of discrete subject learning objectives. It is essentially an interactive approach to learning, engaging pupils to share their ideas and communicate these to a wider audience. Opportunities for the students to evaluate and reflect about what they have done are integral to the process and help to consolidate learning. Pupil autonomy and independence are other key features of the approach. Wallace, Humphries and Evans (2019) demonstrate how the model is particularly suited to the more able in their report based in a Welsh context. The wheel provides support and direction as required to ensure pupils maintain their focus on the purpose of the task. As a process, it takes time to practise and refine but provides opportunities for sustained learning. It embraces both critical and creative thinking strategies.

For RE teaching and learning, the TASC process can address many of the weaknesses that Realising the Potential (Ofsted 2013) raises about clear focus and enquiry-based learning. Teachers can use TASC to develop childrens' skills in their questioning, knowledge and understanding of religions as well as giving opportunity to make connections and contrasts with their own experiences.

TASC is a flexible model, particularly useful for Religion and Worldviews Education in a range of contexts, including international settings where RE may be configured differently to the UK context. Examples of how it has been and could be used within the RE classroom illustrate the potential for cross-curricular links. It is acknowledged that this is only one of many approaches that can be used to promote effective RE learning in the classrooms, but certainly one that should be considered.

ACKNOWLEDGEMENTS

Grateful thanks to the staff at Allithwaite CE primary school, particularly the RE co-ordinator Mrs Lucy Stanway, and to the Year 5 and 6 pupils who trialled the TASC approach in the RE lessons.

REFERENCES

Alhusaini, A. (2018) Using the TASC model to develop gifted students' creativity: Analytical review. *Journal for the Education of Gifted Young Scientists*, 6(3), pp. 11–29. Retrieved from https://dergipark.org.tr/en/pub/jegys/issue/39595/457048

Anderson, L. W., Krathwohl, D. R., et al. (eds.) (2001) *A Taxonomy for Learning, Teaching and Assessing: A Revision of Bloom's Taxonomy of Educational Objectives*, New York: Longman.

Bloom, B. S., et al. (1956) *Taxonomy of Educational Objectives: The Classification of Educational Goals. Handbook 1 Cognitive Domain*, New York: Longmans Green.

Moss, F. (ed.) (2013) *RE IDEAS: GOD*, Birmingham: Christian Education Publications.

OfSTED (2013) *Realising the Potential* (p. 130068), Manchester: OfSTED. Retrieved from www.ofsted.gov.uk/ resources/130068

Religious Education Council (2013) *A Curriculum Framework for Religious Education in England*, London: Religious Education Council for England and Wales.

RE Today (2012) *Opening up Community*, Bedfordshire: Newnorth Print Ltd.

Rivett, R. & Blaylock, L. (2006) *A Teacher's Handbook for Religious Education*, Birmingham: Christian Education Publications.

Sternberg, R. J. (1985) *Beyond IQ: A Triarchic Theory of Human Intelligence*, Cambridge: Cambridge University Press.

Vygotsky, L. S. (1978) *Mind in Society: The Development of Higher Psychological Processes* (Cole, M., et al. eds.), Cambridge, MA: Harvard University Press.

Wallace, B. (2001) *Teaching Thinking Skills Across the Primary Curriculum*, London: David Fulton Publishers Ltd.

Wallace, B. (2009) Developing problem-solving and thinking skills in the mainstream curriculum. Retrieved from www.tascwheel.com

Wallace, B. (2015) Using the TASC thinking and problem-solving framework to create a curriculum of opportunity across the full spectrum of human abilities: TASC–thinking actively in a social context. In Videgor, H. and Harris, C. (eds.) *Applied Practice for Educators of Gifted and Able Learners* (pp. 111–130). Brill. E-Book (PDF)ISBN: 978-94-6300-004-8

Wallace, B., Humphries, W. & Evans, K. (2019) On demonstrating the development of the Thinking Actively in a Social Context (TASC) problem-solving approach in schools in South Wales (UK). *Gifted Education International*, 35(2), pp. 152–160.

Webster, M. (2010) *Creative Approaches to Teaching Primary RE*, Essex: Pearson Education Ltd.

CHAPTER 6

EFFECTIVE AND CREATIVE PLANNING AND ASSESSMENT

Fiona Moss and Katie Freeman

This chapter aims to help you

- Understand curriculum design and progression mapping
- Appreciate different forms of knowledge in RE
- Understand there is diversity within as well as between belief systems
- Consider how best to plan and assess creative and effective RE
- Address concerns of regulatory bodies (for example OFSTED) about less effective practice in primary school RE.

We hope that this chapter will give teachers food for thought but also through real-school examples to show how this works in the primary classroom.

CURRICULUM DESIGN

Curriculum design is a central factor in ensuring that children experience high-challenge, creative and rigorous Religious Education within our schools. Many SACRE agreed syllabi and those designed by multi academy trusts draw on the importance of spiral curriculums; these carefully crafted structures enable pupils to build upon prior knowledge as they move through each year group, so that they know more and remember more.

Although these syllabi are designed by SACREs, trusts or external agencies, it is also important that the leader responsible for Religious Education uses their professional judgement to craft this structure into a curriculum that will enthuse and support all learners in the school within which they teach. It is vital that teachers have the subject knowledge, expertise and confidence to look through the syllabus, structure the units of work, and ensure that the units are placed at times that will support the children to build upon prior knowledge, vocabulary, skills and prepare them for future content that they will encounter as the curriculum progresses.

DOI: 10.4324/9781003361480-8

Our previous research outlined that well-sequenced curriculums are also structured to help pupils integrate new knowledge into their existing knowledge and make enduring connections between content, ideas and concepts. When pupils encounter new content in RE, their prior knowledge has an impact on what they learn. Prior knowledge that pupils need in order to learn new content may include, for example, vocabulary, concepts, narratives and/or factual knowledge.

(OFSTED 2021)

It is the role of the subject leader to ensure that teaching is ordered so that pupils build on and embed previous knowledge and understanding; for example learning about belonging by pupils in early years might be built on by looking at baby welcoming ceremonies or the importance of communities celebrating religious festivals. In Year 2 (see Table 6.1) they may learn about Muslim people for the first time in an in-depth way but build on learning in earlier years about Eid celebrations. Learning about Muslim people allows them to compare and contrast the understanding many Christians have about who God is with what they have learnt about the Shahadah. Whilst the focus in the example is principally on two religious worldviews in the thematic unit, at the end of the year pupils can use their learning about Muslims and Christians and perhaps compare them to a dharmic worldview or a non-religious worldview in the units on celebration, depending on the content studied.

When sequencing pupils' learning and building on prior learning, subject leaders should also consider what pupils have encountered across the school curriculum; for example, learning from English in analysing texts, inference, context and meaning. A pupil's own experiences are also relevant. A pupil living in Leicester will bring different experiences to one growing up in a part of rural Devon. Each child will also bring their own unique worldview (see Chapter 2) which can add different perspectives to the content being studied.

As a high-quality resource for the teaching of Christianity in schools, 'Understanding Christianity' exemplifies the use of core concepts such as 'Salvation', 'People of God', 'Incarnation', 'Gospel' and 'Creation' to support children revisiting core knowledge within a spiral curriculum structure and ensures that they revisit and build upon it (Pett, S et al. 2016). For example, in Foundation Stage, children might learn about the Christian belief that God made the world (see Figure 6.1). In Year 3, they would then learn about the Christian belief that God made a perfect world, but sin caused human beings to be separated from God. By Year Five, the children will learn that different Christians interpret the creation story in different ways. This approach supports children in retaining knowledge, building upon it and finding out about the diversity of views within one worldview. Other religious and non-religious worldviews can be taught using

■ **Table 6.1** Overview of Year 2 long-term plan for RE

Year 2	Who is a Muslim and how might they live? (part 1)	Why does Christmas matter to Christians?	Who is a Muslim and how might they live? (part 2)	What is the 'good news' Christians believe Jesus brings?	What do different communities celebrate?	What makes some places sacred to believers?

The wise men were important because they helped Jesus. (Dawson).

I think Jesus is important because God is his Daddy. (Ada).

Jesus is important because he is the baby. He is many's baby (Chloe).

The wise men are important because they gave Jesus gold. (Daniel).

Baby Jesus is important because he cries. God is his Daddy and many is his mummy. (Jake).

The wise men are important because they are very old. It took two years for them to get to Jesus. (Albie)

■ **Figure 6.1** 4–5 year olds work on the concept of incarnation displayed in the class floor book.

this approach and the work on Big Ideas by Barbara Wintersgill clearly reflects this (Wintersgill 2019).

Although syllabus writers have spent time planning and considering why each unit should be placed at particular points within the syllabus overview, it is vital that teachers and leaders can explain why they have followed the advice of the syllabus writer or why they have chosen to reorder the units. Leaders within schools should have thoroughly engaged with the design process and considered how their curriculums will support pupils to both know more and remember more. Whilst cognitive learning is clearly essential, it should be noted that knowledge is also about understanding and the impact of beliefs and personal knowledge (see section below on three different types of knowledge). A good curriculum will also support development of things such as analysis and reflection (Figure 6.2).

CURRICULUM BREADTH

Across their time in education, pupils should encounter Christianity and the other principal religions in Britain as well as non-religious worldviews, but this does not mean that all of these should be encountered in the primary school. Indeed, to try and do this might mean a surface level interaction with many worldviews rather than an in-depth understanding of some worldviews. In their research review, the OFSTED say,

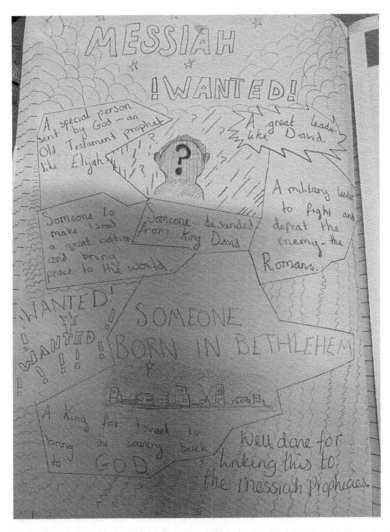

▪ **Figure 6.2** Work from a Year 5 pupil showing the building of understanding from reception. Here the pupil is showing they understand how the prophecies from the old testament provided clues that caused people to label Jesus as the messiah.

> *When subject leaders and teachers consider whether the representations that pupils acquire through the RE curriculum are 'collectively enough', they might take into account the conceptual impression of 'religion' and 'non-religion' that pupils will develop. At the very least, subject leaders can ensure that the planned representations express the variety of religion and non-religion (for example, ways of living found in Abrahamic traditions, dharmic traditions and non-religious traditions).*
>
> (OFSTED 2021)

The breadth and scope of RE is discussed in Chapter 12.

THREE DIFFERENT TYPES OF KNOWLEDGE

When planning how RE will be taught at your school, consider how you will give pupils opportunities to explore and understand both the knowledge you are sharing as well as the different ways of knowing. OFSTED explained these three different forms of knowledge in their recent RE research review (OFSTED 2021). Teaching and learning activities and the assessment of these activities should demonstrate pupils' engagement with:

- Substantive knowledge, that is the factual and conceptual content of the curriculum
- Disciplinary knowledge or ways of knowing, that is, the methods, procedures and tools that are part and parcel of RE
- Personal knowledge, that is, pupils' own worldviews and how they shape their encounters with the content of RE.

In 2018, The Commission on RE published its final report. Within this report, the commissioners recommended the move towards teaching Religious Education using a 'worldviews approach'. This work has now been developed and will go onto develop further through the Religious Education Council publication *Religion and Worldviews in the Classroom: Developing a Worldviews Approach Stephen Pett A Draft Resource for curriculum developers (2022).*

DIVERSITY WITHIN AS WELL AS BETWEEN BELIEF SYSTEMS – USING APPROPRIATE RESOURCES AND VOCABULARY

Publications by Freathy et al and OFSTED support our proposition that it is essential that the vocabulary and resources used in class exemplify diversity within as well as between belief systems. Part of the pedagogy of teaching with this approach is the greater focus on teaching about the diversity within the different worldviews that children will study. In their research report 'Worldviews and Big Ideas: A Way Forward For Religious Education?', Rob Freathy and Helen C John state that:

> There is no monolithic form of Christianity (or Hinduism/African Traditional Religion/Buddhism, and so on), no monolithic Christian worldview, no single template for a 'Christian', only particular forms or expressions of Christianity in particular locations, amongst particular communities and for the individuals who populate those communities. That taken on board, plurality is the key; should we be talking about Christianities, not Christianity and archetypal Christians; Islams, not Islam and archetypal Muslims; and so on, using geographical, temporal and other contextual qualifiers as appropriate? Should we be introducing students to the intersections between contexts, cultures, and perspectives, not bounded, monolithic 'religions' and 'worldviews'?

> (Freathy and John 2019: 8)

The reference here to learning about 'Christanities' or 'Islams' is key in the thinking about how to develop a worldviews approach to Religious Education. In many classrooms, we might hear opening statements such as 'Muslims pray five times a day' or 'Christians baptise their babies'. This generalisation in our language can lead to pupils not fully understanding the diverse nature of the worldviews (both religious and non-religious) that they study.

In my own classroom, I am also aware that this means that children who do identify as following a worldview may not see themselves or their families within the topic that we are studying. Simple shifts in the language that we use within our classrooms can help to change this view. For example, why not change sentence starters to 'Many Muslims pray at the set five times for prayer, but some Muslims choose to pray at other times …' or 'Some Christians choose to baptise their babies, whereas others …'. This shift in language helps children to understand from an early age that there is diversity within the lived reality of the worldviews that they study.

We can take this one step further by supporting children with their responses in RE. By teaching the children in Foundation Stage stem sentences such as 'Many Hindus think that...' or 'Some Muslims celebrate …' we can help children to understand the diverse nature of the traditions that they study.

It is also important to think carefully about how we resource our lessons. Showing children the same puja tray, or photograph of it, may lead them to think that all puja trays are the same and that all Hindu aarti is the same. By showing a diverse range of photographs and resources, we bring diversity into our classrooms. We must also consider the images that we use when studying places of worship in our classrooms. Are they reflective of our local, national and global communities?

For example, Plymouth doesn't have what some may consider to be a 'traditional' looking mosque. The mosques that children who live in this city see are house mosques or large buildings that have been converted into Islamic centres. Children from Plymouth may never have seen a mosque with a tall minaret or walked inside and seen a huge prayer hall with a domed ceiling. It is therefore important that our pupils see images that reflect the mosques and other places of worship that they see around them, finding out about how the call to prayer is said if it is not heard from the minaret. The children should also see images of mosques from other major cities that do have these features and have the opportunity to talk about how the lived experience of believers from these different places may vary (see Chapter 9 visits and visitors).

The use of resources such as 'Picturing Islam and Picturing Christianity' from RE Today services are a simple and helpful step to ensuring that children are accessing a greater diversity of images linked to belief and practice. Examples include Moss 2021a, 2021b, 2021c, 2022a, 2022b, 2022c, 2023.

This approach for an intentional focus on diversity of religion and belief in the teaching of Religious Education does have its challenges, and the most identified one is primary teacher subject knowledge. As primary school teachers, we teach over ten subjects a week and are required to have an in-depth knowledge of each one. We also know that approximately 40% of primary school teachers trained in the last five years had three hours or less of specific Religious Education training on their ITE courses (NATRE Primary survey 2022). This can lead to the fear that many primary school teachers have about teaching Religious Education because they are worried about getting something wrong and offending someone. Adding in an additional layer of representation of the diversity within the traditions that we study in this new approach could indeed spark more fear in these teachers, but see Chapter 1 for confidence building! Also, the 'Ask the Expert Activity' below provides a solution.

> *Ask the Expert Activity:*
> *As teachers of RE or indeed any subject, we need to be braver about admitting that we don't know everything. A journey with a class of pupils to find out the answer to a tricky question can be an excellent learning opportunity for the pupils entrusted to our care. In one of my previous schools, a colleague had a box in their classroom that was labelled 'Ask the Expert'. Each time a child asked her something in RE that she didn't know the answer to, they would drop the question into the box. At the end of the term, she would invite a panel of speakers from the worldview the class had studied into school and the children would pose their questions to them. This opportunity was a powerful subject knowledge tool for the pupils (who would remember the experience and the newly acquired knowledge) and the teacher who would be able to use the information and answers to the questions when she taught the unit again in the future.*

Subject knowledge in Religious Education is vast, ever changing and diverse. As teachers, we cannot be expected to know everything, but we must also ensure that our schools invest time, funding and place importance on the development of this key resource so that children will leave our classrooms knowing more and remembering more.

INTRODUCING NEW VOCABULARY

Teachers should also consider the use of vocabulary, how the children will encounter it and how progression of the acquisition of this key vocabulary is evident within the curriculum as a whole. It is vital that children understand the vocabulary that they encounter and that it prepares them for future learning. For example, in Year 1, amongst other key vocabulary, children may encounter words such as Mezuzah, Shema and Torah. They are taught to say these words using an 'I'll say it, you say it' pedagogy and then move on to using these terms within their spoken and written responses. This vocabulary then lays the foundations for when they revisit Judaism in Year 3 where they will find out about Jewish homes and places of worship. The vocabulary is reused and built upon whilst also adding in further key words.

Planning for vocabulary progression, development and use has formed a key part of my own curriculum design journey at my school. It is often tempting as the curriculum designer to plan for the teaching of lots of new vocabulary. As designers, we must plan this carefully as by giving the children too many new key words can cause cognitive overload. Within my own curriculum design journey, I have found that ten carefully chosen words per topic supports children to know and remember more.

Some simple ways that teachers can help children to develop their knowledge and understanding of key vocabulary are clearly sharing key vocabulary with the children through their knowledge organisers or planning sheets, highlighting key words in a different colour within PowerPoint slides used for the lesson, vocabulary games, word banks, stem sentences and modelling the vocabulary so that the children can repeat it back.

REMEMBERING MORE/ASSESSMENT

Earlier in this chapter, we looked at the structure of the curriculum and how a spiral approach to its structure can help pupils to build upon their prior learning, helping them to know more, understand more and remember more. The content of the curriculum must intertwine with this structure so that teachers and pupils are clear about what they need to know and what needs to be built on. The nature of a spiral curriculum means that children will study a concept in detail. For example, Samsara might be studied in Year 4 but may not be revisited to build upon until perhaps Year 5 or 6. So how do we support children in referring to their previous learning so that they can build upon this and remember more? Remember when OFSTED refers to knowledge, they are not only referring to substantive knowledge but to disciplinary and personal knowledge too.

One popular idea to support children in recalling their knowledge is low stakes quizzing. Some schools support children by giving them a close activity within which they can fill in the blanks and share their knowledge. Others have sticky knowledge quizzes at the start of each lesson, and some use knowledge organisers to discuss and recap over key themes from previous units.

One way of making quizzing fun and supportive for children is to revisit a slide, picture or prompt of key information for each lesson within the previous unit of learning. The children then rapidly share their knowledge using the slides or pictures as prompts. When they revisit the concept later in the curriculum, the teacher can share the quiz slides again, prompting the knowledge so that the children can easily recall it before building upon it in a new unit. This technique is based on metacognition research and supports children in building schema.

Many schools do use these quizzing strategies to support children to remember more or to recap over their learning from previous units. Whilst this strategy is helpful, it is also important that there are a variety of retrieval ideas to support children to remember and understand. Some ideas that teachers might wish to try with their classes are in role hot seating questions, key picture recall or labelling an image. Games such as lingo bingo, give me five (where a child has to name, for example, five things that a Hindu might do at Diwali, although, of course, not all Hindus might do the same five things), articulate, Pictionary or Just a Minute provide strategies that are effective whilst also being enjoyable.

It is important to note that these low stakes retrieval strategies are not to be recorded in a mark book or aggregated to show pupils progress over time but instead support pupils to know and remember and understand more.

The use of quizzing or indeed any strategy that supports recall of acquired knowledge means that teachers and pupils need to be sure of the substantive knowledge that they want the children to acquire within the unit. One way of supporting the children in understanding the knowledge that they need to be able to recall at the end of the unit is to give them a 'Sticky Knowledge' sheet at the start of the topic. These sheets list the content for the topic so that children are able to track and remember the content. These are the key pieces of knowledge in the unit; learners will have encountered much more. In the example, learners heard about different prayer practices from different traditions within Islam. An example of this can be seen in Figures 6.3 and 6.6.

Other schools may choose to share this by using a knowledge organiser which contains other key information such as concepts, vocabulary, artefacts and practices.

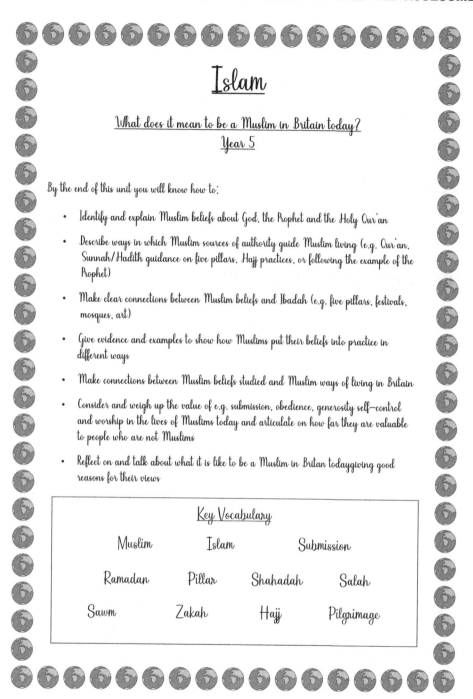

Islam

What does it mean to be a Muslim in Britain today?
Year 5

By the end of this unit you will know how to:

- Identify and explain Muslim beliefs about God, the Prophet and the Holy Qur'an

- Describe ways in which Muslim sources of authority guide Muslim living (e.g. Qur'an, Sunnah/Hadith guidance on five pillars, Hajj practices, or following the example of the Prophet)

- Make clear connections between Muslim beliefs and Ibadah (e.g. five pillars, festivals, mosques, art)

- Give evidence and examples to show how Muslims put their beliefs into practice in different ways

- Make connections between Muslim beliefs studied and Muslim ways of living in Britain

- Consider and weigh up the value of e.g. submission, obedience, generosity self-control and worship in the lives of Muslims today and articulate on how far they are valuable to people who are not Muslims

- Reflect on and talk about what it is like to be a Muslim in Britan todaygiving good reasons for their views

Key Vocabulary

Muslim	Islam	Submission	
Ramadan	Pillar	Shahadah	Salah
Sawm	Zakah	Hajj	Pilgrimage

■ **Figure 6.3** 'Sticky' knowledge sheet for a Year 5 Islam unit.

However, it should be noted that knowledge organisers are only one way of doing this and are only effective if they are regularly used as a tool to help pupils remember and engage with key content.

A good knowledge organiser (KO) is a one page document that sets out the most important, useful and, to use a current term, 'powerful knowledge'.

The knowledge organiser needs to be carefully constructed so that it can be used by pupils to remember and understand the key concepts in any unit being studied. Knowledge organisers can also be useful to teachers enabling them to keep focussed on the most important knowledge and understanding in a topic. A knowledge organiser will not contain all that is taught in a unit; much more will be taught to support pupil understanding and to place the learning in a wider context.

A knowledge organiser could be one of the tools to help pupils move knowledge and understanding from their short to their long-term memory. More work on knowledge organisers has been done by Gillian Georgiou (Georgiou 2022).

PLANNING FOR WAYS OF KNOWING

Earlier in the chapter we referred to three forms of knowledge in RE. Ways of knowing is described by OFSTED in their research review as:

> *'Ways of knowing' is an area of development that is currently emerging within RE. There seem to be 2 main forms of 'ways of knowing' that pupils can learn in the curriculum:*

- *Knowledge of well-established methods and processes and other tools of scholarship that are used to study and make sense of global and historical religion/non-religion*
- *Knowledge of the types of conversation (or 'modes of enquiry' or 'scholarly discourses') that academic communities have about religion/non-religion'.*

(OFSTED 2021)

When concentrating on this emerging area of 'ways of knowing', teachers need to try to be more deliberate about the methods, procedures and tools that are part and parcel of RE and are how we encounter and engage with the substantive knowledge. As part of NATRE membership, the Primary Curriculum book series *Big Questions Big Answers* (RE Today Services) and their new *Exploring Primary* series shares practical ways of teaching with different disciplines such as theology, philosophy or sociology. However, it is also important to make clear to the learners which tools they are using and whether those tools give them the whole picture. For example, if pupils are learning about Shabbat and read two interviews with two seven year old girls about their Shabbat practice, what do they learn?

■   Is this a good way of learning about Shabbat
■   Can they assume it will be like this in all Jewish households
■   What else could they do?

Perhaps they could ask more people or look at some data? This ensures learners understand the diversity within belief systems. Learners could look at sacred text such as the Torah to find out what the origins of a day of rest might be. Pupils probably won't have time to go on and discover more, but they are more aware of the tools they are using and that they do not have a complete picture and cannot assume that things are the same for all followers of the same religious or non-religious worldview.

As they get older, they will also learn that some ways of knowing or disciplines are useful to find out one thing, but others are better for finding out other things. If pupils want to find out *how* different people celebrate Christmas, tools of sociology or religious studies such as surveys, data, photographs and interviews might be useful. However, if they want to find out more specifically about *why* Christians celebrate Christmas, pupils will need to study biblical text and use some tools of theology.

PLANNING

Whilst we know learning can happen in moments of inspiration (a sudden question or opportunity grabbed in the school day), teachers do need to use a clear planning process to facilitate effective learning in RE. The temptation is of course to use an engaging strategy that you have seen in action, but in order to counter the critique of RE as 'providing poor and fragmented curriculum planning' (OFSTED 2013), we must consider how sequences of learning are constructed. These sequences of learning need to build on pupils' knowledge and understanding and skills.

A series of recent agreed syllabi have used planning processes to support and encourage teachers to plan clear sequences of learning. Bedford Borough, Central Bedfordshire and Luton, Gloucestershire, York and Devon are four recent examples of agreed syllabi which have suggested a planning process moving from Agreed Syllabus to scheme of work for your school and ultimately your class of learners.

This process of planning enables a teacher to focus on key questions that will build on pupils' prior knowledge, unlock the pupils' interest and have a clear RE focus. Following a planning structure creates an emphasis on knowing more and remembering more rather than only on the engaging strategies used in teaching.

Assessment

Any assessment in any subject should be *meaningful* and *manageable*. In the first instance, teachers need to understand what knowledge, understanding and skills the chosen curriculum requires (Table 6.2).

Once they understand this, they can give good formative feedback within lessons on what the pupils know, understand and can do, what they don't know or don't understand and what they need to do next. The examples of retrieval practice referenced earlier in this chapter are examples of formative assessment.

This requires teachers to do what we always do: listen to, observe and study what pupils say and do in lessons; in other words, formative assessment or 'assessment for learning' (Black and William 2006). This will allow us to give good verbal feedback to pupils as whole classes, groups and individuals, and occasionally give written formative feedback as well. All this formative assessment is done in lessons, and it informs our ongoing practice, as we need to adapt our planning depending on what we discover.

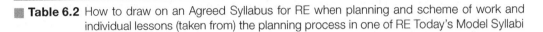

■ **Table 6.2** How to draw on an Agreed Syllabus for RE when planning and scheme of work and individual lessons (taken from) the planning process in one of RE Today's Model Syllabi

Step1: **Unit/key question**	■ Select a unit/key question from the questions in this syllabus
	■ Make sure that you can explain where this unit/question fits into key stage planning, e.g. how it builds on previous learning in RE; what other subject areas it links to, if appropriate
Step 2: **Use learning outcomes**	■ Use the learning outcomes from column 1 of the unit outlines in this syllabus, as appropriate to the age and ability of your pupils
	■ Being clear about these outcomes will help you to decide what and how to teach
Step 3: Select specific content	■ Look at the suggested content for your unit, from column 2 in the unit outlines
	■ Select the best content (from here, or additional information from elsewhere) to help you to teach in an engaging way so that pupils achieve the learning outcomes
Step 4: **Assessment:** **Write** **specific pupil outcomes**	■ Turn the learning outcomes into pupil-friendly 'I can', 'You can' or 'Can you…?' statements
	■ Make the learning outcomes specific to the content you are teaching, to help you know precisely what it is that you want pupils to know. Be able to understand and do as a result of their learning
	■ These 'I can'/'You can'/'Can you…?' statements will help you to integrate assessment for learning within your teaching, so that there is no need to do a separate end of unit assessment
Step 5: **Develop** **teaching** **and learning** **activities**	■ Develop active learning opportunities, using some engaging stimuli, to enable pupils to achieve the outcomes
	■ Be clear about the knowledge you want them to gain, integrating it into their wider understanding in RE and life. Be clear about the skills you want pupils to develop
	■ Make sure that the teaching and learning activities allow pupils to process the knowledge and understanding, thinking hard and practising these skills as well as showing their understanding
	■ Consider ways of recording how pupils show their understanding, e.g. photographs, learning journey, wall or class book, group work, annotated planning, scrapbook, etc.

There are many strategies that support this formative assessment, but it is important to remember that as you listen, watch, quiz, question, check for misconceptions, scribble notes, etc., you don't need to provide evidence for every bit of pupils' attainment (Moss 2019). Many teachers use floor books, particularly in Key Stage 1, which show examples of learning as a class. In Key Stage 2, some have individual books alongside floor books that could be looked at when a subject leader needs to monitor pupil learning.

Assessment for accountability or summative assessment in RE should not be overly different from summative assessment in other foundation subjects. We should also always remember that we spend at least five times more curriculum time on English than on RE and so should not be spending as long assessing RE as we do assessing English. Summative assessment is looking to see how pupils have progressed over time. Whilst

■ **Figure 6.4** Page from class floor book. In this lesson, the children learnt about the Christian creation story. They found out that Christians believe that Adam was given the job of naming all the animals. The children drew different animals, shared their names and explained who Christians believe first named them.

summative assessment is important, it should take second place to what is going on in the classroom between pupil and teacher. It is the weekly in the moment conversations about what pupils know, understand and can do (in other words formative assessment) that will improve learner knowledge, understanding and progress.

Throughout the study of a topic or concept in RE, the class teacher should be assessing the knowledge that children have acquired and remembered (Figure 6.4). One simple way of doing this is through higher order questioning. In my own classroom, I have developed this further in the form of a sticky knowledge quiz. Before encountering new learning within a topic, the children will have a series of slides from previous lessons within the unit that they will work through, rapidly answering questions and sharing their knowledge with the rest of the class. At the end of the topic, the children will share what they know within a sticky knowledge quiz activity, recording their knowledge on a quiz sheet like the one seen below in Figure 6.5.

Although this is a good way to gain knowledge of a child's learning within a topic, it is vital that this is tracked through each lesson by using higher order questioning and marking questions that the children can feedback to. Another strategy that I like to use in my lessons is hot seating. Within these activities, the children can be asked questions

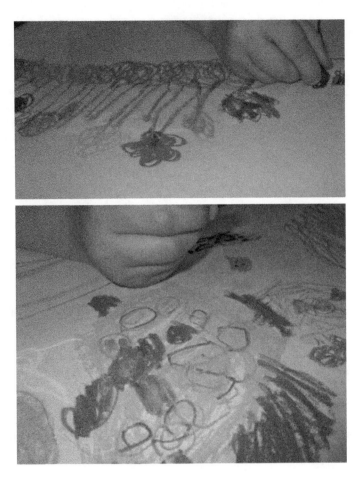

■ **Figure 6.5** After hearing the Christian creation story, the children were asked to think about the different things that were made on each day. They chose a day, drew something that was made on that day and then talked through the story of creation using their class images.

in role as a character. For example, children might answer questions in role as Abram (later known as Abraham) after learning about his call from God within a unit of work on Christianity. Whilst the other children in the class might ask the child in the hot seat questions about the story, the teacher can use this opportunity to ask their own questions and ascertain the child's understanding of the story.

SUMMARY

In this chapter, we have shared some key ideas that are needed to underpin effective and creative planning and assessment for developing knowledge and understanding. A curriculum needs to support all learners to know and understand more about the diversity of religion and worldviews. It needs to ensure that pupils remember their learning,

What do Hindus believe?

Assessment

What is the Trimurti? How does the Trimurti link with Samsara?

What is atman?

Why might a Hindu use the greeting 'Namaste'?

What is Dharma and how does it change throughout a Hindu's life?

What do you know about worship in Hindu Dharma?

What is an Ashrama?

Draw a diagram to explain the concept of Samsara, remember to add notes to share your understanding.

What are Murtis and what do you know about them?

What is Moksha?

Your next steps are...

■ **Figure 6.6** End of unit assessment for a Year 6 unit on the Hindu Dharma.

short-term understanding, encounters and understanding in the long term to help them reflect on their own personal worldviews and to take their place in their community and the wider world.

REFERENCES

Benoit, C., Hutchings, T. and Shillitoe, R. (n.d.). WORLDVIEW A Multidisciplinary Report. [Online] Available at: https://www.religiouseducationcouncil.org.uk/wp-content/uploads/2017/07/5-REC-Worldview-Report.pdf [Accessed 1 Feb. 2023]

Black, P. and Wiliam, D. (2006). Developing a theory of formative assessment. In J. Gardner (Ed.), *Assessment and learning.* (pp. 81–100). London: Sage

Blaylock, L. (2015). *Picturing Christianity.* RE Today Services

Blaylock, L. (2020). *RE in Action.* RE Today Services

Blaylock, L. and Pett, S. (2020) *Picturing Islam, Picturing Muslims.* RE Today Services

Freathy, R. and John, H.C. (2019) Worldviews and Big Ideas: A Way Forward for Religious Education?: Nordidactica. *Journal of Humanities and Social Science Education: Nordidactica* 4, 8

Georgiou, G. (2022). Lincolnshire Locally Agreed Syllabus for Religious Education Using Knowledge Organisers in RE: Guidance and Exemplars Using Knowledge Organisers in RE. [Online] Available at: https://www.lincolndiocesaneducation.com/_site/data/files/users/4D1CE8C496F3BAF3306403EE0ADC1BF0.pdf [Accessed 1 Feb. 2023].

Moss, F. (2019). *Assessment in RE: A Practical Guide.* RE Today Services

Moss, F. (2021a). *Big Questions Big Answers Investigating Environment.* RE Today Services

Moss, F. (2021b). *Big Questions Big Answers Investigating Worldviews.* RE Today Services

Moss, F. (2021c). *Big Questions Big Answers Investigating God.* RE Today Services

Moss, F. (2022a). *Big Questions Big Answers Investigating Good and Evil.* RE Today Services

Moss, F. (2022b). *Big Questions Big Answers Investigating How We Live.* RE Today Services

Moss, F. (2022c). *Big Questions Big Answers Investigating Worship.* RE Today Services

Moss, F. (2023). *Exploring Jewish Worldviews.* RE Today Services

NATRE Primary Survey. (2022). Analysis of the provision of RE in primary schools available at www.natre.org.uk/uploads/Free%20Resources/NATRE%20Primary%20Survey%202022%20final%20(002).pdf [Accessed 10.03.24].

Ofsted (2013). *Religious Education: Realising the Potential.* GOV.UK. [Online] Available at: https://www.gov.uk/government/publications/religious-education-realising-the-potential.

Ofsted (2021). *Research Review Series: Religious Education.* GOV.UK. [Online] Available at: https://www.gov.uk/government/publications/research-review-series-religious-education/research-review-series-religious-education.

Pett, S., Blaylock, L., Christopher, K., Diamond-Conway, J., Matter, H., Moss, F. and Yarlett, E. (2016) *Understanding Christianity: Text Impact Connections; Resource Pack.* RE Today Services

Religion and Worldviews: The Way Forward A National Plan for Re Final Report. (2018). [Online] Available at: https://www.religiouseducationcouncil.org.uk/wp-content/uploads/2017/07/1-Final-Report-of-the-Commission-on-RE.pdf [Accessed 1 Feb. 2023].

RE: Online. (n.d.). Putting Big Ideas into Practice in Religious Education. [online] Available at: https://www.reonline.org.uk/resources/putting-big-ideas-into-practice-in-religious -education/.

RE Today Services (2021). *City of York Agreed Syllabus for Religious Education.* RE Today Services

RE Today Services (2019). *Devon and Torbay Agreed Syllabus for Religious Education.* RE Today Services

The Religious Education Council of England and Wales. (n.d.). Draft Resource. [Online] Available at: https://www.religiouseducationcouncil.org.uk/projects/draft-resource/ [Accessed 1 Feb. 2023].

Shillitoe, R. (n.d.). Evaluation Study of Understanding Christianity Final Report. [Online] Available at: https://www.understandingchristianity.org.uk/wp-content/uploads/2020 /12/Understanding-Christianity-Evaluation-Study-Report-October-2020.pdf [Accessed 1 Feb. 2023].

Tharani, A. (n.d.). The Worldview Project Discussion Papers. [Online] Available at: https:// www.religiouseducationcouncil.org.uk/wp-content/uploads/2021/01/The-Worldview -Project.pdf [Accessed 1 Feb. 2023].

Wintersgill, B., Cush, D. and Francis, D. (2019). Putting Big Ideas Into Practice In Religious Education. RE Today Services

CHAPTER 7

SPIRITUAL DEVELOPMENT THROUGH CREATIVE RE

Sally Elton-Chalcraft, Penny Hollander and Georgia Prescott

Creative RE provides many opportunities for children's spiritual development because it involves children in exploring their own inner ideas, beliefs and feelings in response to learning about religious beliefs and concepts. Creative RE allows for individual reflection and expression through art, music, drama, poetry and other forms of creative writing. Opportunities for awe and wonder are provided through visits to places of worship (see Chapter 9) or through individual responses to religious art or music (see Chapter 8 in this volume). As teachers we need to be aware of children's spirituality and give avenues for them to explore and express this.

This chapter will explore:

- Definitions of spirituality and aims of spiritual development.
- The place of spiritual development in RE and collective worship, including 'Ows' – spiritual development through encounters with the difficult aspects of life.
- Individual experiences – stilling and guided visualization.
- Collective experiences – visits and residential trips.

DEFINITIONS AND AIMS OF SPIRITUALITY

Before considering how to support children's spiritual development, firstly we must have some understanding of what spirituality is and why we should be supporting children's spiritual development.

What is your definition of spirituality and why should we be supporting children's spiritual development?
Before reading any further (resist peeking ahead!)

1. Write your definition of spirituality.
2. Why should we support children's spiritual development.
3. Discuss with a peer/group of peers (perhaps write words/phrases on a big piece of paper).

DOI: 10.4324/9781003361480-9

One of the authors of this chapter has explored perceptions of spirituality (Elton-Chalcraft 2002) asking student teachers and in-service teachers for their definitions of spirituality. The authors have continued to ask groups for their definitions and, probably similar to the lists you have compiled in response to the questions above, diverse and innumerable forms of spirituality are often suggested.

Some examples of definitions of spirituality

> Inner peace, metaphysical, something more than the physical, beautiful scenery, relationships, morals, faith, God, destiny, personal, innate, mysterious, other worldly, search for meaning

While each group's list is always unique and seemingly different to another group's definition, nevertheless four main themes can always be found, see Table 7.1 – the inner, the social and moral, the environmental and the transcendental (Elton-Chalcraft 2002). Myriad and diverse definitions, or forms of spirituality, can usually be categorised into these four dimensions of spirituality which have been recognised by other authors such as Fisher (1999) Hay and Nye (1998) and partly in del Castillo and Sarmiento (2022).

Teachers may struggle to find appropriate activities to develop children's spirituality because they struggle to agree on a consensus definition for spirituality. Elton-Chalcraft (2002:313) suggests a metaphor which likens spirituality to a hologram having dimensions of height, breadth, depth and hue but is not tangible and can come in various forms – a piece of jewellery, a woman's face, a part of machinery. Similarly, spirituality is also intangible but has four dimensions – inner, social and moral, environmental and transcendental but may have totally different forms. Like a hologram, spirituality is multifarious – your own spirituality may be very different to the writers of the chapters of this book and certainly our individual spirituality will be different to those of a different culture, religion, age, gender, country, political stance etc. Table 7.2 attempts to capture these myriad forms of spirituality which, nevertheless, could be categorized into the four dimensions.

■ **Table 7.1** The four dimensions of spirituality (adapted from Elton-Chalcraft 2002; Hay and Nye 2006; Prescott 2014)

Inner dimension – *Looking inwards* to your self

Self: Our feelings/experiences/what is important to us. An inner quest for meaning, creativity/ inspiration, feelings of elation.

Social and moral dimension – *Looking outwards* to others

Others: The way we interact with others and our important relationships. Choices about how to live life, ethics and values.

Environmental dimension – *Looking downwards* to the Earth.

The world: Responses to the physical world/ appreciating what is amazing about the world and nature, and how that fits into our world view.

Transcendental dimension – *Looking upwards* towards God/the transcendent

One's place in the universe: Response to the 'Ultimate', the divine/a sense of 'the other'; destiny, religion/faith/belief system.

■ **Table 7.2** Examples of different forms of spirituality categorized into the four dimensions

---

Different forms of spirituality categorized into the four dimensions

■ Anuj, nine year old Indian boy, offering flowers at the Ganesh shrine in his wealthy Bengaluru home (**transcendental dimension**) in the hope that he will do well in his school test and make his parents proud.

■ Sarah, ten year old white, Cumbrian girl, in the crowd at Wembley watching Carlisle win on penalties 5–4 in the play offs in 2023 may experience the (**inner dimension**) feeling of elation, as she screams in unison 'YEH' with her equally excited, divorced dad in mutual (**social and moral dimension**) happiness together with the other.

■ Martha, 4 year old Afro Caribbean girl from Derby, gathering different sized stones and leaves to make an Andy Goldsworthy (art in a natural environment 2014) art work in the local park observing intently (**environmental dimension**) the impact of the gentle rain on her sculpture.

So if there are myriad forms of spirituality 'out there', even if they can be categorized into the four dimensions, this raises multiple questions for the teacher.

■ Should teachers be responsible for spiritual development? Isn't this a job for parents/the child's faith community/someone else/left to the child to undertake without intervention?

■ Do all humans have the capacity to be spiritual?

■ Which forms of spirituality (if any?) should we be nurturing in our children?

■ How can teachers nurture children's spirituality authentically?

We would argue that all humans are spiritual. In fact, spirituality could be defined as what it is to be 'truly human'. We agree with Heelas (2008:2) that 'human flourishing' is under threat from a wide range of restrictions and regulations and, to be truly human, to be truly spiritual, is to be liberated from the 'iron cages' of 'mainstream society and culture, with their measurable and narrow criteria of what it is to be a "successful" human' (Heelas 2008:3). Especially within the English education system where external regulatory bodies (OFSTED grades and SATS results) are often cited as measurements of success, we should remember that other governmental documents can be found which encourage developments of children's creativity and spirituality (OFSTED 2013 RE realising the potential).

We would agree with Wright (2000) that education is often viewed in the West as 'nurturing', hence the call for teachers to 'support children's spiritual development' (OFSTED 2013). However, we would also agree with Wright's (2000) insistence on supplementing the nurturing with a critical stance, recognising that 'spirituality is a vital yet fundamentally controversial issue' (2000:139).

So before we proceed to suggest creative activities for developing children's spirituality in each of these four dimensions, it is necessary to advocate aims for spiritual development which should underpin any activities.

Wright (2000) argues that teachers must balance nurture with critical thinking. We have translated these two almost conflicting pedagogies of spiritual learning into aims:

1) Nurturing a child's preferred spirituality (according to their preferred web of belief/belief system – see Chapter 1) in terms of the inner, social and moral, environmental and transcendental dimensions.
2) Inviting children to critically challenge their own and others' definitions of spirituality and grapple with pluralism, difference and the human desire for truth, conflicting views of ethical behaviour and lifestyle.

But are these two aims achievable? We would argue yes, and we offer some practical activities below which should ensure each child in your class is aware of their own spirituality and develops critically and mindfully as a successful human being. It is also important that we give children the opportunities to have their spiritual voices heard and not dismissed or silenced by adults (Adams et al. 2008).

In their research with a small group of RE subject leaders in the West Midlands of England, Hill and Wooley (2022) explore these teachers' aspirations for the interaction between RE and spirituality (also referred to as meaning-making). Findings suggest an intention to both promote learning but also apply that learning to real life experience. So developing a spiritual dimension to religious education requires a focus on values and pedagogy with

> a move from the abstract or theoretical and from knowledge acquisition towards increased engagement, making a personal response and considering what difference can be made as a result. As such, a spiritual dimension to learning cannot be passive.
>
> (Hill and Woolley 2022:280)

In her article discussing the place of spirituality in RE in policy documents, Hannam explains that 60 years ago it would have been commonplace for spirituality to be faith nurture in religious affiliated schools. Indeed it is still the same in many countries today where religious education is synonymous with faith nurture and spiritual development is seen as an extension of faith nurture. However in the secular context in which many teachers in many schools find themselves, we would argue that spiritual development does not need to be rooted in religious faith. The activities in this chapter are suitable for a myriad of contexts faith based and secular. We agree with Hannam (2022) that RE is not merely about knowledge transmission and so spiritual development is complex and relates to the 'messiness of human experience' and focusses on what spirituality does rather than what it is. For Hannam, the child should be brought to a state of attention – this might also be described as mindfulness which is becoming popular in the psychological and counselling sphere of supporting those with mental health issues. A calming down and bringing to attention is found to be beneficial in preparing for the day ahead. The activities described later in this chapter – stilling and guided visualisation – do just this. Hannam (2022) also talks about discernment of value and why things matter. So spiritual development is a way of being rather than a way of knowing, and an ability to discern what is of value and why something is important.

Castillo and Sarmiento from Catholic institutions in the Philippines offer an interesting perspective on spiritual development in the religious context where they describe the challenges and possibilities of integrating spiritual modelling as an approach to religious education taken from the social cognitive theory of Albert Bandura. The ideas they present include an emulation of characteristics of people deemed to be positive spiritual role models. For many countries such a role of religious education is not uncommon, and much can be learnt from this in secular contexts because the role models for spiritual development do not have to be drawn solely from religious individuals. There are numerous philanthropists whose example could be emulated and this relates to Hannam's point about discernment. Particularly in the current climate of TikTok and social media influencers, children can consider role models to emulate – for example Marcus Rashford, Greta Thurnberg, Richard Attenborough and possibly Taylor Swift, and whose influence to avoid for example Andrew Tate and perhaps Kim Kardashian. But debates with your class can provide opportunities for a collective discernment of which characteristics are to be valued or not – we would not advocate a teacher imposing their own value judgements.

EXPLORING SPIRITUALITY WITH CHILDREN – WINDOWS, MIRRORS AND DOORS

In this section we provide some lesson ideas supported by the theoretical rationale in the section above. For teachers looking to include a spiritual dimension into their lesson planning, it might be useful to consider the visual image of a doughnut! Liz Mills (2002) developed the concept of the Spiritual Ring Doughnut to represent the whole child. The outer ring is the tangible (mind and body) with the hole representing the intangible (spirit). If there was no hole there would not be a doughnut. The exploration and development of that 'hole' is what makes us whole as human beings. The idea of the doughnut can be explored with children and also the ideas of windows, mirrors and doors.

Liz Mill's work also built on that of David Smith (1999) in developing the concept of 'spiritual windows' through 'Windows, Mirrors, Doors'. These three openings for spiritual development can be included in different curriculum areas.

Discussing with children the wonders of the created world is both relevant to RE lessons and other curriculum areas, particularly science, and provide the 'wows'. This links with the environmental dimension, see Table 7.1. Also delight in their achievement or feeling supported by family, friends or God relates to the personal, social and moral and transcendental dimension respectively, see Table 7.1. Conversely, the things that are difficult about life, suffering, war and poverty are also part of the world in which we live. They are the 'Ows'. It is important to consider how we provide children with the space, tools and frameworks to deal with these 'Ows'. This also relates to the four dimensions, for example – personal dimension, poor mental health, social and moral falling outs with family/friends, environmental – climate crisis. The window provides an encounter for learning about the world in which we live. Mills says that in providing such opportunities children are learning about life in all its fullness, also identified in Ofsted 2021.

Taking this into the children's own experience, a group of primary school teachers created a reflective display for their classrooms to help children express their own 'Ows' in life and to move from this to a 'wow', see Table 7.3. The concept and practice of using displays as a focus for spititual development is discussed further in Prescott 2012.

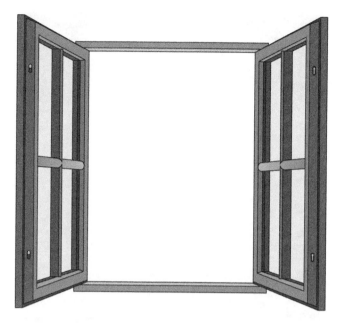

■ **Figure 7.1** Windows: Learning about life – Encounter. Provide opportunities to look out on the world, to gaze and wonder at what is there.

■ **Figure 7.2** MIRRORS: Learning from life – Reflection. Provide opportunities for children to reflect on their own experiences, to look inwards and meditate on life's big questions, exploring their own insights and those of others. They are learning from life.

A Unique Spiritual Identity

Every human being is unique and as teachers we have a responsibility to aid children's spiritual development by giving opportunities for them to pursue a quest for meaning, values by which to live and to develop a sense of truth and mystery.

■ **Figure 7.3** Doors: Learning to live life – TRANSFORMATION. Give children opportunities to respond, to do something and go through the door; creatively expressing, applying and developing further their thoughts and convictions. In doing this they are learning to live by putting into action what they believe and value.

■ **Table 7.3** Ows and wows

Ows and wows in RE

Teachers developed a display presenting the notion of 'ows' and 'wows', aiming to help children to know that life contains both and that a journey can be made between a place of 'ow', and a place of 'wow'. A central signpost clearly shows a journey. The cross at the bottom is to ensure that the message is one of forgiveness, redemption and the centrality of Christ (this was in a church school – but a candle could be used in a non-religious context).

Each activity offers children a space and time to own their feelings and act on them both personally and on behalf of their friends:

- ■ Write down your 'ows' leave them in the 'ow' box.
- ■ Write down your 'wows' and put them in the 'wow' box.
- ■ Take a notelet and write a 'ray of hope' message of encouragement for a friend.
- ■ Use the 'rays of hope' messages as a prompt to help you move from 'ow' to 'wow'.
- ■ Say something kind, take time to think, give someone a smile, do something for someone else.

Rickett A and S, Holloway D. (2012) have used the 'Windows, Mirrors, Doors' principles to map out a series of grids to give children a progression of **experiences** to aid spiritual development across the different age ranges. They give practical examples within four areas of spiritual learning: self, others, the world and beauty, beyond (church schools may wish to make this more specifically linked to God or the Divine, but the process is the same). These headings link with our four dimensions of spirituality.

In each section there are suggestions to provide for learning about life – ENCOUNTER (*WINDOW),* learning from life – REFLECTION (*MIRROR*) and learning to live life – TRANSFORMATION (*DOOR*).

Another way to express this is to encourage children to look INWARDS, OUTWARDS, DOWNWARDS, UPWARDS.

Questions to Discuss

Some examples from Rickett et al. (2012) synthesised with (Elton-Chalcraft 2002) include:

Self/Inner Dimension

What makes me happy?
Who am I?
What do I deserve in life?
Where does your identity come from?

Others/Social and Moral Dimension

What makes a good friend?
How do I treat others?
Why should I care for those who may be in need but I have never met?
Why should I accept different values and beliefs from my own?

World and Beauty/Environmental Dimension

What makes a special place?
Respond to a stimulus and verbally express reaction to something wonderful.
Diversity within world environments.
What is a perfect world?

Beyond/Transcendental Dimension

Puzzling questions – what does God look like? Where is God?
What is the purpose of the earth?
Is there life after death?
Lat Blaylock from REToday has produced many practical activities to aid children's spiritual development. On the NATRE website www.natre.org.uk in the 'Spirited Arts' section, there are examples from both the 'Art in Heaven' section and spirited poetry in the 'Galleries' section. A few of these are illustrated below and show children's engagement with questions relating to themselves, others, the world and God.
How We Should Live

My Hope for the World

Speranza (Age 10)

My Art in Heaven work is about hope for the world. Because I want peace to come to the world. I want everyone to stop arguing and to make the world a better place. My picture is called 'My Hope for the World'. My name means hope in Albanian. And the words on the picture mean hope in other languages.
http://www.natre.org.uk/spiritedarts/index.php

MY BEATITUDES

Aiden Tompkins, age 8

Blessed are those who starve and thirst
For they understand God's feeling.

Blessed are those who appreciate others' respect and love
For they will respect and love back.

Blessed are those who tolerate the world
For they listen to each other.

Blessed are those who are responsible for their actions
For they are responsible for God.

Blessed are those who care for their neighbours
For they care for God's love.

Blessed are those who trust their neighbours
For they trust God and the world.

Blessed are those who feel friendship in others
For they will be friends with the world and God.

Blessed are those who show happiness to the world
For they show happiness to God.

http://www.natre.org.uk/spiritedarts/index.php

How we should treat our friends

KEEP A PROMISE

Anna Beresford, age 5

If you keep a promise
You will keep a friend
You will keep your friend
From beginning to end

Do not break a promise
This you should not forget
Please don't break a promise
Or your friend might get upset

We should always try to keep
The promise that we make
Like the one I made at rainbows
Which I really don't want to break

Promises are special
To you and to your friends
Friendships keep you together
This is what God recommends

What is life like

Celebrating Life, Celebrating Love!

Kieran Age 8

LIFE AND LOVE ARE DANGEROUSLY EXCITING

My picture is of lots of lightning striking across the sky. The lightning is like life and love. It can be exciting and beautiful, but it can also be really scary and dangerous.

---

http://www.natre.org.uk/spiritedarts/index.php

STILLING AND GUIDED VISUALISATION

Mary Stone's book *Don't Just Do Something Sit There* (1995) and Stone and Brennan (2009) have helped teachers design opportunities for spiritual development. Stilling means 'being still' both physically and mentally, beginning with exercises of self control and moving on to guide the mind into visualisations about a particular theme (eg wonder at the natural world, focussing on a leaf, a stone etc) or a particular event or story from religious tradition (eg Jesus' parable of the tax collector, the Buddha's first visit outside his palace, Moses' experience at the burning bush etc).

Stone and Brennan (2009) describe guided visualisation as using the imagination to recall an event, an object or a situation, which for the purpose of creative RE helps develop deeper reflection. The child is led through a story sequence, for example, in the role of a bystander and the teacher narrates using 'you' to ensure the child is actively involved (Stone and Bennan 2009:5). Guided visualisation is inclusive because it does not involve reading or writing and most children find it enjoyable. The teacher's narrative, in the guided visualisation, introduces children to historical contexts through engaging children's awareness of the sights, sounds, smells and textures of the situation. So when the teacher tells the story of Buddha leaving his luxurious lifestyle in the palace, the child takes on the role of the charioteer who takes Buddha outside the palace gates. The child, through guided visualisation, observes Buddha's reaction to the world outside the royal enclosure when he saw an old man, a sick man and a corpse. Through guided visualisation, the child can reflect on Buddha's feelings and gain insight into the impact this experience might have had on the Buddha. (Story can be found at http://www.buddhanet.net/e-learning/buddhism /pbs2_unit01.htm which the teacher can retell in the guided visualisation style).

The visualisation (see Tables 7.4 and 7.5) takes the child through a journey as a leaf by appreciating and entering into the natural world (Stone 1995:18–20).

■ **Table 7.4** How to begin and end a stilling/visualisation session – adapted from Stone (1995)

How to begin and end a stilling/guided visualisation session

Before you begin, ensure the room is quiet and the children have been suitably briefed about spending some time in silence, ideally with their eyes closed (this does take some practice and perseverence, but after a few weeks most children begin to enjoy stilling). Ensure your voice **tone is gentle and relaxing** – children should pick up on the cue that there is a different atmosphere. Make sure you pause frequently to enable the children to think deeply

i.	I wonder if you can sit in an 'alert' and 'relaxed' position? Is your back straight… your feet on the floor… your hands in your lap, in a cupped position? Can you shrug your shoulders to relieve tension?
ii.	While you are sitting in an alert and relaxed position, can you let your eyelids very gently close…
iii.	Now breathe in and out slowly and gently, perhaps counting in your head one, two, three as you breathe in and one, two, three as you breathe out and feel any tenseness in your body release.
iv.	We are going to go on an imaginary journey… Take children through the guided visualisation…
v.	Now we are going to leave our imaginary journey… and slowly return to the classroom.
vi.	Feel the hardness of your chair… and the sounds inside and outside the room.
vii.	When you are ready slowly open your eyes… and have a good stretch.
viii.	Would you like to make a comment about the visualisation?
ix.	What did you find out today?

Discuss the visualisation. Possibly (but not always) the children could be asked to paint, sculpt, discuss, write a poem, design a group poster etc to express their responses to the guided visualisation.

■ **Table 7.5** Journey of a leaf stilling/guided visualisation session – adapted from Stone (1995:18)

Stilling and guided visualisation

The environmental dimension of spirituality: Journey of a leaf

1.	I am going to give one of you a leaf… Examine and 'get to know' your leaf. Look at the patterns, the veins, the colours, the texture…
2.	This leaf given to you by a tree is unique… There never has been one exactly the same and there never will be… If I were to ask you to put it on a pile with everyone else's leaf would you be able to pick out your leaf? Good… But now just place it in front of you.
3.	*(Steps i–iv above)*
4.	Now you are going to imagine you are that leaf… Feel what it is like to be that shape… That weight… Those colours…
5.	Imagine you are on top of a tall tree… Attached to a twig… Feel the gentle wind on both sides of you… Listen to the splash of the raindrops on you… Feel the rain.
6.	Now go back in time to when you were a bud… Feel what it was like to be tightly closed up… Feel the warmth of the spring sunshine… Feel the life force from the tree surging through your veins… Feel yourself uncurling… Facing the sun…
7.	All through summer you feel yourself growing… You have a marvellous view… What can you see?
8.	Autumn approaches and you feel a difference… The strength of the sap surging through your veins ceases… Your colour begins to fade… A gust of wind blows you from the twig on which you have spent the whole of your life…
9.	You finally settle on the ground… What happens to you now?
10.	*(Steps v–ix above)*

Depending on age group – children could discuss what it felt like to 'be' a leaf.Does this have an impact on how they now view leaves and the natural world?Can they explore how different religious groups view the environment? For example

■ Many Christians view humans as 'stewards' looking after the world and using resources wisely, so God created the natural world for humans to care for, but also enjoy.

■ Many Hindus do not see the divine as separate from nature. The natural world (living and non-living things) are part of the Divine and so many Hindu rituals are designed to harmonise humans with the natural world.

THE POWER OF COLLECTIVE EXPERIENCES

When head teachers are asked how their school provides opportunities for spiritual development, one of the things they often talk about is their residential trips and visits outside of the classroom (see also Chapter 9). The power of these collective experiences is not to be underestimated in terms of how they can help children to develop spiritually. They usually include the first two dimensions – inner, social and moral, and often can also include environmental and transcendental dimensions, depending on the context and nature of the trip.

> The bonding that takes place during a residential or on a day trip out of school is both strong and subtle. Children learn different things about each other that they may not have learnt in the classroom. Hidden strengths and talents as well as sometimes humbling challenges alter set preconceptions of what someone is like.
>
> (Prescott 2014)

Children begin to see each other in new and different ways. A confident child may not be as brave or strong outside of the classroom and may be unwilling to try new activities and in need of support from their peers to succeed. Conversely, a quiet child can be very confident and surprise their classmates with their inner strength, bravery or abilities. The previous perceptions of them are expanded and developed. A child who can be very challenging in the classroom is sometimes utterly engaged on school trips and contributes with enthusiasm. The class experiences things together and bond together more strongly as a group because of it. At leavers' assemblies at the end of Year Six, day and residential trips are often relayed as amongst their most memorable experiences from their time at primary school.

Trips give children new encounters and opportunities and they can grow through these. The sense of achievement at trying something new like canoeing or sailing or conquering their fears going for a night walk is huge. Many of the outdoor education trips and residential visits will involve the environmental dimension of spirituality, as they include children being in the outdoors and experiencing it in new and different ways. The 'wow' moment at reaching the top of a mountain and seeing the world from a different angle can be very powerful, as can the amazement at seeing the minute and intricate details of nature in a flower or a spider's web. Likewise, for a child from a rural area, the first experience of a city environment can provoke a sense of awe and wonder.

Within the transcendental dimension, RE has a significant part to play through helping children to experience a range of places of worship, both in their own locality and further afield. You do not have to be a Christian or a Muslim to feel awe and wonder at the beauty of a mosque, or the grandeur of a cathedral. We should allow children the chance to be still and absorb the atmosphere of a place of worship in a multi-sensory way (Stone and Brennan 2009).

Pauline Lovelock (2011), who spoke movingly about showing children round the Julian Shrine in Norwich and giving them experiences of stilling there, recorded one child as saying:

> *I lit a candle and I felt all shaky – but I'm not a Christian. That never happens in football.*

If we provide children with these kinds of inner and, at times, transcendental experiences, and a way to express their responses afterwards, we are going some way to *'allowing their spiritual voices to be heard'* (Adams et al. 2008).

IGNITING A SPARK AND INTERDISCIPLINARY RE

A head teacher we know had a saying on the wall in her office which read, *'Every child has a spark; it is our job to ignite it'*. This is a powerful statement which encapsulates what being a teacher is about and also what spiritual development consists of. If we get to know our children and encourage them to develop by supporting them through challenges and giving them a wide range of experiences and opportunities, we are helping to nurture their inner being at the deepest level. A good school is one where children seem to be 'alight' with their enthusiasm for life and learning. We can almost feel the sparks in the air (Prescott 2014). Creative RE has a real role to play in ensuring this happens.

Another plea we have is for teachers to see the interconnectedness of RE with other subject areas and academic disciplines, already mentioned in Chapter 1. Young children are by nature multi-disciplinary, no child would look at a tree and think: biology – photosynthesis; art – leaf prints; RE – spiritual journey; geography – shelter and biodiversity; maths – height, weight; good and nutrition – apple tart; and so on. Rather a primary teacher would encourage a child to investigate a tree by combining and drawing on all these elements.

Adams (2022) talks about avoid silos in RE. This is particularly important in developing children's spirituality where the teacher can draw on their knowledge of psychology and counselling to develop mindfulness (the self/inner dimension), sociology to consider how humans interact with each other (others/the social and moral dimension), environmental sciences (world and beauty/environmental dimension) and philosophy/RE (beyond/transcendental dimension).

So supporting children's spiritual development is not exclusively in the RE domain but rather it spans the whole experience of school. A child's spiritual development is more a way of thinking and being, but in this chapter, in an RE book, we have endeavoured to illustrate how our subject can support this important part of a child's development.

REFERENCES

Adams, K. (2022) Religious education, children's spirituality and the problems of academic silos. *Journal of Religious Education* 70: 217–222. https://doi.org/10.1007/s40839-022 -00167-9.

Adams, K., Hyde, B. and Woolley, R. (2008) *The Spiritual Dimension of Childhood*. London: Jessica Kingsley Publishers.

Blaylock, L. (2002) *Reflection, Inspiration, Engagement. Spiritual Development through RE 31 practical activities.* SACRE Conference RE Today. Lancaster.

del Castillo, F. and Sarmiento, P.J. (2022) A systematic review on spiritual modeling: Opportunities and challenges in religious education. *International Journal of Christianity & Education* 26(1): 6–17. Available at https://journals.sagepub.com/doi/ pdf/10.1177/20569971211038968 (Accessed on 14 May 2023).

Elton-Chalcraft, S. (2002) Empty wells: How well are we doing at spiritual well-being? *International Journal of Children's Spirituality* 7(3): 309–328.

Fisher, J. W. (1999) Helps to Fostering Students' Spiritual Health. *International Journal of Children's Spirituality* 4(1): 29–49.

Hannam, P. (2022) Reflections on the place of spirituality in policy making for religious education. *Journal for the Study of Spirituality* 12(1): 78–85. DOI:10.1080/20440243. 2022.2062823.

Hay, D. and Nye, R. (2006) *Spirit of the Child*, Revised ed. London: Fontana.

Heelas, P. (2008) *Spiritualities of Life: New Age Romanticism and Consumptive Capitalism.* Oxford: Blackwell.

Hill, Ellie and Woolley, R. (2022) Religious education and its interaction with the spiritual dimension of childhood: Teachers' perceptions, understanding and aspirations. *Religions* 13(4): 280. https://doi.org/10.3390/rel13040280.

Lovelock, P. (2011) *Can You Feel the Silence?* Presentation at the Westhill Trust Seminar Leeds 2011: Spirituality and RE: Imagination, spiritual development and the RE Curriculum.

Mills E. (2002) Spiritual development; The doughnut and the hole. Available at: www .crackingre.co.uk/htdocs/crackingre/secure/teach?Supp/donut.html.

NACCCE (National Advisory Group for Creative and Cultural Education) (1999) All our futures: Creativity, culture and education. Available at: http://www.cypni.org.uk/ downloads/alloutfutures.pdf (Accessed on 20 February 2014). www.natre.org.uk/ spirited arts for examples of both Art in Heaven and Spirited Poetry.

Ofsted (2013) RE realising the potential. Available at: http://www.ofsted.gov.uk/resources/ religious-education-realising-potential (Accessed on 20 January 2014).

Ofsted (2021) *Research Review into Religious Education.*London: Department for Education.

Prescott, G. (2012) Spirituality in the classroom: Interactivity and imagination. *RE Today* 29(1): 46–48.

Prescott, G. (2014) *From Unconscious Incompetence...? A personal journey to understanding spiritual development.* Birmingham: RE Today.

Rickett, A., Rickett, S. and Holloway, D. (2012) *Progression in Spirituality Salisbury Diocesan Board of Education.* Salisbury: Diocesan Board of Education.

Stone, M. (1995) *Don't Just Do Something, Sit There.* Norwich: Religious and Moral Education Press.

Stone, M. and Brennan, J. (2009) See RE: Stories from Christianity - Guided Visualisations for Children Aged 7–11. Norwich: Canterbury Press.

Wright, A. (2000) *Spirituality and Education: Master Classes in Education Series.* London: Routledge.

RELIGION AND WORLDVIEWS THROUGH THE ARTS

Linda Whitworth, Saima Saleh and Janet Orchard

This chapter aims to:

- Extend thinking about creativity in Religion and Worldviews education by considering interpretations of creativity in relation to the arts.
- Consider the importance of process in creativity and how pupils may examine and express their own worldviews through exploring a variety of art forms.
- Assist teachers in recognising their own worldviews and consider how to enable pupils to encounter the worldviews of others.
- Encourage teachers to develop children's exploration of music, drama, art and technology in relation to RW.
- Encourage engagement with religious and cultural art forms, artefacts, symbolism and meaning-making.
- Explore cross-curricular and interdisciplinary learning involving RW, considering understanding which enriches children's substantive knowledge and personal schemata.
- Provide a case study to draw together the different elements explored in this chapter.
- Assist Early Careers Teachers in considering cultural and religious inclusivity and sensitivities which may emerge in the primary classroom.

INTRODUCTION

Thinking about Creativity in the Context of This Chapter

In this chapter we discuss the value of promoting 'creativity' in RW lessons, recognising it as a term with a range of alternative meanings. Being creative may describe a way of life, a means by which to express feelings, beliefs, and ideas, individually and collectively, as well as concerning the production of a variety of art forms. Creativity is a vital element of human experience we maintain, across cultures and communities worldwide.

DOI: 10.4324/9781003361480-10

Here we investigate the positive contribution played when connections are forged between Religion and Worldviews (RW) and Art, Music, Dance, and Technology, as examples of key areas of artistic human achievement in relationship to religious and/or human inspiration and interpretation. The chapter takes the form of a dialogue between three voices, led by a narrator, Linda, an experienced primary teacher educator, with two interlocuters, whose comments are presented in speech boxes: Saima (an experienced classroom teacher) reflects on the practical implications of creativity in Primary RE, while Janet, (a former RE teacher, now a university-based researcher) identifies possibilities and challenges from a theoretical angle. We take this creative approach to respect the distinct voices of practitioners and academics on matters of classroom practice, respecting creative processes as both individual and collaborative; having three voices enables both dialogue and expression of individual perspectives.

Interpretations of Creativity in Relation to the Arts

From extensive discussion of creativity over many years, two main interpretations emerged by the late 20th/early 21st centuries, often referred to as ‘*Big-C*’ (Csikszentmihalyi, 1998, 80) and ‘*little-c*’ creativity (Craft, 2001). Taking *Big C* creativity first, this idea refers to skilled practitioners in what is termed ‘high’ or elite artistic performance, whether in fine art, music, dance, or drama, who are recognised as ‘masters’ of their skill (Kaufman and Beghetto, 2009). Examples of recognised ‘*Big-C*’ creatives include Rembrandt, J.S. Bach, Jane Austen, Ravi Shankar, Rumi, or Dame Margot Fontaine. *Big C* creativity (Merrotsy, 2013) is highly prized, attracting status and financial support. ‘*Big-C*’ creatives are revered for perpetuity as part of a ‘cultural canon’, rather than popular during their lives, so that once their reputation is established, they should be subjects of a broad and balanced education so that pupils see, hear, and interact with their creative masterpieces.

Enabling pupils to experience *Big C* religious and cultural expression is important, while recognising strong Western influences on the established canon. This should be noted when using masterpieces of religious art, for example, by Leonardo da Vinci and Michelangelo, which tend to be European and Christian. An argument for using them sensitively is to empower children who might not otherwise access them, thus engaging them productively and imaginatively with high art forms. However, it is also clearly important to widen pupils’ experience of *Big C* art forms, reflecting *Big C* cultural diversity in illustrations chosen for lessons.

In contrast, *little-c* creativity relates to everyday aspects of creativity available to all (Merrotsy, 2013), moments or acts of creativity occurring day-to-day. Harder to define than *Big C* contributions, *little-c* creativity is of considerable importance to anyone seeking to express their feelings and ideas in creative forms. Merrotsy (2013) cites Stein (1987) as a key thinker concerned to recognise everyday creativity, including by schoolchildren. In RW, *Little-c* creativity promotes imaginative thinking, using prior knowledge and understanding to make new connections or schemata. Take, for example, creating a mini-world or expressing personal views and feelings through artistic means; or making a table into a cave or house and making stories or objects to accompany such play. Interpreting one’s ideas through verbal, physical or other expression, including art, music, or dance, can bring excitement, frustration, joy and/or contentment in things attempted and/or completed. Creativity can refer to a process as well as a product. There is huge value in opportunity to think creatively in lessons, even though it can be less easy to define and plan for.

Imagination can be taken to mean the capacity to suppose, or to think "beyond actuality into the sphere of the possible" (White, 2002). Imaginative teachers take a conventional model of practice and translate it to a different one, for example taking an idea from a television programme and applying it to classroom practice in an original way. Being imaginative and creative in this *little-c* sense takes something that exists already and translates it to a different acceptable purpose (White, 2002). The point about having an 'acceptable purpose' is important, although getting the balance right is tricky and leads to the occasional mistake. Inappropriate connections that don't make any sense to other people won't work in the classroom. Sound your creative ideas out first with others you trust before setting your heart on implementing them, and keep things simple. For me, when things have gone wrong, on reflection I have over-complicated things, been too ambitious or over-elaborate.

Janet

Kaufman and Beghetto argue for a more complex four c model of creativity, by introducing two further categories: *'mini-c'* and *'pro-c'*. Although contested (Runco, 2014), the value of the four c model for primary teachers is how it emphasises being creative through the process as much as the result, especially in educational settings. *'Pro-c'* (2009, 2) identifies a distinction between increasing competence and enduring skill when considering how a skilled practitioner becomes a master or proponent of *Big C*. Given the tangential relevance to mainstream primary classrooms, it will not be considered further here, but would be important in primary departments of specialist arts institutions and the individual tuition of younger children. However, 'mini-c' reminds teachers to invest time and effort in 'creativity inherent in the learning process' (Kaufman and Beghetto, 2009, 1). We consider this briefly next.

LEARNING THROUGH THE PROCESS OF CREATIVITY

Providing opportunities to become immersed in making can be inherently valuable when teachers are mindful to encourage process as well as product. *Through* the process, for example, when pupils are taught to play a variety of percussion instruments in Music, they can be helped to channel a range of events or emotions, their own or other people's, with whom they might then better empathise. These might then be developed into a score, and/or used to illustrate a story, combining a range of knowledges and skills.

Saima:
"If we listened more to pupil voice, we would know that they value learning tasks that enable them to empathise with others in ways that are meaningful, have high impact and are fun!" This quote from a past pupil, Lucy, summarises it well:

> *"It's important to learn about the religious and non-religious worldviews of others because we get to understand more about what's important to them. When we learn in a fun way, it goes in better and we remember it. We can then think about it afterwards and think about what difference what we've learnt could make to us and our lives".*
>
> Lucy

Whether working as an individual, or collectively, the creative process helps pupils to develop and express their identity through a dialogue between the internal or personal self, and public shared experiences (Chappell et al., 2016). Such outcomes, albeit small-scale, represent uniquely valuable opportunities for self-expression, enabling pupils to develop through opportunities to experiment multiple times – sometimes successfully, others not. Learning to feel dissatisfied with one's creative efforts, and to manage those feelings constructively, may be just as important as experiencing a sense of satisfaction.

> Providing children with creative lessons is so important: it helps pupils to be engaged and active in their learning, making it memorable. In order for our curriculum to be more connected, it's important to find links between subjects in a meaningful manner, where creative lesson activities overrule rigid worksheet-based lessons (often just factual learning), which mean little to most pupils.
>
> Saima

> Being creative in lessons and across whole school activities matters to a child's intellectual as well as personal development. It is heart-breaking to see it marginalised in formal education today. RW is not the only subject that can redress the balance, but its unique contribution is worth exploring.
>
> Janet

RECOGNISING YOUR OWN WORLDVIEW AND ENCOUNTERING THE WORLDVIEWS OF OTHERS

To encourage you to see opportunities for creativity in the RW classroom, we will now consider how the ideas about creativity we have discussed can be extended into classroom practice. But before we do that, we think it is really important to begin by asking you to reflect on your own sense of aesthetics in order to recognise the influence of your own worldview. As teachers we need to understand what influences us so we can recognise our own preferences as we teach and deliberately extend beyond them. What is beautiful, attractive, moving, or conversely ugly or repellent to you, and why? What criteria inform your judgements? Note that these can be highly subjective.

The questions in Table 8.1 are designed to help you in this process:

Table 8.1 *Big C* and *little-c* questions

- What *Big C* art forms are you most drawn to and why? If none, why not?
- How do you express yourself creatively in the *little-c* sense? If not, why not?

The next process is to consider the different personal and organised worldviews which influence your pupils, who may share some common cultural references with their teachers as well as differences resulting from age, stage of development and culture. Ask them in general terms what they have seen and heard and what is beautiful or exciting to them.

Then, consider their prior learning. The following questions in Table 8.2 may help this process:

Table 8.2 Identifying previous learning

- What cultural and social influences and experiences may some of them have?
- Have they previously visited artistic venues or attended cultural events which may have influenced their understandings?
- Have they already encountered creativity in other curriculum areas in school, e.g. art, music, drama, and technology and do they link to planned for or potential learning in RW? What have they learned already in RW that connects to arts subjects?
- What skills have they already begun to develop that enable them to express their creativity? Do they participate in after-school or weekend activities which include artistic, religious, or cultural references?

Next, consider Religion and Worldviews and the distinctive contribution it makes to the curriculum by referencing a wide range of cultural and ideological perspectives on creativity and the arts. How might different pupils bring their own experiences, cultures and beliefs to their RW learning? While artistic and cultural references should be included across the curriculum, in RW pupils should become increasingly aware of diverse forms of artistic expression in special or sacred settings. Such learning assists pupils in recognising who they are and what they understand (Thapa, 2020). RW at its best will enable children to understand the considerable variety of human expression of faith and belief, within and between religious and non-religious communities, so it is important to ensure curricular planning avoids caricature and stereotypes in representing the 'other'.

> The opportunities to explore culture and meaning in RW across the full range of diverse identities represented in the UK, are an important contribution the subject can make to children's worldview literacy, as well as their wider social, moral, and cultural awareness.
>
> Janet

Festivals and celebrations of communities represented in the school can be a good starting point to explore the place of the arts in creative expression and, in schools which value creativity, teachers can use these wider resources to enrich their teaching. In schools situated in culturally diverse areas, their RW curriculum often draws on their pupils' lives to ensure inclusive learning. It is important that all teachers should expect to introduce pupils to the cultural and religious diversity which is increasingly part of Britain's identity.

USING ARTEFACTS TO EXTEND THINKING ABOUT RELIGIOUS AND NON-RELIGIOUS PRACTICE

We now consider pedagogical strategies associated directly with teaching RW with arts subjects by using artefacts. Using religious and other significant objects generates opportunities for pupils to engage with both the creativity of others and develop their own creative ideas. Many religions use artefacts in regular observance, including aids to prayer and special clothing. Exploring religious artefacts and the symbolism behind them offers an excellent route into navigating metaphorical language. All schools should be encouraged to acquire them, as using a three-dimensional object can be more powerful than a two-dimensional image.

It is important to handle artefacts sensitively, so their use should be researched in advance. For example, some objects should be observed from a distance without contact, while others are intended to be held by observers. Explain the need to show respect for the beliefs and practices of others as well as taking good practical care of the objects themselves. Schools which use 'Show and Tell' as a part of their weekly routine will already have created class rules for talking and listening as well as handling valued objects.

Teachers should model how to care for artefacts while teaching about them. They should aim to establish an atmosphere which anticipates something interesting for the pupils. It can be helpful to have a beautiful box or bag from which the artefact is lifted, using gloves of the kind a museum curator might wear. Artefacts can be placed on a table covered with cloth to indicate care and respect. In some circumstances it would be appropriate for pupils to wash their hands and sit quietly while the artefact is produced. In EYFS/KS1 it is particularly helpful to have objects which can be handled and passed around. For many pupils this first contact with a significant object can inspire multiple questions and comparisons with their own experiences.

An issue for teachers can be to understand the place of the artefacts in religious observance. It is important not to stereotype religious practice when introducing a religious object. Not all members of a religion will have the same artefacts, nor will they have the same interpretations. Teaching about artefacts is an excellent way to encourage pupils to understand varying interpretations which enrich a deeper understanding of the place and practice of religion in individuals' and communities' lives.

Here is an example of an artefact, key words (Figure 8.1) and pupils' key questions (Table 8.3) that Saima has used in her classroom. Saima reflects on her teaching experience in the speech box.

■ **Figure 8.1** Exploring Sikh symbols © Saima Saleh 2022.

■ **Table 8.3** Questions drawn up by a group of children in Saima's class, working together to create an assessment task

---

Questions about living a Sikh life

1. What are the 5 K's?
2. Why is Kesh important to many Sikhs?
3. What is this? (Kara) Why is it important to many Sikhs?
4. What is this? (Kachera) Why is it important to many Sikhs?
5. What is this? (Kirpan) Why is it important to many Sikhs?
6. What is this? (Kangha) Why is it important to many Sikhs?
7. Where do you find a Kirpan on a Sikh person's body?
8. Which of the 5 K's do you think is the most commonly worn and why?

My pupils had to work collaboratively to compose and agree on a set of questions that would be useful as an end of unit quiz. I had requested that they think about how 'lived experiences' would play a part in the questioning.

Quizzes make a fun way of reinforcing learning and, when the pupils themselves have to formulate the questions, they are made to reflect and think creatively on how to do this, recognising what they have learned and deciding what should be assessed. This enables them to recognise the different facets of knowledge that they think are valuable. This group of children then went on to record a short video of the answers, which they were keen on teachers using as a classroom resource.

Saima

SYMBOLISM AND MEANING-MAKING

Symbolism is an aspect of creativity which connects both *'Big C'* and *'little c'*. Exploring symbols broadens understanding. Major art works sometimes include symbols, like a dove or olive branch to represent peace, or light to indicate understanding (e.g., 'The Baptism of Christ' by Piero della Francesca or 'The Light of the World' by William Holman Hunt). Asking pupils to construct their own symbols allows them to invest objects or characters with new meanings, using clay, modelling materials or Lego to express ideas. *Little-c* creativity of this kind requires teachers to engage with a broader range of teaching approaches, being creative themselves as a model for pupils and finding imaginative ways to engage them. In return, for both the teacher and pupils, there can be considerable pleasure in planning and teaching lessons which inspire and resonate with pupils' interests, extending their chance to experiment with meaning.

Creatively Encountering Religion and Worldviews Through Music, Art, Drama and Technology

In this section we encourage you to explore RW through the lenses of various artistic disciplines and create valuable opportunities for pupils to consider both their own understandings of the world and the understandings and cultural products of others.

The RW curriculum is locally determined in England, so it is important to establish early on which locally Agreed Syllabus is used at your school. Some Agreed Syllabuses and schools have developed their own distinctive explorations of the relationship between RW and the arts suited to their local context. An example can be seen in this knowledge organiser from the Norfolk Syllabus Year 5 Enquiry 2 'How has belief in Christianity/ Islam impacted on music and art throughout history?' which shows how RW is using information about Art and Music to develop its own learning. (Norfolk SACRE, 2019)

https://view.officeapps.live.com/op/view.aspx?src=https%3A%2F%2Fwww.dioceseofnorwich.org%2Fapp%2Fuploads%2F2021%2F08%2FYr5Enquiry2.docx&wdOrigin=BROWSELINK

The National Curriculum (DfE, 2013) framework for each arts subject sets out the aims and content of what should be learned and identifies specific skills and knowledges.

Each of the subjects seeks to develop an increasingly complex and skilled understanding and capacity for expression from ages four to eleven. These should be clearly traceable through a school's schemes of work across the year groups and should enable teachers to plan series of lessons which enrich children's substantive and personal schemata. Helping pupils build within and across subjects enables them to own their learning more holistically.

We review the potential of promoting RW in four discrete 'carrier' subject areas next.

EXAMPLE 1. PURPOSE OF STUDY – ART

Art, craft and design embody some of the highest forms of human creativity. A high-quality art and design education should engage, inspire and challenge pupils, equipping them with the knowledge and skills to experiment, invent and create their own works of art, craft and design. As pupils progress, they should be able to think critically and develop a more rigorous understanding of art and design. They should also know how art and design both reflect and shape our history, and contribute to the culture, creativity and wealth of our nation.

(DfE, National Curriculum, 2013)

Exploring Belief in Jesus Through Art

One frequent use of art in the RW classroom involves paintings which reflect on the story of the historical Jesus, for example using images found on Christmas cards or in art galleries and churches. Not only is it important to choose pictures which are appropriate to the ages and understandings of the pupils, Christianity is a global religion, so representations of Jesus should be introduced from different countries, continents, and cultures at an early point, to illustrate this global dimension. There are a number of resources which have been developed over the last 25 years, including Margaret Cooling's excellent *'Jesus through Art'* (1998), which provide suitable material for primary-age pupils. RE Today has published a series called *'Picturing Jesus'* (2001, 2003) and *Picturing Jesus: Fresh Ideas* (2010) which contain a range of global images of Jesus and teaching ideas. Different global representations of the Nativity can be found at *Paintings of the Nativity From Around the World – BAME Anglican (wordpress.com)*.

USING AN EXAMPLE OF *BIG-C* CREATIVITY IN A LESSON ABOUT THE NATIVITY

Our suggestion is that by the time pupils have reached 10–11 years old, a painting such as 'Mystic Nativity' by Botticelli might be introduced to discuss Christian understandings of the story. This is best viewed on a computer screen to appreciate its rich colours. Draw pupils' attention to the repeated image of olive branches throughout the picture symbolising peace. Notice the pattern of the angels' clothing, showing reference to rhythm by using three colours. From an artistic perspective the relative size of each of the figures can be considered. What is the artist trying to say about who and what is important? Note the figures at the bottom of the painting and consider why they might have been included. Consider theological understandings of the nativity and the power of Jesus. The image can be downloaded from the National Gallery website, which also has information about the picture to support teachers. https://www.nationalgallery.org.uk/paintings/sandro-bot-ticelli-mystic-nativity.

There is a further detailed interpretation offered by the BBC https://www.bbc.co.uk /sounds/play/m0012qxq. This explains the background of the painting and considers the likely messages intended by Botticelli. These layers of symbolism can be interpreted with pupils, according to their backgrounds and ages.

EXAMPLE 2. PURPOSE OF STUDY – MUSIC

> Music is a universal language that embodies one of the highest forms of creativity. A high quality music education should engage and inspire pupils to develop a love of music and their talent as musicians, and so increase their self-confidence, crea-tivity and sense of achievement. As pupils progress, they should develop a critical engagement with music, allowing them to compose, and to listen with discrimina-tion to the best in the musical canon.
>
> (DfE, National Curriculum, 2013)

Growing confidence in and experience of self-expression through music can be harnessed in RW as Julian Stern (2004) illustrates:

> Religious education (RE) is a vital subject in the inclusion of pupils and staff alike, as it brings together ways of life and communities, the personal and the social. Music, embedded in religious and other ways of life, adds a communicative dimen-sion that strengthens inclusive RE … and … can be used as a form of community-making of the most comprehensive (i.e. inclusive) kind.
>
> (2004, 112)

Carefully chosen examples can evoke emotional and meditative responses in pupils with-out a need for verbal explanations and with recognition of their own cultural and religious roots. Music is a wonderful opportunity for pupils to engage with the worldviews of oth-ers through exploring interpretation. However, in some religions, some adherents do not listen to music and teachers should carefully explain why this is the case. For example, Otterbeck and Ackfeldt (2012, 229-230) state

> Muhammad is said to have encouraged occupational songs and songs at weddings, but he is also reported as having prophesied that music is one of the signs of the moral chaos toward the end of time. The discussion has resulted in music being divided into different types.

Meanwhile, the following quotations, taken from Hussain and Cooper-Davies (2024), offer three (authoritative) sources suggesting more receptive views from within Islam:

> Musical instruments were played in front of the Prophet (to welcome him) during his first arrival in Medinah and Abu Bakr wanted to tell off those who were playing the instruments but the Prophet stopped him saying: Leave them alone O Abu Bakr

so that the Jews (of Medinah) will also learn and know that our religion is relaxed and accommodating!

(Al Qurtubi)

Whoever says that all music is prohibited, let him also claim that the songs of birds are prohibited.

(Al Ghazali)

Listening to music, attending musical gatherings, and studying music of all genres and instruments is allowed as long as it is not accompanied with immoral and sinful acts, or used as a way to invite people towards haraam (prohibited) behaviour, and it does not preoccupy a person away from observing the obligatory acts of worship.

(Grand Mufti of Al Azhar University, Egypt, 1980)

As we point out later in example 3 below, some faith groups also consider dance to be inappropriate. Teachers need to be aware of different perspectives and this highlights diverse practice within as well as between different religions.

Teaching about Cantors in Judaism

With its intersecting liturgical and cultural roots, music can be heard in synagogues and homes as part of religious and family life across many forms of Judaism. As a religion prac- tised in many parts of the world, moreover, Jewish culture reflects the influence of a variety of places as well as times. When pupils are learning about the Torah and its place in Jewish worship, one appropriate strategy might be for pupils to hear portions of the Torah recited and prayers sung. The haunting, highly evocative sound of a cantor at their most expert illustrates the 'communicative dimension' to music used in RW to which Stern refers.

Pupils can learn about the role of the cantor (chazzan) in Orthodox and Reform Judaism and listen to prayers sung for the High Holy Days. In some traditions cantors can be men or women, so this is a good opportunity to teach about different groups and practices within the faith. Cantors can also have a role in training adolescents for their Bar/Bat Mitzvah and, if they have been ordained, can take the role of a rabbi in services. Examples of reciting text can be a useful introduction to learning about these services.

EXAMPLE 3. DANCE

Although the current Purpose of Study for Primary Physical Education does not specifically include dance, it does list it in the subject content across the primary phase which states 'perform dances using simple movement patterns' for younger children and 'perform dances using a range of movement patterns' for older ones (DfE, 2013). As well as engaging pupils in movement, dance can contribute to RW in providing *little-c* and *mini-c* opportunities to create dances which illustrate stories or opportunities or see dances performed as part of cultural and religious celebrations.

Using Dance to Explore the Idea of Movement and Balance

Dance can be explored, for example, in the Hindu tradition. In Figure 8.2, Shiva is por- trayed as dancing in the *Nataraj* pose (Nata means dance and raj means king), portraying

■ **Figure 8.2** Shiva in Nataraj pose © Elton-Chalcraft, 2023.

the continuing cycle of death and rebirth. In Hindu belief, Shiva is one of three main gods composing Brahman, the supreme god. This image of Shiva, the god of destruction, shows him in perfect movement and balance. The statue's pose was developed around the ninth to tenth centuries CE in Southern India and has become a universally recognised Hindu image.

Pupils can be encouraged to question the meaning of the *murti* (statue) and the symbolism it conveys. Why is dance seen as central to maintaining the balance of the world? Is the movement of the world continuous? How might the world be out of balance? What aspects of balance can they explore though dance and why is balance important within movement and stillness?

While some religions promote dance as part of their religious expression, teachers should also explore carefully with pupils a few reasons why some faith groups regard dancing as inappropriate or unacceptable. We pointed out similar issues with music in the previous section. Reasons which may be given to censure dance include a perception that it is too uncontrolled, or inappropriately sensual. Dancing potentially contravenes accepted cultural behaviours, especially if it involves both men and women dancing together. These might be interesting views to discuss with children.

Are any pupils in the class learning dance as part of their community's cultural and religious education, at Saturday schools or after-school clubs? It can be affirming for them to share these experiences. For example, Hindu and Sikh pupils learning cultural and religious dance outside school can be given opportunities to discuss, perform and share their skills. Such events can celebrate diverse religious and cultural heritages and create opportunities to invite guests into school.

■ **Figure 8.3** Kalta Minor Minaret in Khiva Uzbekistan© D. Whitworth 2017.

EXAMPLE 4. PURPOSE OF STUDY – DESIGN AND TECHNOLOGY

> Design and technology is an inspiring, rigorous and practical subject. Using creativity and imagination, pupils design and make products that solve real and relevant problems within a variety of contexts... Through the evaluation of past and present design and technology, they develop a critical understanding of its impact on daily life and the wider world.
>
> (DfE, National Curriculum, 2013)

Food technology can involve pupils learning about different religious food requirements as well as festivals and their related celebrations. Many involve making decorations as well as the preparation of special, and often symbolic foods, which pupils can create or sample, subject to necessary safeguards. By focussing on design, pupils can explore different artefacts – for example, Muslim prayer mats (investigating their manufacture, patterns and the meanings underpinning them). Tiles may be interpreted, for example on mosques (see Figure 8.3), to promote learning about the significance of repeated patterns and use of symmetry. Designing their own patterns can be a thought-provoking follow-up activity, in which pupils appreciate the attention to detail and religious and cultural mores which lies behind these beautiful designs.

CROSS-CURRICULAR AND INTERDISCIPLINARY LEARNING IN RW

We now consider different models for teaching creatively. Although the National Curriculum and Basic Curriculum in England separate subjects out for study, notions of creativity discussed in Chapter One and presented in this chapter also encourage elements of cross-curricular and interdisciplinary thinking. At different times in British educational theory there have been advocates for both cross-curricular as well as single subject learning (Rose, 2009; Alexander, 2010; Barnes, 2018; Scottish Government, 2019; Welsh Government, 2021). Critics raise concerns about 'watering subjects down', in a 'mishmash' of unstructured learning, but there should be opportunities for creativity when pupils amalgamate learning from different areas and use it to interpret and extend their views of the world. Substantive knowledge is an important part of the current Ofsted inspection framework (Ofsted, 2021), requiring clear understanding of the nature and content of each subject and how they are developed through lesson planning. However, piles of discrete, unconnected subject knowledge can be equally challenging to make sense of and do not reflect how some learning can be applied in the real world. Through drawing together threads from arts and humanities subjects, as well as literature and language, pupils can see a rich tapestry of human development, focussing on what is valuable and worth sustaining and developing.

As discussed in Chapter One, a balance is needed between a perceived need for pupils to understand what different subjects contain and the underpinning philosophies they hold, on one hand, and carefully thought-out, well-planned opportunities to connect across a range of subjects using interpretive skills on the other. Such connections can be particularly powerful in subjects which have humanity as their core, including History, Geography, RW and Citizenship, but also those which explore the products of humankind's creative endeavours. Art, Music, and Dance have traditionally been seen as the prime areas.

Given a lack of time available in many primary schools for foundation subjects, one practical way to enrich the curriculum is to link those subjects together through theme or topic work. (Barnes, 2018; Banks and Waters, 2022). Learning that references knowledge from other areas of the curriculum encourages children to be more imaginative and strengthens their understanding because they learn to use it creatively (Kidd, 2020). There is a place for both single subject and cross-curricular learning in a creative curriculum.

As Mick Waters says:

> Teachers who are true subject enthusiasts know that their subject discipline is a living thing to be enjoyed and explored as it unfolds in the modern world. The best educated, however, are not limited by subjects but possess that critical skill of making those vital connections between disciplines.
>
> (Waters, 2013, 288, cited in Kidd, 2020, 43)

There are a variety of approaches to managing cross-curricular learning creatively. Some schools have stand-alone weeks where certain subjects are prioritised. Others teach using topics which include a two or more subjects. Often one subject takes the lead, with other subjects used to develop the learning about the topic or theme. Planning should show careful mapping of each subject to identify coverage.

A further step is a move towards interdisciplinary learning. This has been indicated for example in the Scottish primary curriculum (2019), where RE is called 'Religious and Moral Education', or in the Welsh curriculum (2021) where pupils are taught 'Religion, Values and Ethics'. This approach echoes the way that children learn, developing schemata and making connections to create new knowledge. Interdisciplinarity encourages pupils to use what they have learned in a variety of contexts and manipulate their knowledge to make sense of new understandings.

DIWALI – A CASE STUDY

In the following section we bring together everything we have discussed through the chapter and apply it to one case study, focussed on the festival of Diwali or Deepawali, which promotes learning in RW linked to our featured 'creative' subjects of art, music, technology, and dance. By way of context, the festival of Diwali is celebrated during the autumn term by Hindus, Sikhs, and Jains to mark the beginning of a new year. Dates for celebrations in different religions can be found at https://www.reonline.org.uk/festival -calendar/ as they vary each year and deviate from the standard 'Western' calendar, following a lunar rather than solar calendar.

Schools often teach Diwali to the four to seven age group, where pupils typically learn the Hindu story of Rama and Sita and sometimes make *diya* or *diva* lamps from clay and decorate them to represent the lights placed by the people of Ayodhya to welcome Rama and Sita home from exile (see Figure 8.4). It is important to recognise that the **making** of lamps is Design and Technology and not RW.

The RW element lies in the consideration of the religious story, the engagement with the continuing experience of believers in decorating their homes and the symbolism evoked in the festival. Older pupils can learn greater intricacies in the story as well as

■ **Figure 8.4** Picture of commercial diya lamps © L. Whitworth 2022. Note the central diya is designed to express good luck and prosperity.

develop a deeper understanding of the impact it has on the lives of believers, seen in the pictures and murtis of Rama and Sita created by devotees, in illustrated story books or found in Hindu mandirs and family shrines. Traditional pictures may include other characters from the story such as Lakshman (Rama's brother), and Hanuman. Rama is often recognisable because of the bow he carries and the blue/mauve skin tone of the picture/murti indicating he is an avatar of Vishnu.

Pupils should be encouraged to examine the pictures or murtis carefully to identify the symbols and links to the story which are shown in them. This will enable them to recognise their meaning (see Figure 8.5 and Jessica's explanation of her picture). Older pupils can study pages from the *Mewar Ramayana* (also known as the *Jagat Singh Ramayana*), commissioned by Maharana Jagat Singh in the 17th century and digitalised by the British Library, accessible on-line at https://www.bl.uk/Ramayana. This beautiful example of an illustrated Ramayana commissioned in India offers a good introduction to the story. It also contains cultural references to dress, architecture, and the landscape of the time, a style of Indian art which might otherwise not be studied.

The Hindu celebration of Diwali also includes welcoming Lakshmi, the Hindu goddess of wealth, to a house or place of worship. *Rangoli* patterns are often created at the entrance, traditionally made with dry coloured materials. There can be carefully managed moments of synthesis between DT and RW through the process of making a *rangoli*, if pupils are given time to create complex patterns and explore symmetry or repeat patterns. This exercise is not intended as an act of worship, but the effort and care in creating a design can encourage pupils to consider the experiences of believers.

■ **Figure 8.5** Rama is banished Copyright NATRE Spirited Arts.

Rama Is Banished

Jessica Aged 9
I believe that the most important turning point in this story is when Rama is banished from the kingdom, because if that hadn't happened the story wouldn't have happened at all.
I have drawn the king crying because he is upset that Rama was banished. Rama is sad because he has been banished. I have drawn my picture in the Madhubani Indian style using pencil crayon.

Celebrations of Diwali may include music and dance forms which tell the story. Those found in Java and Bali include a style called Kecak which involves dance and chanting, e.g. Kecak Dance, Bali – Tale of RAMAYANA – Entry of Hanuman – YouTube Kecak Dance, Uluwatu Temple, Bali – YouTube . There are also Javanese and Cambodian shadow puppet performances of the Ramayana which could be explored through a combined unit in DT and RW.

Finally, Saima provides an end of unit activity showing how applying creative principles to assessment generated an imaginative opportunity to engage a whole class in producing narrative music to represent the Ramayana story with primary-aged pupils.

How Can Hindu Stories Help Many Hindus to Make Sense of Their Beliefs?

Be able to interpret a story from the Hindu scriptures drawing out and explaining key beliefs and consider their value in communicating religious ideas.
Main expressive activity:
In groups, children to be given a traditional Hindu story The Ramayana

■ What can you learn about Hindu beliefs from this story?
■ What does this story tell you about the god it is about?
■ Most Hindu stories involve good overcoming evil. What were the qualities that the god showed?
■ What message does the story teach?
■ Is there a Hindu festival associated with this story?
■ Are there any similarities in this story to any other religious or non-religious story that you know?
■ How could a Hindu today use this story to help them fulfil their duty?

At the end of the topic on Hindu Dharma with a Year 4 class, I asked pupils to reflect on their learning about the story of Rama and Sita, where the theme of light overcoming darkness, good overcoming evil, was the main objective to be portrayed. I love using music in my lessons across the curriculum as I feel that learners of all abilities are able to connect with it and through it as a medium. After having discussed what the story was about and having drawn out a story map, pupils then had to decide which instruments they would choose to portray the story and send the right message to their audience.

Then pupils were given 20 minutes to rehearse their work before presenting their pieces to the rest of the class. I was so proud of the children's results because it showed how much thought they had put into their work. When presenting their compositions, the rest of the class listened and watched in avid silence: they were really absorbed in what they were hearing and consequently, were able to identify various parts of the story and justify why they thought the music matched each piece.

I wanted my class to think about how they could use music to enhance the feelings encountered by each of the characters within the story. I told them that the aim was to tell the story just through sound in order to evoke emotion and develop the story of Rama and Sita. This was their first experience of narrative music, one which could also lend itself to creative writing within the unit. This lesson worked especially well with my pupils who needed greater learning adaptations. As there were no words required in the final piece, they had the freedom and time to spend thinking about how a range of sounds could be made to portray various points in the story. What thrilled me most was the pride which my pupils took in performing their pieces. Using music to deliver a narrative was an effective way of communicating with the audience: a powerful one which seemed to supersede the use of any dialogue.

Saima

Saima's example powerfully demonstrates some of the aims of this chapter on RW through the arts. It recognises how the learning opportunities given to her class encouraged them to reflect on their own learning and interpret it through musical performances. The creative activity is inclusive and allows pupils to express their understanding of the story through performing and listening. It allows for personal and group interpretation and considers sound as a symbol for characters and events in a religious context. The engagement the pupils show underlines the value of connecting RW to other subjects which encourage interpretation. It provides an example of how to engage pupils sensitively and inclusively. The story is repeatedly rehearsed and understood, so that it can be recognised in the performances of different groups. There is both intellectual and emotional engagement through performance and pupils expressed their enjoyment and pride in and through participation. This demonstrates how powerful creative RW can be and how it enables pupils to remember and reflect through their own expression.

SUMMARY

■ **In RW children benefit from looking at the creativity of others and having time and materials to express their own creativity, both in terms of process and product.**

▨ Representing religions and worldviews through creative arts needs to recognise and represent the diversity within and between religions and worldviews sensitively.

▨ Using arts subjects in RW requires recognition and development of the knowledge and skills being introduced across all subjects to enhance RW learning.

▨ Pupils remember learning which is enjoyable and engages them. This is very important in RW lessons which can be made more stimulating through planning and teaching which engages with different art forms.

▨ Schools can develop their RW curriculum by building up relationships with local religious communities which will enable them to understand the experiences of believers and how these can be expressed in artistic forms.

▨ Teachers should be brave in planning and teaching RW creatively. Both teachers and pupils benefit from working creatively.

▨ Teachers should seek out collaborative CPD opportunities in RW to develop their own understanding of being creative in the classroom and how this can be developed with pupils.

A Last Word on Creativity in Teaching

Once you are beyond the basic survival stage in teaching, engaging with educational ideas and theory is hugely important if you are to sustain creative practice in your classroom practice. There are many opportunities to access seminars on line, read blogs and watch podcasts by academics where reading isn't practical. Carefully planned classroom-based research will support you to have your own ideas and to try them out; look out for opportunities to join in projects or apply for teacher fellowship schemes. Carefully thought-through curricular experiments, reflected on critically afterwards, will give you added purpose. As a teacher myself, listening to and learning from well-read and thoughtful mentors gave me permission, in my own mind at least, to 'think otherwise' and for myself. What did I want to do, given the aims of my lessons and the young people I was teaching? More than just my opinion, ideas from those people whose authority I respected supported me to think for myself, rather than accepting the curriculum without question. Imagine becoming a creative teacher and you will find room to foster creativity.

Janet

REFERENCES

Alexander, R. (2010) *Children, Their World, Their Education: Final Report and Recommendations of the Cambridge Primary Review*, London: Routledge.

Al-Haq, S.J.A.-H.A.J. (1980) *Fatwa on music by the Grand Mufti and Shaykh of Al-Azhar*, The Islamic Text Institute http://islamictext.wordpress.com/music-azhar-fatwa/.

Banks, C. and Waters, M. (2022) *A Curious Curriculum, Camarthen*, Wales: Crown House Publishing Ltd.

Barnes, J. (2018) *Applying Cross Curricular Approaches Creatively*, Abingdon: Routledge.

Chappell, K.A., Pender, T., Swinford, E. and Ford, K. (2016) 'Making and being made: Wise humanising creativity in interdisciplinary early years arts education', *International Journal of Early Years Education*, 24(3), 254–278. DOI: 10.1080/09669760.2016.1162704.

Cooling, M., Walker, D. and Taylor, J. (1998) *Jesus through Art*, Norwich: Religious and Moral Educational Press.

Craft, A. (2001) 'Little c creativity', in Craft, A., Jeffrey, R. and Leibling, M. (eds.), *Creativity in Education*, London and New York: Continuum, pp. 45–61.

Csikszentmihalyi, M. (1998) 'Letters from the field', *Roeper Review*, 21(1), 80–81.

Department for Education (2013) *National Curriculum in England: Key Stages 1 and 2 Framework Document*, https://assets.publishing.service.gov.uk/media/5a81a9abe5274a2e8ab55319/PRIMARY_national_curriculum.pdf.

Hussain, Z. and Cooper-Davies, C. (2024) 'Ijtihad in the RE classroom'. *Journal of Beliefs and Values* DOI: 10.1080/13617672.2024.2312337.

Kaufman, J.C. and Beghetto, R.A. (2009) 'Beyond big and little: The four C model of creativity', *Review of General Psychology*, 13(1), 1–12.

Kidd, D. (2020) *A Curriculum of Hope: As Rich in Humanity as in Knowledge*, Carmarthen: Independent Thinking Press.

Merrotsy, P. (2013) 'A note on big-c creativity and little-c creativity', *Creativity Research Journal*, 25(4), 474–476.

Norfolk SACRE (2019) 'Norfolk agreed syllabus: A religious education for the future', Norfolk-religious-education-agreed-syllabus-2019.pdf (dioceseofnorwich.org).

Ofsted (2021) *Education Inspection Framework* Education Inspection Framework (EIF), GOV.UK. www.gov.uk.

Otterbeck, J. and Ackfeldt, A. (2012) 'Music and Islam', *Contemporary Islam*, 6, 227–233 https://link.springer.com/article/10.1007/s11562-012-0220-0.

Rose, J. (2009) *The Independent Review of the Primary Curriculum: Final Report*, Nottingham: DCSF.

Runco, M.A. (2014) '"Big C, little c" creativity as a false dichotomy: Reality is not categorical', *Creativity Research Journal*, 26(1), 131–132.

Scottish Government (2019) 'Curriculum for excellence what is curriculum for excellence?' | Curriculum for Excellence | Policy drivers | Policy for Scottish education | Scottish education system | Education Scotland.

Stein, M.I. (1987) 'Creativity research at the crossroads: A 1985 perspective', in Isaksen, S.G. (ed.), *Frontiers of Creativity Research: Beyond the Basics*, Buffalo, NY: Bearly, pp. 417–427.

Stern, J. (2004) Marking time: Using music to create inclusive religious education and inclusive schools, *Support for Learning*, 19(3), 107–113.

Thapa, S. (2020) 'Assessing intercultural competence in teacher education: A missing link', in Westerlund, H., Karlsen, S. and Partti, H. (eds.), *Visions for Intercultural Music Teacher Education*, Springer. https://link.springer.com/content/pdf/10.1007/978-3-030-21029-8.pdf?pdf=button.

Waters, M. (2013) *Thinking Allowed: On Schooling*, Carmarthen: Independent Thinking Press

Welsh Government (2021) 'An introduction to the curriculum for wales (updated)', https://hwb.gov.wales/curriculum-for-wales/introduction/.

White, J. (2002) *The Child's Mind* (1st ed.). Routledge. https://doi.org/10.4324/9780203453445.

CHAPTER 9

VISITS, VISITORS, PERSONA DOLLS AND INTERFAITH DIALOGUE

Rebekah Ackroyd,
Sally Elton-Chalcraft
and Imran Kotwal

This chapter aims to

- Critically explore the theoretical and empirical basis for using visits, visitors and interfaith dialogue with 3–11-year-olds.
- Creatively explore the practicalities of how, when and where to organise visits, visitors and use persona dolls with 3–11-year-olds.
- Provide an exemplar of being a Muslim visitor to a primary school setting.
- Highlight key considerations to minimise the risk of superficial engagement and interaction with the lived experience of different religions and worldviews.

INTRODUCTION

Organising a visit or hosting a visitor is arguably one of the most memorable aspects of learning in Religion and Worldviews (R&W). It is likely to be a time-consuming task for the teacher of R&W, as well as often taking up substantial learning time for children. In order to make the most of such opportunities, it is therefore important that teachers are clear about what will be gained from the visit or visitor, and how it will make an effective contribution to children's learning in R&W. In this chapter we set out the rationale and theoretical basis for using visits, visitors and encouraging interfaith dialogue. We then look at the practicalities of arranging visits and visitors in order to help make the most of these exciting learning opportunities. It is our intention to illustrate the gamut of possibilities which are available when one thinks creatively about visits, visitors and interfaith dialogue in R&W.

Throughout the chapter we use the term R&W, and sometimes just Worldview, because we seek to be inclusive of the fact that whilst visitors and visits might involve

DOI: 10.4324/9781003361480-11

engaging with institutional religions, visits to official places of worship do not represent the totality of opportunities for learning. Following the thinking of Ruth Flanagan and Linda Whitworth in Chapter Two of this book, a worldview can be understood as denoting a wide range of factors which influence how someone sees, understands and interacts with the world. This opens up the possibility of including a wider range of perspectives which children might learn from through visits and visitors, including but not limited to humanist, atheist and agnostic worldviews.

WHY USE VISITS, VISITORS AND INTERFAITH DIALOGUE?

The use of visits and inviting relevant visitors into schools is widely regarded as a positive teaching strategy for R&W. This is highlighted in the final report from the Commission on RE (Commission on RE, 2018, p. 76), a commission by the non-governmental Religious Education Council for England and Wales. The report points to the benefits of including lived experiences in R&W. The advantages identified of doing so include the chance for children to learn about the breadth of experiences which can exist within a Worldview, as well as helping them to understand that not all followers of a Worldview adopt all the practices and beliefs recognised at an institutional level. Slightly more recently, the national regulatory body for education in England, the Office for Standards in Education, Children's Services and Skills (Ofsted) published a research review of Religious Education (Ofsted, 2021). In this, they note that visits and visitors can provide important opportunities for children to learn about different aspects of religion, including historical and cultural elements. On the topic of visitors, the Ofsted report (2021) also points to the interesting different insights which children might glean from hearing faith accounts from both religious leaders and individual followers. However, the report also argues that learners will need to have key prior knowledge in order for them to gain the most from the visit. This shows the importance of teachers planning for visits so that they enhance other learning that children have been engaged with and occur at a logical point during a scheme of work, rather than relying on visits as the sole means of learning about a particular Worldview. Indeed, as Teece (2010) points out, children learning from a visit to a Sikh gurdwara can only be fully realised if it is accompanied by careful teaching about key Sikh beliefs in order for children to be able to make more fulsome connections between their own experiences and what they experience during the visit.

In the UK, a range of guidance, including a publication from the National Association for Religious Education (NATRE), the professional association for RE/R&W in the UK promotes the benefits of using visits and visitors. NATRE have produced a helpful code of conduct for such occasions (2014) and well as further guidance on visits and visitors being available via their website. The curriculum guidance for Humanities in Wales (Llywodraeth Cymru Welsh Government, 2022) which includes the subject Religion, Values and Ethics (RVE), also independently affirms the suggestion that learners visit places of worship and special places, observe cultural activities, engage with religious artefacts and meet people who can share their personal experiences of faith and belief. Meanwhile in Scotland, the curriculum for excellence (Education Scotland, 2011, p. 217) identifies the benefit of using visits to places of worship as a means of enabling learners to gain insights into Scotland's cultural heritage and identity as part of the subject of Religious and Moral Education (RME).

Theoretical Background: Place-Based Learning

Having established that the use of visits and visitors in R&W is positively regarded it is important to consider the theoretical basis for the benefits of using visits and visitors in R&W. Firstly, it should be noted that visits and visitors represent opportunities for learning outside of the classroom. One pedagogical theory underlying learning outside the classroom is that of place-based learning. Vander Ark, Liebtag and McClennen (2020) observe that from their earliest moments, children learn from what surrounds them. They chart how from the mid-19th century, a growing desire to increase access to education led to a shift from learning being place-based, to classroom-centred. However, Vander Ark, Liebtag and McClennen (2020) argue that place-based learning can make vital contributions to helping children to connect to their communities, as well as promoting agency and equity. This is because place-based learning takes children outside of the confines of their normal rules and routines, helping them to develop their own sense of identity and providing access to different types of opportunities for all learners. Vander Ark, Liebtag and McClennen (2020, p. 12) thus identify four specific ways in which place-based learning can help to build community, highlighted in Table 9.1.

Other advocates of learning outside the classroom like Sedgwick and Karsh (2012, p. 3) have argued that "teaching children outside a classroom, almost regardless of what we are teaching, increases the vitality of learning". This suggests that visiting a place of worship, for example, is likely to have implications for learning even once children return to the confines of the classroom. It can be powerful because of the rich experience which it provides for children. One example of this is seen in Lundie and Conroy's (2015, p. 281) ethnographic research which captures how a visit to a Hindu temple by pupils from a Muslim-majority school provides the chance for learners to encounter first-hand a culture which they have previously experienced only through "crude cultural stereotypes". Their research captures how during the course of the visit, the learners shifted from exhibiting visible signs of fear and discomfort and became increasingly relaxed and engaged with the temple. Writing in the context of America on this topic, Kunzman (2006) does, however, note the importance of visits providing the opportunity for learners to interact positively with followers of the religion during the visit. Doing so, Kunzman (2006) suggests, affords the chance for learners to experience the importance of the religion to adherents and mitigates against the risk of reinforcing stereotypes.

Table 9.1 Ways that place-based learning can help to build community, adapted from Vander Ark, Liebtag and McClennan (2020, p. 12)

1.	It creates bonds between different places and people, reflecting other emphases in early years education and beyond about helping children to understand how they can learn and work together.
2.	It helps children to build a personal connection to their community.
3.	It contributes towards building social capital, for instance, by expanding the social networks that learners have.
4.	It promotes contribution by helping children to make meaningful contributions to their communities in the present, rather than seeing education as preparing future citizens.

Taking children outside the classroom encourages learning which is not centred around pen and paper, but which provides opportunities for children to draw on all five of the senses: sight, sound, taste, touch and smell. A good example of this is highlighted in Kindermann and Riegel's (2018, p. 136) research about 8year-old children visiting a Catholic church as part of Catholic Religious Education in Germany. The vast majority of children participating in the visit had a positive experience. Many of them noticed non-visual sensory aspects of the church including the smell of wood and the sound of the organ. This highlights how teachers can consider the breadth of different experiences children might be able to have whilst on a visit. Chapter Eight (on using arts in R&W) in this book provides further prompts for thinking in this direction.

Theoretical Background: Exploring Robert Jackson's (2004) concept of "Fuzzy Edgedness"

As well as being an example of place-based learning, using visits and visitors in R&W also draws on many of the principals of Robert Jackson's (1997) interpretive pedagogical approach to the subject. Jackson (1997, p. 130) argues for a pedagogical approach to R&W where teachers start with the language and experiences of believers and then look at learners' experiences, before "oscillat[ing] between the two". Jackson's (1997) interpretive approach to R&W thus gives primacy of place to the experiences of believers, rather than, for example, focussing on sacred texts or abstract beliefs. Jackson (2004, p. 87) argues that an advantage of this approach is that it can take account of the variabilities within religious traditions and enable children to explore their "fuzzy edgedness". We understand this as meaning that it is beneficial for children to learn about the diversity within religions and worldviews, and from the perspectives of different followers of the Worldview. Thus, using visits and welcoming visitors could enable children to gain first-hand experience of the insider accounts of religions and worldviews which are at the centre of an interpretive approach to R&W.

A further aspect of this, highlighted by Jackson (2000), is the possibility of using children's experiences of religion as the insider accounts. Jackson (2000, p. 132) has developed a set of books for children aged 5–14 which provide insider accounts of religion from the perspective of children. Other possibilities for this include the use of video clips and story books which highlight a child's experience of and engagement with a particular worldview. Jackson's interpretive approach thus also highlights how teachers might make use of children's own experiences of different religions and worldviews in the classroom. Ackroyd's (2023) research for her PhD found that teachers identify allowing peers to share their own stories as one key approach which can be used to help promote mutual respect and tolerance for different faiths and beliefs. Such moments might even arise spontaneously within the classroom, which teachers in her research felt could increase the authenticity of the account and enhance engagement between peers in the classroom. However, if doing so, it is important not to put children in the spotlight; do not force them to share their accounts if they do not want to and remind other children that their experiences may differ from other adherents of the religion or worldview.

Positionality: No-One Stands Nowhere

Considering inviting a visitor to your classroom or taking your learners out on a visit also requires you to consider where the people you meet might be coming from in terms of their own positionality. The move towards the use of the term Worldviews in preference to Religious Education has seen the Theos Think Tank seek to raise awareness of how we all occupy different positions and have different views of the world. This is explored in an engaging video created by Emily Downe (2021). As well as reflecting on your visitor's positionality, in addition, you will need to carefully plan how you will make your learners aware that visitors may hold particular positions, which may differ even from other adherents of the same religion or worldview. This might provide a valuable learning opportunity for your learners to become more aware of their own positionality too.

Salter's (2020, p. 298) interview-based research with four faith practitioners from different Christian denominations helps to illustrate the significance of positionality. Salter asked participants who are leaders in four different Christian denominations (which she terms 'faith practitioners') about how they would prefer to represent Christianity during a visit to their church. Salter's research highlights how the faith practitioners all said they would be concerned to talk to visitors about the different institutional aspects of their churches such as key doctrines, artefacts and the physical building, because this provides an important context to their particular denomination's traditions. In addition, faith practitioners said they would ideally also talk about their personal experience of Christianity and explain the importance of their faith and relationship with God. These personal experiences and insights, Salter (2020, p. 300) argues, do not exist in the public domain and so they can be helpful for addressing the authenticity gap in how religions are represented. This is because they focus on the individual account of the person, rather than generalisations about a religion. Salter (2020, p. 299) also emphasises the importance of the role of the teacher, who must be able to make clear to children that a faith leader's presentation is their version of the religion, and not representative of whole tradition.

The findings from Salter's (2020) research about the importance of giving children the chance to learn from other people's experiences are echoed in Lundie et al.'s (2022) action research project about enhancing RE in primary schools. This research includes some insights gathered from asking 96 children aged 8–11 about what they hope to learn from visits and visitors. The children identify the importance of hearing someone speak about their worldview, gaining an overview of the services they go to, understanding how the visitor's religion is different to others, learning about the way they live their life and other things linked to this such as charity work. Most of the children were also interested to ask questions about the person's religion but did not feel comfortable with challenging the person's beliefs. Although children did want to try foods and clothes, their enthusiasm for doing so connected to understanding how the believer lives out their beliefs in the rest of their life. Overall, 79% of the children felt that visits and visitors were helpful for understanding a faith (Lundie et al., 2022, p. 145).

DIALOGUE AND DISCUSSION

As demonstrated in the discussion so far, arguably one of the most valuable things making visits and welcoming visitors offers children is the experience to hear and engage with someone who holds a particular Worldview, be this religious or non-religious. This can thus be considered as contributing to an opportunity for children to experience and engage in interfaith dialogue. Regarding the meaning of dialogue, drawing on insights from physicist David Bohm, Senge (2006, p. 223) suggests that the term 'discussion' reflects the idea of a topic being "analysed and dissected from many points of view",

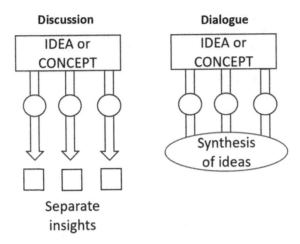

Discussion

Dialogue

Separate insights

▨ **Figure 9.1** The difference between dialogue and discussion informed by Senge's (2006) description.

but where ultimately you want your own view to win through. In contrast, a 'dialogue' which originates in the Greek of 'dia' meaning through and 'logos' meaning the word or the meaning, denotes instances when the purpose is to "go beyond any one individual's understanding" in order to gain insights that would not be arrived at without the group exploration (see Figure 9.1). Interfaith dialogue could thus be understood as being about providing children with occasions on which they can exchange ideas with a range of people in order to collectively deepen their understanding of different Worldviews.

Research into the use of interfaith dialogue, and more broadly community cohesion and interfaith relations, in the subject area of R&W has identified how different types of dialogue can be used by teachers. Key among these is the Shared Spaces project, run by academics at the University of Bristol alongside NATRE, which has explored how a theory from the field of Psychology called the contact hypothesis might be used in R&W. The contact hypothesis originates in the work of psychologist Allport (1954) and proposes that contact between people who have different opinions under the right conditions might promote positive intergroup relationships. Williams *et al.* (2019, p. 222) and Orchard *et al.* (2021) asked 95 R&W practitioners, including 16 primary teachers, about their use of the contact hypothesis to promote community relations in R&W. 39% of the examples provided use discussion or dialogue and 24% focus on visits with diverse others. However, whilst dialogue and visits are widely reported as being used, Williams *et al.* (2019) find that not all of the approaches which the teachers report actually employ the principals of the contact hypothesis. Williams *et al.* (2019) identify three levels of contact which are represented in the responses, illustrated in Table 9.2. Firstly, Encounter (exposure to diverse views without meaningful discussion, such as a visit to a place of worship). Secondly, Conversation (approaches which allow for discussion about difference, but in which the diverse others are not present). The most effective but least commonly used is Interaction, which refers to teaching approaches which promote exposure to difference and diversity alongside meaningful discussion. It is only this latter approach which embodies the principles of the contact hypothesis. It is therefore wrong to assume that visiting a place of worship alone will necessarily lead to meaningful interfaith dialogue

■ **Table 9.2** Types of contact between diverse others, adapted from Williams *et al.'s* (2019, pp. 221–222) research on R&W teachers' use of the Contact Hypothesis

Types and examples of contact between diverse others in increasing order of efficacy

Encounter	Conversation	Interaction
Meaning: Exposure to diverse views.	Meaning: Discussion about difference but potentially without the diverse other present.	Meaning: Exposure to diversity and difference alongside meaningful discussion.
Example: Visiting a place of worship or watching a video clip that prompts discussion.	Example: Parents discussing different beliefs with their children.	Example: Asking a faith speaker questions about their beliefs.

between children and diverse others. Instead, teachers should give careful thought to what types of dialogue and discussion opportunities might be available for children. For example, before going on the visit teachers might help learners to plan some questions which they might ask to help promote more meaningful Interaction in line with the contact hypothesis.

Finally, it is important to note research has also found that making physical visits to places of worship or welcoming visitors into the classroom in person are not the only opportunities for interfaith dialogue and visiting places of significance to R&W. Some visitors might be willing to visit your classroom virtually using a platform like Microsoft Teams or Zoom. In addition, Vander Ark, Liebtag and McClennen (2020, p. 18) note the potential for using videos, augmented and virtual reality to visit places which might otherwise be inaccessible or high risk to visit. Using Google's Arts and Culture platform might provide a starting point for engaging with these sorts of opportunities and the Cumbria Development Education Centre website also provides a comprehensive list of possibilities (see useful resources at end of this chapter). On the topic of interfaith dialogue, Ipgrave's (2009) research for the Building E-Bridges project connected primary aged children (5–11 years old) from different geographic and religious communities in England with each other via email. Ipgrave's (2009) research found that the teacher plays a significant role in moving the discussion to cover topics which explicitly relate to the diverse religious and cultural identities of the children, as well as that of friendship.

ORGANISING VISITS

In the next two sections of the chapter, we examine a range of practicalities to consider when organising a visit or visitor. The key points to bear in mind are summarised in Tables 9.3, 9.4 and 9.5 and expanded on throughout the chapter. The section ends with an overview of a suggested framework for a visit to a place of worship.

It is important to start by considering what your visit to a place of worship might aim to achieve. Reflecting on this might help you to decide where to go as well as what to do when you are there. At first it might seem tempting to visit a large Mosque or Cathedral in a big city in order to enable children to experience the magnitude and grandeur these places of worship can offer. However, if your aim is for children to gain insights into the

▨ **Table 9.3** Key principles for organising a visit or visitor in R&W

Do	Don't
Take time to explain to children that everyone (including themselves) has a different position or worldview.	Assume that visiting a place of worship will automatically lead to meaningful interfaith dialogue. This is likely to need careful thought and planning.
An individual account of a Religion or Worldview is not necessarily representative of all people who follow the same tradition.	
Encourage children to see the "fuzzy edgedness" Jackson (2004, p. 87) of beliefs systems by recognising the diversity within different Worldviews.	Force children into the spotlight by asking them to share their beliefs and practices unless they wish to do so.
Consider the benefits of visiting places of worship to represent different denominational perspectives, especially those in your local area. For example, a Methodist chapel in Christianity or Shi'ah Mosque in Islam.	Forget to consider the full range of sensory experiences which children might be able to engage with during a visit.
Present the differences frankly to enable learners to develop their understanding.	Make comparisons between religions and worldviews which gloss over key differences between them.
Explore the potential of visits beyond places of worship. Consider how galleries, museums and online visits might present equally beneficial learning opportunities.	Limit opportunities for visits.

experience of different R&W in your local community it is worth considering whether this might be better served by visiting a small, local Mosque or your local parish Church. These are perhaps more likely to be the buildings which believers in your local community attend. The Commission on RE (2018, p. 72) also recommend that where your local area has a significant number of adherents to other worldviews such as Jainism, it might be appropriate to include these in your curriculum because children may encounter them in their daily lives. Visiting local places of worship also has the advantage of being time efficient, thereby potentially enabling you to visit more than one building and hence provide children with the opportunity to compare and contrast them.

You can also consider the possible benefits of visiting places of worship from different Christian denominations such as a Methodist chapel, Quaker Meeting House, or Orthodox Church. If travelling further afield for your visit it may seem to make efficient use of time to visit, for example, a Jewish synagogue and Sikh gurdwara in the same day. If you decide to visit more than one place of worship, it is important to give careful thought to if and how you make comparisons between the two. The risk of making superficial comparisons in the hope of advancing mutual understanding is highlighted by Wright's (2003, 2007) pedagogical approach to RE known as Critical Religious Education. This approach to RE emphasises the importance of learners engaging with the truth claims of different religions, even if at times these are conflicting and may even be irreconcilable. Teachers should therefore be cautious of making broad statements which emphasise similarities between religions, such as saying that a Church and Mosque are both decorated on the inside. In fact, absence of images of people inside the Mosque reflects key Islamic beliefs about avoiding idolatry.

■ **Table 9.4** Key questions and considerations before, during and after a visit

Where and when (practicalities)	During the visit	Following-up
When in the school year will be the most beneficial time for a visit? How does the visit link to your curriculum?	Who will you speak to there? What position are they coming from and how will you explain this to learners?	How will you link the visit back to your curriculum?
Is there an opportunity to visit more than one place in the same day? What possibilities are there locally as well as further afield?	Are there any opportunities for engaging with different sense experiences during the visit, for example, music, artefacts or objects?	Do you have the contact details of anyone you could write to, to thank for the visit?
Have you considered beyond places of worship such as a gallery or museum where learners could explore the religion from a different perspective?	Are any other events significant to the place happening? Are any workshops available?	How will you remind learners that everyone comes from different positions, including themselves?
Ensure any risk assessments are completed. Check for inclusion and safeguarding considerations.	Encourage learners to ask questions and to engage in learning first-hand about topics which they have studied.	What opportunities are there for learners to critically reflect on what they have learnt and how it relates to their own beliefs and ideas?
Make learners aware of any dress code or behaviour requirements.	Are there any opportunities for dialogue and talking to people you meet during the visit?	If you have visited more than one place, can you make meaningful comparisons between them that do not 'gloss over' key differences?

■ **Table 9.5** Possible Framework for a visit to a place of worship

Possible framework for a visit to a place of worship

■ Ensure effective pre-visit learning completed including about positionality and diversity within religions and worldviews.

■ On arrival, allow learners 5–10 minutes to 'soak up' the atmosphere of the place of worship.

■ Give learners three questions to consider about what they are experiencing. For example: what can they see? How many of a certain item? What can they hear? How do they feel?

■ If appropriate to the place visited, provide learners with an opportunity to touch and look at a range of objects and artefacts. There might be a chance to see a ritual happening.

■ Invite the speaker/guide to respond to questions from the learners. Encourage learners to also draw on the pre-visit learning undertaken here.

■ Ask the speaker if anything has not been covered. This could include the speaker giving a tour of key points of interest.

■ If possible, provide learners with some final time alone to seek out other information they are interested in. This might be captured by photos, drawing, poems or short notes.

■ Provide a chance for a final short Q&A session.

■ Thank the speaker!

When planning your visit to a place of worship consider what sort of experiences might be available for children during the visit. Listening to a long talk may not be the most engaging way for children to experience the place of worship, so make sure to discuss in advance what you would like them to gain from the visit and how you hope to bring this about. If someone will show you around, it is worth thinking about who this will be. It need not be the religious leader; a member of a congregation can provide different types of insights for learners. There may be other opportunities to experience different aspects of the place of worship too. For example, might it be possible for children to hear religious music which typically forms part of a worship service? Could it be beneficial for children to experience some quiet time sitting and absorbing the atmosphere of the building? Taking care to respect different religious teachings about who can hold certain objects and in what circumstances, might there be any objects or artefacts which children can hold or look at during the visit?

Visits linked to R&W need not be limited to places of worship. A visit to an art gallery might provide an interesting opportunity for children to look at how different aspects of religion and key religious figures have been represented in art. Alternatively, going to a museum might afford the chance for children to see and experience important religious artefacts. These types of opportunities may also be linked to cross curricular learning opportunities, perhaps with other humanities subjects. If this is the case, it is important to be clear about the specific learning which links to R&W. Lastly, special festivals and events such as interfaith weeks and 'visit my mosque' days can provide opportunities for children to experience one off events and workshops happening in the community. Even if attending with your class proves impossible, children and parents can be informed about such events through the school newsletter.

WELCOMING VISITORS

Organising a visitor may be slightly more straightforward than a visit in that travel will not be needed. This may mean that a visitor can be invited into existing curriculum time allocated to R&W and this may also be a more cost-effective option. Although you may not be going outside the school gates, do still remember to check for relevant health and safety and safeguarding requirements you school has in place for visitors, as well as reminding your visitor to bring any photographic ID or other documents that might be needed.

Think creatively about who might be a visitor for R&W. Some schools of a religious character might already have an established link with a local religious person such as a Christian minister, Imam or other faith leader. If inviting such a person to your R&W class it is important to establish how this visit will be distinctive from other visits made to school which might involve taking assemblies, leading worship or meeting with staff. It is a good idea to speak to the intended visitor in advance in order to agree the length and nature of their visit. This might also be an opportunity to explain how their visit fits into your scheme of learning and what preparatory work children will have done.

Alternatively, you might consider whether parents could contribute to your class's learning. For instance, when studying Diwali, a Sikh or Hindu parent could visit your class to share insights into their personal experiences of celebrating the festival, and the meaning behind different rituals. A speaker from a religious charity, such as Islamic Relief, the Catholic Agency for Overseas Development (CAFOD) or the Salvation Army might make for a meaningful visit if learning about different people's ideas and religion's teaching about charity, poverty and helping people. Likewise, a visitor from a charity like the Street Pastors could provide an informative opportunity for children to learn about how some religious people put their faith into action. These types of visitors can provide valuable and memorable insights and can also help to remind children that authentic sources of authority on a religion can be found beyond speaking to official representatives of religions. At the same time, these visits need careful planning. Prior to the visit it is crucial to remind children of the concept of positionality and to consider what position the invited guest might be coming from. It often works well to have a pre-visit lesson in which you explore the topic to be talked about with the visitor and identify some questions children could ask. It is also very helpful to speak to the visitor in advance so that they also know about your hopes for their visit and how it will relate to other learning already completed.

There are a number of organisations who run workshops in schools or organise for visitors with different worldviews to visit your class. Some organisations such as the Faith and Belief forum run at a national level in the UK and can help to find speakers from different religions and perspectives to visit your class. They also run workshops on topics such as identity, diversity and interfaith dialogue. Other organisations like the Humanists UK can also be contacted directly to organise a speaker to visit your class. In addition, there are a number of local organisations who work to connect speakers and schools and promote interfaith dialogue. Asking your local Standing Advisory Council for Religious Education (SACRE) for their recommendations might be a good starting point to connect with local organisations. Inviting a faith speaker into your school is likely to provide a unique and powerful opportunity for children to hear first-hand about the individual's experiences, as seen in the subsequent example from Imran Kotwal, a Muslim faith visitor.

INSIGHTS FROM A MUSLIM FAITH VISITOR – IMRAN KOTWAL

I have been leading Islam assemblies, workshops, and staff training in primary schools since 2015, and am privileged to have worked with many wonderful schools in the North of England.

Headteachers and RE leaders always make me feel my visit to their school is essential. They introduce me in the assembly as a special visitor, highlighting the importance of learning from people of different faiths and backgrounds. Often, headteachers have invited additional guests to join the assembly such as parents, governors, local vicars and priests, even local newspapers have been present.

My visits go beyond teaching Islam, rather, the school visit complements the excellent work schools are already doing in preparing pupils for modern-day Britain on areas such as promoting British Values, tackling anti-bullying, and challenging hate (including Islamophobia). I work closely with the RE coordinators to work out the best topics to cover each time, so it can be aligned to the work they are doing in the school.

Some schools like me to attend at the start of their learning, to help launch their Islam learning. Others prefer me to visit at the end, to build an extra layer of content and depth to their knowledge.

The format changes from school to school with different approaches to engaging pupils and facilitating learning, but the intention is the same, for the children to meet a person from the faith-community who can share their beliefs and practices from first-hand experience. Only they can answer questions like 'How do you feel during Ramadan?' or 'What's it like going round the Ka'bah seven times? Children are naturally inquisitive with many questions that visitors can answer (hopefully!).

From visiting the schools regularly, I have been able to build relationships with the pupils, to them, I am simply Imran, who lives in Bolton, has four children, and is a big Man Utd fan! The visits can vary in nature, and I have built close working relationships with headteachers and RE coordinators over time, so we share ideas on what topics would be best to deliver, and they have some wonderful ideas on how to create innovative and exciting ways to run the assemblies and workshops.

Some schools like me to teach the same key topic each year, for example at Harrow Gate Primary, I lead a practical workshop for their Year Six pupils about the Hajj (pilgrimage to Mecca). We enact the full pilgrimage with all the rituals and sharing my personal reflections of going for Hajj with my wife. At Westwood Park Community Primary School, I lead Islam workshops during their anti-bullying week, parents are invited to join too and work through activities with their children. I have also had an hour-long interview from Year Six pupils at Silloth Primary School, each taking turns with quick fire questions so they could cover lots of topics at once. I also take part in world religion days where visitors from different faiths come together to show unity and lead different activities while showing respect for all. That's just a whistlestop tour of some of the innovative teaching methods, as well as leading standard sessions and assemblies in schools on the five pillars of Islam and what it's like to be a Muslim in Britain today.

I like to include humour in my assemblies and workshops, which helps tackle misconceptions, results in laughter, and gets pupils engaged in learning. For example, I would have all my Islamic artefacts and special objects in a large rucksack and put this on the table in front of me. I'd ask the pupils what they thought was in the rucksack and begin to take out items like pictures of Mosques, prayer mats, the Qur'an, and finally ask what else I have in my bag. 'A rabbit?'

I've started supporting schools in other parts of the country too. Recently, several small schools came together to share a visit across three days so all staff and pupils could be involved. In fact, since the pandemic, I've been offering schools live virtual Islam assemblies, workshops, and staff training, and this has been popular with schools who otherwise may have struggled to find a Muslim visitor.

My presence in the schools has enabled me to build important relationships with headteachers and RE coordinators. We have established important relationships and I am honoured that they share with me how valuable they feel my visits are. In addition to leading assemblies and workshops with their pupils, I am an adviser to many of them, helping them learn how to deal with sensitive issues like Islamophobia, and helping teachers feel better equipped to teach about Islam, both in an informal manner and through structured staff training where it is requested.

In a few schools, the headteachers have spoken to me about their concern over some parents and carers withdrawing their children from Islam sessions and planned Mosque visits. To tackle this, I have led a separate workshop for the parents and carers to answer questions and tackle any misconceptions. These workshops have been an immense success, with people confessing to their ignorance about the faith and enjoying learning first-hand from a Muslim. Parents are always welcome to attend the assemblies for the pupils too, perhaps it can reassure them we are not preaching, just teaching.

If you are considering inviting someone from the Muslim faith-community to lead an assembly or to run a workshop to complement your Islam teaching, do it! The feedback has been overwhelmingly positive and the learning for the children invaluable. I have been to schools in rural parts of the North of England where I am the first Muslim the pupils have ever met.

To find the right person, you could go with recommendations from other schools or suggestions from the Diocese. If you are contacting the local Mosque, remember the Imam may not speak English, but they do tend to have volunteers who show visitors around the Mosque who may be able to lead an assembly. Also, you're most likely to reach someone if you contact the Mosque in the evening, it is normally closed during the daytime, only opening for the dawn and midday prayers.

Prior to the visit, give your visitor as much information as possible on what you want to achieve from the visit, what the pupils already know from their learning, and how you think the delivery would work best. If it's the first visit and you're unsure, you could ask the visitor for recommendations based on what has worked well at other schools. It's also worth asking if they have any special requests for their visit, for example, I often need somewhere to make wudhu (ritual ablution) as I will be touching the Qur'an in lessons and a private space to pray. Dietary requirements may also have to be considered if the visitor is there for lunch.

As an aside, the teachers are generally fully involved in the visit and learning, however sometimes they use the time to mark books. Personally, I think this is a missed opportunity to learn something new and find opportunities to continue further conversations with the children, not to mention they may miss out on hearing some of the pupils' stories and misconceptions, such as the time one child told me that Allah had 100 names, but a camel ate one, and that's why He now only has 99 names!

It really is a pleasure to be able to deliver these workshops and assemblies, the teachers ensure I know what an important experience they feel it is for pupils to understand first-hand what it's really like to be Muslim. It adds an extra layer of knowledge and depth to the teaching, enriches the subject, and promotes respect and tolerance as well as tackling sensitive issues like racism and Islamophobia.

You can arrange a school visit by Imran Kotwal (in-person or virtually) at www. muslimlearnerservices.org

USING A PERSONA DOLL AS A CLASSROOM 'VISITOR' – SALLY ELTON-CHALCRAFT

A persona doll (like the one in the photographs in Figure 9.2), is a doll who represents a child from a particular community. The teacher 'creates' the identity of the persona doll, building up a picture of a 'real' child in a 'real' family, with 'real' experiences, 'real' preferences and dislikes. The persona doll's identity is fixed. So, for example the persona doll in the photograph (Figure 9.2), Jeetinder, has worked with one of the authors for over twenty years, but remarkably he still remains the same age!

■ **Figure 9.2** Sikh persona doll, Jeetinder, with Sally Elton-Chalcraft his 'creator.'

Jeetinder's character was originally based on an amalgamation of several real children from schools in which the author worked, but once defined his identity remained fixed, as described in 9.6 below and in two publications (Brown, 2008; Warner and Elton-Chalcraft, 2022). Persona dolls have been used in classrooms around the world for a number of years (Persona Doll, 2023; Brown, 2008; van Keulan, 2004; Bowles and Hardy, 2004). One of the most influential proponents of persona dolls is Babette Brown (2001, 2008) and Jeetinder's lived experience is captured in her collection of practitioners' work with Persona dolls (Brown, 2008).

If you use the personal doll approach you will need to purchase a doll from a recognised stockist and then create a persona, for example through Persona Doll Training (2023). While the initial stage is costly and time consuming it can be great fun and your persona doll (or dolls) will provide an authentic and invaluable resource which will be useful for decades. Groups of schools could even purchase a set of dolls collectively and share them as needed. The Persona Doll (2023) training and stockists outline the rationale and advantages of this approach in the classroom. The Persona doll (2023) approach is summed up as:

Participatory
■ Children actively participate right from the start. They express their ideas, thoughts and feelings, and they become the problem-solvers.

Fun
■ A visit to your classroom by a Persona Doll is a special event the children look forward to. Initiate activities based around your doll's persona.

Educational
■ Persona doll stories introduce and celebrate diversity, rich in true-to-life details which broaden horizons and unlearn prejudices.

Adaptable
- Create stories for your Persona Doll to address a wide range of issues which cause exclusion such as racism and gender bias.

Empowering
- Develop personas and stories which empower children to challenge stereotypes and speak up for themselves and others.

Rewarding
- Watch how the children develop empathy, self-confidence, a sense of fairness and critical thinking skills as they bond with the dolls.

Persona Doll Training (2023 homepage)

Getting Started With Your Persona Doll

In a classroom context, the children's interactions with, and questions to, the doll may vary but the doll will always draw on their own (teacher ascribed) fixed identity in their responses. The identity of Jeetinder, a Sikh persona doll, is described in Table 9.6. While it is 'fun' to create your own identity for each persona doll there are 'ready-made' identities available which you could use as a starting point – see the Persona Doll UK (2023) website, Marilyn Bowles and Martha Hardy (2004) 'The little book of persona dolls', and Babette Brown's books (Brown, 2001, 2008).

Using persona dolls can be a useful way for children to learn about 'living as a believer' through the voice of the persona doll (which is really the teacher's background research about the persona doll). The teacher sits the doll on their knee and the persona

---

Table 9.6 Jeetinder's identity (teacher ascribed from a variety of sources including own contacts, website information etc) as described in Brown (2008, pp. 42–45)

Jeetinder:
- Nearly eight years old
- Favourite food – fish and chips, lentil dhal and vegetable curry
- Tejpreet – brother, eleven and going up to big school, likes playing football
- Manjit - sister, fourteen, recently selected her chosen subjects to study for her external exams – including Biology, Chemistry, physics (she aims to be a doctor) and Panjabi (she uses external exam support guides such as Quizlet (https://quizlet.com/en-gb/content/aqa-gcse-panjabi-flashcards). Jeetinder and Tejpreet test their sister Manjit on Panjabi words.
- Speaks English and Panjabi
- Wears a *jurra* (top knot) and has uncut hair because his family are *kalsa* Sikhs. He sometimes gets teased about wearing his *jurra*
- His best friend Jagdeep is a non-*kalsa* Sikh. Jagdeep's family do not wear all the 5 K's
- Enjoys going to local playground with Jagdeep
- He visited the *Gurdwara* (place of worship) to celebrate his baby cousin's naming ceremony

---

doll either uses the teacher as a translator by whispering in the teacher's ear (Brown, 2008) or the teacher actually speaks the words of the doll (Warner and Elton-Chalcraft, 2022). Either way, the children learn first-hand about the life and experiences of the Persona Doll.

Table 9.7 is an example of an extract from a lesson where Jeetinder comes to visit a year 2 class. The format of the lesson follows that described in Chapter 12 (Table 12.3) where the teacher begins with *Shared human experience*, starting from where the children are, there is an exploration and analysis of a *traditional belief system* – Sikhi/Sikhism, and the learners appreciate *individual patterns of belief.* The learners think about their own responses to what they hear. The persona doll visitor, Jeetinder, can also encourage the learners to move from 'bystander' to 'change maker', as described by TED speaker Nova Reid (2019) because of the anti-racist stance Jeetinder adopts (see also chapter 3). The example in Table 9.7 is presented in a format to show the theory behind using a persona doll as a 'visitor' in the classroom and how this is worked out in practice.

Persona Doll Identity Responding to Difficult Questions

Jeetinder has a 'real' identity and so he is considered to be a 'visitor'. Lessons which describe Jeetinder's visit in a classroom with the 'teacher' have been recorded in Babette Brown's book Equality in Action (2008, pp. 42–45). He also makes an appearance in textbook *Professional Studies in Primary Education*, see Warner and Elton-Chalcraft's chapter 'Teaching Race Culture and Ethnicity Awareness' (2022, pp. 319–321). Some student teachers have concerns that the persona doll will ask them a question they cannot answer – despite increasing subject knowledge through reading books, website information getting to know 'real' adherents etc. This is a valid concern but when asked a difficult question Jeetinder (the teacher) replies:

'I'm sorry I am not sure about that – I will ask my mum and dad and tell you later.'

Most children would be content with a persona doll's response 'I'll ask my parents' because an eight-year-old would not be expected to know every aspect of their belief system. So, a lack of 'teacher' subject knowledge is an opportunity to explore answers together and sends a message that teacher and learner are in a community of enquiry thus breaking down barriers of an adult monopoly on knowledge.

As articulated in Table 9.8 (which captures advantages and limitations of each strategy), Persona dolls can provide a more comfortable way into controversial issues – for example the learners can explore different attitudes towards LGBTQ+ in different religions and worldviews. So Jeetinder could talk about his family and friends discussing Jasvir Singh a prominent male Sikh in the Media who spoke about being a devout Sikh and married to a man (Maqbool, 2023). Learners can hear about disagreements between Jeetinder's family and friends, thus gaining an insight into a variety of attitudes and beliefs; they can also be encouraged to explore the Equality Act 2010 and also how their own cultural context informs the development of their own attitudes. LGBTQ+ and Religion is discussed in Chapter Three where intersectionality and discrimination are explored, and also in Chapter Twelve where we consider ways of approaching controversial issues in the classroom.

Table 9.7 Extracts from a Sikh persona Doll lesson AND rationale/theoretical underpinning

Lesson discussion	Rationale/theoretical underpinning
Jeetinder: On my way into your school I had a go on the swing, do any of you play on the playground? *Izaak: Yes I go on the swing too?* *Jeetinder: Can you push yourself? My friend Jagdeep pushes me.* *Izaak: My friend Henry pushes me* *(General discussion about who likes the roundabout, climbing frame etc)* *Jeetinder: Perhaps after school we can play together?*	**Shared human experience** – learners can relate to Jeetinder as a child just like them. Beginning a lesson by starting from 'where the children are' establishes a comfortable and non-threatening environment
Jeetinder: But something not very nice happened – some big boys and big girls teased me for wearing my jurra (top knot), shalwar and Kamize (tunic and trousers) *Mary: Why do you wear them?*	Introduce a **'problem' of discriminatory behaviour** which is directly related to the persona doll's ethnicity or beliefs etc and provoke curiosity
Jeetinder: Because I am a Sikh, and some Sikhs wear the 5 K's – so having uncut hair and wearing a comb is one of the 5 K's *Judith: Do all boys have long hair?* *Jeetinder: Me and my family have uncut hair and wear the kanga (comb) but my best friend Jagdeep is not a kalsa Sikh so he cuts his hair and he wears jeans and a tee shirt, but actually I wear jeans and a t shirt most of the time , I only wear shalwar kamize when I go to a wedding or something, and my mum told me to wear them today!* *Ben: Why don't you cut your hair?* *Jeetinder: Many kalsa Sikhs grow their hair and wear a comb to keep it neat and tidy – this reminds us to keep our lives neat and tidy – but my bedroom is a bit messy.* *Ben: Mine is too, my mum tells me that's why I can't find anything.*	Introduce some **subject knowledge**, learning about the traditional belief system – the kanga (comb) one of the 5K's Draw out the **individual patterns of belief** – Jeetinder's family are kalsa Sikhs and have uncut hair and wear many of the 5 K's, his friend Jagdeep does not wear all of the 5 K's. **Learning from** the belief system of Sikhi/Sikhism the children can relate to their own lives

(Continued)

■ **Table 9.7** Extracts from a Sikh persona Doll lesson AND rationale/theoretical underpinning *(Continued)*

Lesson discussion	Rationale/theoretical underpinning
Jeetinder: Would you like to see another of the 5 k's?	Further learning about the traditional belief system-raising curiosity and inviting predictions.
Shameema: Yes please?	Opportunities for learners to:
Jeetinder: What do you think this is? And what does it begin with?	**Explore, express, interpret, enquire, investigate and analyse.**
Mary: It looks like a bracelet, does it begin with a 'kicking K' too?	Individual patterns of belief – both Jeetinder's family and Jagdeep's family members wear a kara, but it
Izaak: Do boys and girls all wear bracelets	has a different symbolic meaning for different family members. There is diversity within a worldview and
Jeetinder: This bracelet is called a kara and most Sikhs wear it but it reminds us of different things. What shape is it?	even between different family members.
Judith: A circle	Learning from the belief system of Sikhi/ Sikhism the children can relate to their own lives, beliefs and practices
Jeetinder: So in my family it reminds us that God has no beginning or end and is always with us. Jagdeep says it reminds him to do the right thing because in the sweet shop he always looks at his kara on his wrist and it reminds him to not steal the sweets but take them to the counter to pay for them.	
Shameema: In the Qu'ran it says it is wrong to steal	
Jeetinder: Do any of you wear things?	Learning from the belief system and relating to prior or personal knowledge
Judith: My grandma wears a cross	
Jeetinder: Why?	Persona doll can be used as a vehicle to assess knowledge and understanding
Judith: Because she is a Christian	Opportunities for learners to
Jeetinder: Do all Christians wear a cross? What does it mean?	**Reflect, examine, react, respond, consider, apply**
Mary: My uncle wears a cross because he believes in God and Jesus died on the cross.	
Ben: But my sister wears a cross with jewels on and she's not a Christian	
Judith: Some people wear a cross because they are Christian, but some Christians don't wear a cross and some people wear a cross because it's a pretty necklace.	
Jeetinder: That's like Jagdeep and me – we wear the kara for different reasons and some people wear bracelets for fashion.	

(Continued)

■ **Table 9.7** Extracts from a Sikh persona Doll lesson AND rationale/theoretical underpinning (*Continued*)

Lesson discussion	Rationale/theoretical underpinning
Jeetinder: This is another of our 5 K's – can you see what it is?	Approaching issues of diversity with the persona doll provides a **safe context to explore bullying and negative behaviour** followed by group solution creating. Skilful management of the discussion can facilitate a bystander to changemaker standpoint (Reid, 2019)
Izaak: It looks like a knife – that's not a good thing to wear on a necklace, do you stab people?	
Jeetinder: It is a dagger and we don't use it to attack people but instead to …. what do you think? And what does it begin with?	Questioning and discussion supports learners to empathise with discrimination felt by Jeetinder (Van Kuelan, 2004; Brown, 2008; Persona doll, 2023; Warner and Elton-Chalcraft, 2022)
Mary: To defend yourself? Kicking k?	
Jeetinder; Yes –it's a Kirpan to defend ourselves when we are attacked, but not a real fight – just a tiny non-dangerous kirpan on a necklace.	Shared human experience and **group problem solving**
Judith: Phew, I don't want to be stabbed.	It is important for the persona doll to talk about positive experiences and not just be 'the problem doll'. Jeetinder can talk about his successes – e.g. gaining a 25 metres swimming badge when discussing 'keeping fit' in PE and science lessons. So, the persona doll does not just appear in RE lessons but is an **integral part of the children's lives and curriculum.**
Jeetinder: Yes, it's only to defend - But I didn't defend myself when those big boys and girls were teasing me. It's hard to stand up to people when you are bullied, have you been teased?	
Ben: I get teased for wearing glasses it makes me really sad and cross	
Jeetinder: What do you do?	
Ben: I feel really sad and cross because they call me 'geeky four eyes'	
Jeetinder: My dad says the kirpan reminds us to stand up for ourselves – so what can we do when we are teased? Why do people bully us?	
Mary: You should tell a teacher!	
Ben: They probably don't understand I have to wear glasses because I am short sighted.	
Shameema: They probably tease you because they don't understand about the jurra and kara. My sister sometimes gets bullied for wearing a hijab – the scarf some Muslims wear.	
Jeetinder: So, I need to explain to the children that bullied me about why I wear some of the 5 K's – will you help me?	
Most learners: YES	
Jeetinder: If we do some pictures and plays about the 5 K's we could tell them in an assembly, then hopefully they won't tease me anymore.	

▨ **Table 9.8** Advantages, limitations and points to note when using visits, visitors and persona dolls

Approach	Advance planning required and cost	Advantages	Limitations	Suitable for
Visit	-Contact with potential visit locations and advance planning essential -Risk assessments, internal approvals and parental consent usually needed -Medium cost depending on travel needed	-Authentic experience and highly memorable -Provides opportunities for authentic dialogue in line with the Contact Hypothesis (Allport, 1954) -Presents opportunities for varied sensory experiences	-Detailed advance planning, cost, supervision needed -Requires effective learner preparation to maximise learning -To maximise learning, it needs the teacher to find time to prepare the leader/speaker of the place visited with your expectations and context	All ages
Virtual visit	-Teacher research needed to identify suitable resource (see Cumbria Education Development Centre in useful resources) -Low cost, minimal practical limitations as long as good internet access is available	-Can be included as part of a lesson or throughout a unit of work -Potential to explore places beyond your local area -Could work well to complement an in-person visit e.g. by visiting a place of worship from a different denomination	-No opportunities for interfaith dialogue to enrich learners' understanding of what they are seeing -Less engaging for learners and hard to explore beyond visual sensory aspects – no chances for physical interaction -Virtual experiences may be inauthentic and not capture the reality of the place	6- to 11-year-olds
Visitor	-Requires teacher research to identify and speak in advance with the visitor -Requires careful teacher planning for pre and post visitor lessons to explore the visitor's context and identify some potential questions -Cost dependent on speaker fee, which may also involve travel costs	-Likely to be engaging and interactive -The visitor may be able to bring relevant artefacts, objects, artwork etc. with them for learners to experience -Represents a valuable opportunity for genuine interfaith dialogue in line with the Contact Hypothesis (Allport, 1954)	-Requires teacher to explore the concept of positionality with learners so that learners can critically reflect on how the visitor's position and the insights they provide are similar and different to other people from the same and other Worldviews -May need to be scheduled at a particular time and location	All ages

(Continued)

■ **Table 9.8** Advantages, limitations and points to note when using visits, visitors and persona dolls (*Continued*)

Approach	Advance planning required and cost	Advantages	Limitations	Suitable for
Online visitor	-Requires teacher research to identify and meet in advance with the visitor. This could take place online too -Requires careful teacher planning for pre and post visitor lessons to explore the visitor's context and identify some potential questions -Cost dependent on speaker fee, but does avoid any travel costs	-Time efficient as no travel is needed -May enable you to invite a visitor from another country or context who could not physically visit your classroom -Likely to be able to take place within your usual R&W lesson	-Risk of technical glitches during the session may mean interruptions or short pauses in the discussion -It may be more difficult for the visitor to build a rapport with your learners and for learners to have the confidence to ask questions in the virtual environment	All ages
Persona doll	-Teacher research required to create the fixed identity of each persona doll. -After initial outlay of doll purchase and time to research and create identity, the persona doll lessons require minimum preparation.	-Interactive and engaging -Teacher can facilitate the discussion and use their skill to answer questions/ address misconceptions. -A highly anti-discriminatory approach – the teacher can move learners on from bystanders to change makers who learn to challenge discriminatory behaviour (racist, sexist etc)	-During lesson teacher may be unable to answer a learner's question (default – ask the persona doll's parent and report back tomorrow!) -Requires detailed research and knowledge from teacher to create identity but thereafter minimal preparation.	-Early years 3- to 7-year-olds (with care they can be used with 8–11-year-olds) -Can be drawn on in other curriculum areas. Persona doll is a member of the school community

CONCLUSION

In this chapter we have tried to show the benefits and also points to watch when using visits, visitors and persona dolls to support learners. The teacher can use the Table 9.8 to gauge which approach is most suited to the age of the learners, how much preparation is needed and how to mitigate against the limitations. We believe that during the first stages of educating three to eleven years, a learner should encounter a range of first-hand approaches to worldviews including regular visits, visitors and persona doll engagement. These 'first hand' approaches are authentic and memorable and also have the capacity to deepen a learner's understanding of other worldviews and their own personal belief system. But as is the case with all learning it is the skill of the teacher which makes the approach rich or a disaster! This is particularly the case with using visits visitors and persona dolls – so please engage, but with great care and preparation to enhance your learners' experiences.

USEFUL RESOURCES AND FURTHER READING

- BBC Religion website – particularly useful for creating authentic identity of persona dolls: https://www.bbc.co.uk/religion/religions/
- Cumbria Education Development Centre website, with some material by Jane Yates, including a comprehensive list of virtual visit suggestions: https://www.cdec.org.uk/use-our-resources/films-and-virtual-tours/virtual-tours/
- Faith and Belief Forum: https://faithbeliefforum.org/
- Interfaith Week: https://www.interfaithweek.org/
- Muslim Learner Services (Imran Kotwal): www.muslimlearnerservices.org
- NATRE sheets on visits and visitors - available via the website: https://www.natre.org.uk/about-re/guidance-on-resources/visits-and-visitors/
- NATRE Voices of faith and belief in schools guidance and a code of conduct: https://www.natre.org.uk/uploads/Free%20Resources/Voices%20of%20faith%20and%20belief%20in%20schools.pdf
- Persona Doll (2023) *Persona Doll training and purchasing UK* available at https://personadoll.uk/

REFERENCES

Ackroyd, R. (2023) 'Tolerance and mutual respect in three secondary schools in England: How teachers of religious education working with 11–14-year-olds construct and promote these concepts', PhD Thesis, University of Cumbria, Lancaster.

Allport, G.W. (1954) *The Nature of Prejudice*. 25th Anniversary edition. Cambridge/Reading, MA: Addison-Wesley.

Brown, B. (2001) *Combating discrimination : persona dolls in action*. Stoke-on-Trent: Trentham.

Bowles, M. and Hardy, M. (2004) *The little book of persona dolls: using dolls to help children understand the views and feelings of others*. Husbands Bosworth: Featherstone Education.

Brown, B. (2008) *Equality in Action*. Stoke on Trent: Trentham Books.

Commission on Religious Education (2018) *Religion and Worldviews: The Way Forward*. Commission on Religious Education. Available at: https://www.commissiononre.org.uk/wp-content/uploads/2018/09/Final-Report-of-the-Commission-on-RE.pdf (Accessed: 19 November 2019).

Downe, E. (2021) 'Nobody stands nowhere. Theos think tank', Available at: https://www.theosthinktank.co.uk/comment/2021/05/12/worldviews-film (Accessed: 25 April 2023).

Education Scotland (2011) 'Curriculum for excellence', Available at: https://education.gov
.scot/documents/All-experiencesoutcomes18.pdf (Accessed: 26 September 2022).

Ipgrave, J. (2009) 'The language of friendship and identity: Children's communication choices
in an interfaith exchange', *British Journal of Religious Education*, 31(3), pp. 213–225.
Available at: https://doi.org/10.1080/01416200903112292.

Jackson, R. (1997) *Religious Education: An Interpretive Approach*. London: Hodder &
Stoughton.

Jackson, R. (2000) 'The Warwick religious education project: The interpretative approach to
religious education', in Grimmitt, M. (ed.), *Pedagogies of Religious Education: Case
Studies in the Research and Development of Good Pedagogic Practice in RE*. Great
Wakering: McCrimmon, pp. 130–152.

Jackson, R. (2004) *Rethinking Religious Education and Plurality Issues in Diversity and
Pedagogy*. London: Routledge Falmer.

Kindermann, K. and Riegel, U. (2018) 'Experiencing churches as spiritual and religious
places: A study on children's emotions in church buildings during scholastic field trips',
British Journal of Religious Education, 40(2), pp. 136–147. Available at: https://doi.org
/10.1080/01416200.2016.1209458.

Kunzman, R. (2006) 'Imaginative engagement with religious diversity in public school
classrooms', *Religious Education*, 101(4), pp. 516–531.

Llywodraeth Cymru Welsh Government (2022) 'Curriculum for wales humanities', Available
at: https://hwb.gov.wales/curriculum-for-wales/humanities/designing-your-curriculum
(Accessed: 30 September 2022).

Lundie, D. *et al.* (2022) 'A practitioner action research approach to learning outside the
classroom in religious education: Developing a dialogical model through reflection
by teachers and faith field visitors', *British Journal of Religious Education*, 44(2), pp.
138–148.

Lundie, D. and Conroy, J. (2015) '"Respect study" the treatment of religious difference and
otherness: an ethnographic investigation in UK schools', *Journal of Intercultural Studies*,
36(3), pp. 274–290. Available at: https://doi.org/10.1080/07256868.2015.1029886.

Maqbool, A. (2023) 'I am a devout Sikh and I'm married to a man', Available at: https://www
.bbc.co.uk/news/uk-64496456 (Accessed: 7 February 2023).

NATRE (2014) 'Voices of faith and belief in schools guidance and a code of conduct',
Available at: https://www.natre.org.uk/uploads/Free%20Resources/Voices%20of
%20faith%20and%20belief%20in%20schools.pdf (Accessed: 3 October 2022).

Ofsted (2021) 'Research review series: Religious education', Available at: https://www.gov.uk
/government/publications/research-review-series-religious-education/research-review
-series-religious-education (Accessed: 26 November 2021).

Orchard, J. *et al.* (2021) 'Knowledge exchange, intergroup relations and "sharing space": A
community of enquiry for the professional development of teachers of religion and
worldviews', *British Journal of Religious Education*, 43(3), pp. 265–277. Available at:
https://doi.org/10.1080/01416200.2021.1898933.

Persona, Doll (2023) 'Persona doll training and purchasing UK', Available at: https://
personadoll.uk/ (Accessed: 5 January 2023).

Reid, N. (2019) 'Not all superheroes wear capes – how you can have the power to change the
world', Available at: https://www.ted.com/talks/nova_reid_not_all_superheroes_wear

_capes_you_have_the_power_to_change_the_world?language=en   (Accessed   29th February 2024).

Salter, E. (2020) 'Welcome to my church: Faith-practitioners and the representation of religious traditions in secular RE', *Journal of Religious Education*, 68(3), pp. 289–303.

Sedgwick, F. and Karsh, E. (2012) *Learning Outside the Primary Classroom*. London: Taylor & Francis Group. Available at: http://ebookcentral.proquest.com/lib/cumbria/detail .action?docID=981800 (Accessed: 26 September 2022).

Senge, P.M. (2006) *The Fifth Discipline: The Art and Practice of the Learning Organization*. Rev. and updated ed. London: Random House Business.

Teece, G. (2010) 'Is it learning about and from religions, religion or religious education? And is it any wonder some teachers don't get it?', *British Journal of Religious Education*, 32(2), pp. 93–103.

Vander Ark, T., Liebtag, E. and McClennen, N. (2020) *The Power of Place: Authentic Learning Through Place-Based Education*. Alexandria: Association for Supervision & Curriculum Development.

Van Keulan, A. (2004) 'Persona Dolls an innovative approach', in Van Keulan, A., Malleval, D., Mony, M., Murray, C. and Vandenbroeck, M. (eds.), *Diversity and Equity in Early Childhood training in Europe*. DECET Network. Available at: https://cmascanada.ca/wp -content/uploads/2016/01/diversity%20and%20equity%20in%20early%20childhood %20training%20in%20europt%20manual.pdf#page=99   (Accessed   30   December 2022).

Warner, D. and Elton-Chalcraft, S. (2022) 'Teaching for race culture and ethnicity awareness and understanding', in Cooper, H. and Elton-Chalcraft, S. (eds.), *Professional Studies in Primary Education*, 4th ed. London: Sage.

Williams, A. *et al.* (2019) 'Promoting positive community relations: What can RE learn from social psychology and the shared space project?', *Journal of Beliefs & Values*, 40(2), pp. 215–227. https://doi.org/10.1080/13617672.2019.1596582.

Wright, A. (2003) 'The contours of critical religious education: Knowledge, wisdom, truth', *British Journal of Religious Education*, 25(4), pp. 279–291.

Wright, A. (2007) *Critical Religious Education, Multiculturalism and the Pursuit of Truth*. Cardiff: University of Wales Press (Religion, Education and Culture).

CHAPTER 10

REALISING QUALITY RELIGION(S) AND WORLDVIEW(S) EDUCATION WITH *THE RE-SEARCHERS APPROACH*

Giles Freathy

This chapter introduces the internationally-recognized *RE-searchers approach* as a creative and practical pedagogy ideally suited to teaching Religion(s) and Worldview(s) Education. The chapter provides

▪ A rationale for a critical, dialogic and inquiry-led approach based on assertions about the nature of knowledge about religion(s) and worldview(s)

▪ Features of the academic disciplines associated with the study of religions and worldviews and recognition of the impact that the positionality and personal world-view of the knower has on the process of knowledge construction

▪ Information about the cartoon characters used in the approach to personify research methodologies, so that the reader can use them to construct their own learning sequences

▪ Practical ideas on how to plan a sequence of lessons using all four *RE-searcher* characters, ensuring pupils appreciate the representational nature of substantive knowledge and on what cultural environment teachers should seek to establish to promote pupil reflexivity.

Thanks to Rob Freathy and University of Exeter for permitting the use of the material on The RE-searchers approach.

DOI: 10.4324/9781003361480-12

INTRODUCTION

The RE-searchers approach is a critical, dialogic and enquiry-based pedagogy which uses cartoon characters to personify different research methodologies. Pupils are introduced to the characters, their research interests and their preferred approaches to learning about religion(s). These approaches are then used within the pedagogy to learn about the designated focus of the series of lessons. The approach was designed primarily for teaching multi-faith RE in schools without a religious affiliation, but can, and has, been applied in different forms of RE (i.e. mono- or multi-faith) and in different types of school (those with and without a religious character; secondary and primary). *The RE-searchers approach* and its associated literature has drawn international attention and can been seen to have significantly influenced the review of the subject produced by the regulatory body responsible for school inspections in England (Ofsted 2022), where, for instance, schools are encouraged to teach 'ways of knowing' (e.g. Theology, Philosophy, Human Sciences, History…) alongside the substantive content. The approach is entirely compatible with the subject when it broadens its scope to include non-religious worldviews. In fact, the inclusion of non-religious worldviews enriches class reflection on the appropriateness of different *RE-searcher* characters for learning about different groups e.g. can a narrative theologian's research methods be applied to a non-theistic worldview?

Whilst this chapter provides a summary of *The RE-searchers approach* further information can be found in the original texts which are more detailed and are accompanied by a raft of exemplar learning sequences and activity ideas. Notably, these include: *The RE-searchers approach: A New Approach to Religious Education in Primary Schools* (Freathy, G. *et al.* 2015); *The RE-searchers approach: A quick start guide with exemplar units of work and activities* (Freathy, G. 2016) and, a theoretical introduction, *Pedagogical Bricoleurs and Bricolage Researchers: The Case of Religious Education* (Freathy, R. *et al.* 2017). The approach, as articulated in these materials, aims to introduce pupils to disciplinary knowledge and skills evident in academic communities of enquiry involved in theological and religious studies.

THE FOUR METHODOLOGIES

The four methodologies used in *The RE-searchers approach* are personified cartoon characters collectively known as *The RE-searchers* (see Table 10.1). They are: Ask-it-all Ava (an ethnographer who specializes in interviewing and empathising); Debate-it-all Derek (a philosopher who critiques truth-claims and ethical beliefs); See-the-story Suzie (a narrative theologian who specializes in narratives and interpretations) and Have-a-go Hugo (another ethnographer, who prefers participant observation as his method of study). Table 10.1 depicts the characters and combines materials from our prior publications (Freathy, G. *et al.* 2015; Freathy, G. 2016) to present a revised and brief summary of each.

In the approach, pupils learn about the different research methodologies (the characters) as well as learning through them (by way of the associated learning/research activities as like those suggested in Table 10.1). By learning about the different methodologies, pupils are introduced to disciplinary knowledge or 'ways of knowing' in keeping with the recommendations of the recent Research Review for Religious Education conducted

■ **Table 10.1** *The RE-searcher* characters in brief

Ask-it-all Ava (Interviewer / Empathiser)

Ava likes talking to representatives of religion(s) and worldview(s) groups about what they believe and do. She listens carefully to those she interviews to learn how people's backgrounds, families, communities and traditions shape their lives. She compares these answers with her own, those of other members of the group and those of religion(s) and worldview(s) traditions in general.

Suggested research/learning activities:

Understanding people's interpretations of the world through talking to them

■ Interview a member of a religious/worldview community in-depth or analyse a transcript derived from one.

■ Prepare questions for future interviews or surveys, by reflecting on what they know and don't know based on their prior knowledge and knowledge of Ava's values.

Making comparisons within and between religions

■ Ask the same few questions to several representatives from either multiple religious / worldview positions or from within a single tradition, to explore the diversity of responses to Ask-it-all Ava questions.

■ Compare pre-existing responses gathered from religious / worldview communities.

Reassessing my own beliefs, values and behaviour in the light of talking to people

■ Complete reflective logs/journals/blogs/diary entries/etc. to consider the extent to which the beliefs, values and behaviours they have encountered were similar to, or different to their own; what they have learnt and whether their beliefs, values and behaviours changed as a result of the research.

(Continued)

■ **Table 10.1** The RE-searcher characters in brief (*Continued*)

Debate-it-all Derek (Philosopher / Critic)

Derek is interested in what is true and what is right. He asks himself and others Big Questions such as: 'Is there a God?', 'What happens after we die?' and 'What is good and evil?' He likes to think on his own and with others about where religion(s) and worldview(s) agree and disagree to decide which views he agrees with (if any) and always seeks to give good reasons and provide evidence for his beliefs.

Suggested research/learning activities:

Exploring their own and others' beliefs

- Practice spotting assumptions about what is real; what causes what & what people should do in written or spoken accounts from Religious traditions and worldview stances.

- Select artworks which best represent their beliefs (or those of the belief system they are studying) and justify their choices.

- Reflect on beliefs according to how well they cohere with their own or how well they match the belief system in focus.

Critically evaluating truth-claims and the reasons/ evidence supporting them

- Reflect on their beliefs e.g. whether they know them to be true, think that they are true, have heard them to be true, would like them to be true, believe them to be true, guess that they must be true etc. and reflect on the meaning of verbs such as know and believe.

- Rank different types of evidence according to how trustworthy they are and justify their choices.

- Practice spotting apparent contradictions in paired statements.

(*Continued*)

■ **Table 10.1** The RE-searcher characters in brief (*Continued*)

See-the-Story Suzie (Narrator / Interpreter)

Suzie is interested in stories that carry significance for religious and worldview groups. She likes to compare stories and different versions of the same story.
She likes to develop her own interpretation of these stories and explore her own responses and reactions. Suzie likes to engage with the characters, the story-line and different interpretations of the same story. She suggests ways in which people's lives might be affected by the way they understand these stories.

Suggested research/learning activities:

Get to know the story

- Learn the story from a particular religious tradition or worldview through films, books, paintings and other representations (experiencing a range of versions of the story where possible).

- Create a flow diagram of events from the story and recall it with an ever-reducing number of cues.

Interpret the story for themselves

- Add speech/thought bubbles to images to attribute thoughts and feelings to characters displayed.

- Discuss which characters are the heroes and villains; which actions could be considered good and bad; what 'themes' (e.g. love, sacrifice, forgiveness, rebirth and creation) are covered in the story.

Reflect on how the stories from their own lives inform their interpretations

- Recall and share stories (real or fictional) from their own lives which have similar characters, events and themes as those in the religious stories studied.

- Explain why the stories from a particular religious tradition or worldview do or do not make sense to them drawing on stories from their own experience to explain their reasons.

Encounter other interpretations

- Read a range of different interpretations of the same story from a particular religious tradition or worldview.

- Order interpretations according to the extent to which they are agreed with, justifying their rankings with reference to the stories.

(*Continued*)

■ **Table 10.1** The RE-searcher characters in brief (*Continued*)

Have-a-go Hugo (Experiencer / Participant)

Hugo likes to take part in activities that are significant to religious and worldview communities. He does this to try to understand members and to see what it feels like to join in. He believes that feelings are more important than beliefs when trying to understand members. He is interested in what people feel to be true in their hearts rather than what they believe to be true in their heads. He wants to know or imagine what it feels like to belong to the communities and to be able to sympathise with the follower.

<u>Suggested research/learning activities:</u>

Participating in and experiencing religious practices and activities

■ Observe and makes notes on a significant live or recorded (non)religious event (e.g. a meal, rites of passage ceremony, practice or charity event).

■ Participate (or simulate participation) in an event of this kind.

■ Take part in an activity symbolically akin to a religious one e.g. washing dirty hands for baptism; abstaining from eating a doughnut to simulate fasting.

■ Interpret and appreciate religious art or music.

Getting in touch with the emotions and feelings of participants

■ Monitor, record and express their feelings and emotions whilst participating in any of the aforementioned activities.

■ Imagine what they would do if they were to participate in a Religious or worldview activity e.g. making a choice about what they would give up if they were observing Lent.

■ Seeing things from different points of view

■ Explore interpretations of the activities and events studied, including their own and others' interpretations, within and outside of the classroom, and religious and secular responses.

■ Speculate how someone with a particular worldview might interpret a given stimulus/event.

■ Explore the relationship between the interpretation of an event/stimulus and the feelings/emotions which correspond with them.

by the regulatory body in England (Ofsted 2021). However, the approach goes beyond learning about 'disciplinary knowledge' by enabling pupils to learn in the style of each of the characters. In doing so, pupils learn to conduct their own enquiries and are invited to compare the relative merits and affordances of the different approaches. In doing so, they can become knowledgeable about research methodologies and methods; skillful in the application of them and discerning when considering how and when to adopt particular ones as part of a broader enquiry into a topic. For instance, See-the-story Suzie's concern for narrative may not be appropriate for the study of a worldview that does not see itself in narrative terms, e.g. scientific humanism.

The determination to re-frame learners as researchers is a response to the challenges posed by having to teach contested, complex, diverse, multifaceted and evolving subject matter, such as religions and non-religious worldviews. Freathy and John (2019, pp. 22–23) argue that we need to welcome the 'messiness, contestation, fluidity and uncertainty' inherent in this subject, instead of trying to deny it and think of it as a problem. The proposed solution here is to reconceive the teacher and pupils as co-researchers (Freathy, G. *et al.* 2015) into religion(s) and worldview(s), who encounter, as far as possible, the diversity and complexity of the subject matter through the interrogation of sources using research methods in the context of an enquiry cycle (Freathy G. *et al.* 2015, p. 10). One of the key roles of the teacher in this conception of the subject is therefore to select the sources of information/foci of inquiry that will enable pupils to develop an ever more sophisticated representation of the topics covered. As a result of presenting subject knowledge solely in the form of sources of information for interrogation and/or hypotheses generated following an enquiry process, pupils will come to know that the substantive knowledge of the curriculum is only ever a representation and reconstruction of religious and non-religious traditions and concepts, rather that the 'things in themselves'.

SPANNING DISCIPLINES

The use of multiple RE-searcher role models is justified by the fact that the academic disciplines that share a concern for knowledge generation about religion(s) and worldview(s) are multiple and various (i.e. characterised by a diversity of relevant disciplines, methodologies, interpretative frameworks and research methods). The solution proposed is that pupils should be taught about the diversity of approaches, using the four (or possibly more) contrasting research methodologies selected from the myriad available. In Freathy R. *et al.* (2017) we argue that the utilisation of multiple methodologies is important not only to more accurately reflect the multi-disciplinary nature of the field of study, but also to avoid favouring one approach over others. Research methodologies and pedagogies are constructed based on philosophical assumptions about what the content of the subject is like and how (and to what extent) that subject may be known (e.g. through interpretation or debate). For instance, the teacher who favours the teaching of religion(s) and worldview(s) by way of philosophical enquiry will be – knowingly or unknowingly – promoting the idea that religion(s) and worldview(s) are first and foremost a set of beliefs best interrogated by critical analytical reasoning. Such a position, is at best contested and at worse, clearly wrong, given the emphasis on religion as a way of life and culture within the dharmic traditions, for instance. Thus, favouring one approach over others' risks indoctrinating pupils and marginalizing others who could/may hold legitimate views at odds with those championed by the teacher's preferred approach.

Inclusion of multiple approaches not only improves balance, but also facilitates academic rigour (through the multi-perspectival analysis of content). Freathy and John (2019, p. 15) dismiss claims that the inclusion of multiple methodologies and their associated focuses would result in a 'dilution' of subject content, arguing that this approach permits the inclusion of vastly differing ways in which even a singular institutional worldview varies across denominations, countries and cultures. The inclusion of ethnographic approaches, for instance, enables the inclusion of the 'lived experience' and the 'real religious landscape' (Dossett 2019, p. 8). This inclusion is of particular importance to ensure pupils establish an appreciation of the diversity of ways people manifest and evolve their worldview and support the important task of challenging stereotypes (CoRE 2018, p. 36).

Moreover, the introduction of multiple contrasting perspectives enables the development of pupils' criticality in this matter. When utilised as roles to be stepped in and out of (like the putting on a costume), the characters function as a distancing technique that separates the approach taken from the teacher so as to permit pupils to: a) see it as distinct from the teacher and b) facilitate evaluation of it as a distinct approach. Pupils can be taught to assess through their evaluation what each approach to the study of religion and non-religious worldviews reveals and simultaneously obscures, so as to be ready to 'call out' those who attempt to impose a singular view on the matter.

The approach also provides a solution to another enduring problem facing the subject. There is no vantage point from which objective or neutral knowledge can be established or taught. A researcher's, teacher's or pupils' social identities, beliefs, attitudes and values will shape, limit or, perhaps, determine what they can learn from any given encounter with an object of study of how they engage with it (Freathy, R. & John 2019, p. 13). What we attend to; what questions we ask; what information we collect and how we interpret our findings betrays our 'positionality'. Expressed differently, our worldview is evident in all aspects of our enquiries and importantly in our outcomes. Whilst we can monitor the influence of our worldviews and our attendant biases, our ability to do so is delimited by the extent of our self-awareness, in the terminology of the Ofsted review (2021), our 'personal knowledge'. This is problematic for the teacher because we cannot teach content without imposing the worldview and values of the knowledge producer on the pupils, as well as our own. The authority of any knowledge source should not be accepted uncritically and nor should the teacher ever stop monitoring how their inevitable biases are shaping the pupils' encounters with the content. Moreover, we should not be surprised to find that pupils are challenged by lesson content that 'jars' with deeply held assumptions or by the prevalence of (mis)conceptions that differ from how we believed the taught content would be understood. *The RE-searchers approach* explicitly invites pupils to monitor the impact of the self on knowledge construction; their developing worldview and its impact on their engagement with subject content and with different research methodologies.

Spanning disciplines is also discussed in Chapter Seven where Elton-Chalcraft, Prescott and Hollander discuss advantages of drawing on a range of approaches for spiritual development and RE in general, thus avoiding silos.

ACADEMIC ATTRIBUTES, SCHOLARLY VALUES AND LEARNER'S PERSONAL WORLDVIEW

In contrast to other conceptions of the subject, in *The RE-searchers approach* there is no attempt to form pupils' worldviews, beyond promoting academic attributes (such as open-mindedness, rigour, criticality and reflexivity) and scholarly values (such as integrity, honesty, fairness, respect and responsibility) (Freathy, R. *et al.* 2017, p. 8). This is because, in the context of study of religions and worldviews, pupils' worldviews are only relevant insofar as they shape or are shaped by their engagement in the study of religions and non-religious worldviews. They must be included because personal reflection and reflexivity are integral to what it means to engage in scholarly study (Larkin *et al.* 2019). Without treating the pupils' worldviews as objects of study, the subject fails to live up to the rigorous, critical and 'scientific' engagement expected of any academic field (Freathy & John 2019, pp. 15–16). Through this process of reflection, pupils can be given the opportunity to consider how/whether their own worldview and their own identity: changes; contains multiple layers; is influenced (perhaps unknowingly) by external ideas and influences (Dossett 2019, p.8) and is aligned (or not) with the institutional worldviews (religious and non-religious) studied (Ahs *et al.* 2016, p. 212).

CLASSROOM ACTIVITY – 'MANTLE OF THE EXPERT'

In this section, I present classroom ideas which combine *The RE-searchers approach* with features of a system of learning known as Mantle of the Expert (MoE). MoE was originated and developed by Dorothy Heathcote (1926–2012) a drama educator in the UK (Aitken 2013 cited in Hatton & Aitken 2018, p. 34). In the approach learners are framed as experts in an imagined responsible team and are invited to carry out a high stakes commission for an important, fictional, client (Heathcote & Bolton 1995; Aitken 2013 cited in Hatton & Aitken 2018, p. 126). Over the course of a sequence of lessons, the class - in their collective role – are required to operate as a "supportive, interpretative, and reflective community" (O'Neill in Heathcote & Bolton 1995, p. viii) engaging in manufactured challenges and/or problems manifest in the course of their inquiry or project (Sayers 2011, p. 21).

MoE has been an unacknowledged influence my writing of exemplar materials for *The RE-searchers approach*. For instance, in Mr. Stricken's Nativity Nightmare (Freathy, G. 2016, p. 82), Mr Stricken, a fictional primary school headteacher requests help from the class to conduct research into Jesus' birth narratives to assuage the concerns of his board of governors that his self-penned nativity play is going to be "historically accurate" and reflect the "true meaning of Christmas". Similarly in the unit of work, Let's Talk about Love (Phillipson, N. & Wegerif, R. 2016), the class are provided with a narrative where the class is invited to participate in the pilot of a TV programme about 'Religion for Children' involving the four *RE-searcher* characters.

As well as adding purpose to the sequence of learning activities, features of MoE can be adopted to underline the relevance of religions and worldviews to contemporary public and private affairs and to show how knowledge and understanding of religions and worldviews can be developed. The use of real-life contexts can further highlight the applicability and transferability of knowledge and skills associated with the study of religions and worldviews.

In the following four examples, it is possible to imagine projecting the class into a scenario selected from current affairs to intercede in the role of a decision-making body.

Example One: Removal of Earth Goddess statue

The scenario: *"Religious leaders in a Cornish tutown have called for a statue to be removed or for its name to be changed because of its 'spiritual significance'. The £80,000 ceramic art Earth Goddess was put up in St Austell in June to 'celebrate the area's heritage'. A letter was sent by seven religious leaders to the town council, saying the statue was 'offensive to God'." (BBC, August 2022)*
The commission: *The class are asked by the local council to work as consultants investigate what the artwork represents, why it has provoked such a reaction and whether it should be removed.*

Example Two: Removal of Crucifix

The scenario: *"A vicar has defended a decision to remove a crucifix from the outside of the church. Critics of its removal say that the effect is to play down the significance of Christ's sacrifice on the cross. But parents had commented that children had been scared by the ten-foot crucifix's distinctive image. The main motivation behind removing it was to replace it with "a symbol of hope rather than hopelessness" (adapted from The Church Times 2009).*
The commission: *After a lot of news coverage and protests, the vicar asks the class to use their research skills to investigate whether they think he made the right decision.*

Example Three: A Hindu Prime Minister openly discussing his faith

The scenario: *"Rishi Sunak [became] the UK's first Hindu prime minister. Sunak is a practising Hindu, although he has rarely talked publicly about his faith. Two years previously, when Sunak was chancellor, he lit candles to mark Diwali on the doorstep of No 11 Downing Street at a time when Covid restrictions remained in force. My faith, he said, 'gives me strength, it gives me purpose. It's part of who I am,' he said. (The Guardian 2022).*
The commission: *The class are commissioned by the Conservative party to consider whether Rishi Sunak should explain how his religious faith shapes his choices ahead of a future General Election.*

Example Four:

The scenario: *"A Buddhist temple on the edge of Beijing has developed a robot monk who can chant mantras and explain basic tenets of faith. At 2ft high, Xian'er is encased in saffron-yellow robes and has a shaved head. His purpose is to reach out to people who are more connected to their smartphones than their inner being. Master Xianfian, a (human) monk at Longquan and Xian'er's creator, said artificial intelligence could be harnessed to spread Buddhist wisdom in China. 'Science and Buddhism are not opposing nor contradicting, and can be combined and mutually compatible,' he told Reuters."* *(The Guardian 2016)*
The commission: *The class are invited to investigate whether a robot could/should, replace a Buddhist monk.*

What role in the news event could the class play as a commissioned team undertaking an investigation where they need to research a religion or worldview?

Can you think of any examples of local, national or international news items involving a religion or a worldview that would engage learners and support curriculum learning with a topic that is appropriate to your pupils?

PREPARING TO USE THE RE-SEARCHER CHARACTERS

Whether a scenario such as those suggested above is used or not, a critical, dialogic and enquiry-based approach requires pupils to consciously adopt and reflect upon multiple research methodologies. With *The RE-searchers approach*, the RE-searcher characters personify four such methodologies. Whilst it may be necessary to introduce one character at a time within sequences of lessons (e.g. six lessons simultaneously exploring a topic and getting to know Ask-it-all Ava), the richer and more rigorous sequences of learning involve switching between characters and considering where this is beneficial within

---

■ **Table 10.2** Teacher Planning prompts for RE-searchers

See-the-story Suzie Planning Prompts

Is there a story connected to this topic for which there is more than one interpretation?

Will exploration of these interpretations support pupils' understanding of curriculum concepts pertinent to the chosen topic?

Ask-it-all Ava Planning Prompts

Do you have access to living representatives (or the perspectives thereof) of the religion or worldview that are the focus of your topic?

Do you know (or can you find out) how these people's backgrounds, families, communities and traditions shape their lives?

Have-a-go Hugo Planning Prompts

Is there a practice associated with the featured religion or worldview and relevant to the topic that pupils could observe/undertake/emulate in some way?

Will the activity support reflection on feelings and personal meanings that could conceivably support empathetic engagement with members of the focus group?

Debate-it-all Derek Planning Prompts

Is there a 'big question' related to the topic related to questions truth-claims or ethical dilemmas?

Are you aware of contrasting answers to the 'big question' existing within and/or between different worldviews and religions, notably the religion or worldview explored in this topic?

Where such resources are available, it is possible to combine them with activity ideas detailed in Table 10.1, to produce learning activities that align with each of the research methodologies. Depending on knowledge, experience and capability of your class, teachers can increase or decrease the level of challenge of any of these activities by making adjustments to them. Teacher can alter the level of support made available to individuals or groups and change how open or closed the research activity is (i.e. how pre-determined the knowledge is that pupils are expected to engage with and learn as a result of the enquiry activity).

---

lessons. To facilitate such a sequence of learning it is necessary to be pragmatic and to consider what resources you will need to support authentic encounters with the religion or worldview when using each character. Typically, if you can ask yourself the questions in Table 10.2 affirmatively, then you have all that you need to support a rich and rewarding sequence that will enable an exploration of the defining features of each RE-searcher. Examples of how this works in a series of lessons is shown in Table 10.3.

▪ **Table 10.3** Series of Lessons for Example 1: Removal of an Earth Goddess Statue

---

The scenario 'Example One' – Removal of an Earth Goddess statue sould be built into a sequence of learning using resources such as those suggested like this:

Lesson One: Introduction to the scenario; exploration of pupils' initial thoughts and feelings; opportunity for pupils' to develop curious questions and consider ways and means the answers could be sought.

Lesson Two: Exploration of four perspectives on the piece of art from the scenario ('Mother Earth' by Sandy Brown) through Ask-it-all Ava interviews or role play hot-seating interviewees espousing different points of view from inhabitants of St. Austell such as:

▪ A conservative view (detailing the first two commandments from the Old Testament and arguing that England is a Christian country at risk of losing touch with its identity).

▪ A liberal Christian view that recognises the plurality of religions and worldviews and the shared nature of a public space.

▪ A member of the public who has reservations about the appearance of the sculpture, but appreciates that the sculpture is made with local clay.

▪ A pagan representative who celebrates the arrival of the artwork on the basis that is demonstrates a reverence and love for Mother Nature.

Lesson Three: Exploration of the story of Moses, the Ten Commandments and the Israelites' golden calf in the style of See-the-story Suzie enquiry focussing on seeking to empathize with the characters in the story.

Lesson Four: Continuation of the See-the-story Suzie work. A comparison of two Christian interpretations of this story, where one perspective suggests the story is about human tendency towards sin and the other suggests it is about God's mercy. Exploration of how a Christians' interpretation of this story might shape their views on whether the artwork should be removed.

Lesson Five: Share an interview with the artist with the pupils where she explains that the inspiration for her piece was her own mother and her experience of her farming parents being disappointed that she was a girl. Create or meditate on artwork, as Have-a-Hugo might, depicting either a woman who is important in their lives or a parent or carer who is important to them. Pupils reflect on what the artwork means to them and how it feels to share their reflections on this with others.

Lesson Six: Pupils learn about Debate-it-all Derek and how to disagree without being disagreeable. Pupils rehearse their new techniques whilst debating the merits of the four different views of the sculpture explored in Lesson 2. Pupils vote on whether they will recommend to the council whether the sculpture should be removed and justify their conclusion.

Representation: Religion(s) and Worldviews

In order to investigate a scenario like those suggested in Tables 10.2 and 10.3 with pupils – or indeed any topic selected for a sequence of learning – a teacher may wish to introduce substantive knowledge to enable pupils to ask informed questions. Given that there are no uncontested accounts of the nature of individual religions or worldviews (Freathy & John 2019, p. 13), there are challenges associated with teachers determining what or whose knowledge to use when teaching pupils about a topic. The solution I suggest here is that where we introduce knowledge to pupils, we also indicate the source of the information and invite pupils to investigate its validity through their own research activities. Doing this highlights that knowledge does not exist separately from social contexts. Where it is not possible (or appropriate) to identify a single source that is fit-for-purpose, age and topic appropriate, texts can be created and attributed to a fictional source. - I have done this before using characters such as 'Dr. Know' and 'Professor Why?' who take it upon themselves to furnish the class with background information. Whilst this does not carry the authenticity of engaging with genuine sources of information, the attribution of the knowledge to an individual (who may be flawed or biased) can be used to support pupils in adopting a critical stance in a way that they might not should the information be presented by the teacher alone. An exciting opportunity – worthy of further investigation – is how Artificial Intelligence Large Language Models (such as Chat GPT) could be used to 'harvest' and represent knowledge to pupils for them to explore and test through a critical, dialogic and enquiry-based pedagogy. Moreover, the potential for such an activity to enhance pupils' understanding of the limitations of AI and how to get Large Language Models to produce better answers is very exciting.

Have you ever been challenged by a pupil about the accuracy of the information you are teaching about a religion or worldview?

Was this the religion or worldview of the pupil raising the challenge?

How did you (or would you) manage this?

Do you think attributing the substantive knowledge to a real or fictious source/person and inviting pupils to test the validity of the claims is a solution to this problem?

How and when might you choose to do this?

CREATING A REFLEXIVE CLASSROOM CULTURE

One of the reasons why it is important to recognise that all knowledge in this subject cannot be separated from the social context within which it has been generated, is because the positionality of the researcher and their attendant beliefs, values and purposes shape

– if not determine – what knowledge they seek; how they find it out and how they interpret the findings (Freathy, R. & John 2019, p. 13). A researcher's concern for and reflection on how they, being themselves, are shaping the knowledge they produce is called reflexivity. The role of the self in knowledge production and learning has implications for how we present and engage with accounts of religions and worldviews, but also for how we think of ourselves and our pupils as knowledge producers and curriculum learners. What we and our pupils choose to focus on; what aspects we attend to; how we engage with the content, whether we engage with the content and how we interpret it when we do, will be shaped to a lesser or greater degree by who we are. The pupil's prior experiences, knowledge, attitudes, values, expectations (amongst other factors), impact on what they will take away from their learning episode. Given the centrality of the learners' positionality and worldview in determining what understanding(s) pupils achieve and their readiness to undertake different forms of study, it is suggested that the developing pupils' worldview should be considered an object of study alongside that of the religion or worldview in focus and the research methodology selected for the enquiry (Freathy, R. *et al.* 2017). The aim of supporting pupils' reflections on their worldviews should not be to foster these in any particular direction, but to enable a level of critical engagement that permits pupils to see, recognise, monitor and manage their bias in such a way that improves their ability to investigate and understand religions and worldviews (Freathy & John 2019, p. 13).

To achieve this, Larkin *et al.* (2019) suggest that teachers should invest time and energy into creating a classroom culture where pupils' reflection upon their worldview, their modes of engagement with the substantive knowledge and the sources of information they encounter are supported through the creation of time and space(s) for each. The prompts below may help a teacher looking to adopt a critical, dialogic and enquiry-based pedagogy, such as *The RE-searchers approach*, to consider whether they have created the appropriate classroom culture to sustain the approach. Specifically, they support consideration of whether pupils will be adequately supported in their reflection on their worldview and its impact on their learning.

- Are pupils in your classroom given time and space to reflect on what they believe, the nature of these beliefs and the reasons they have for holding them? Do your pupils feel safe to reflect on these areas independently, with you and/or with their peers?
- Would pupils in your class feel confident and safe enough to explain their thoughts and feelings about topics covered in the subject?
- Would pupils in your class feel confident and safe enough to explain their thoughts and feelings about the methodologies selected to engage with the subject matter? e.g. How did you find being Debate-it-all Derek today? What did you think to be the strengths and weaknesses of the approach?
- Are the class sufficiently used to reflection to enable you to challenge and support them in making links between the thoughts and feelings they experience during learning activities/enquiries and that which they have articulated about themselves and their worldview?
- Are pupils ready to consider how they can use the knowledge they have about themselves to make decisions about their learning and to monitor how their learning is being affected by who they are and the beliefs they hold?

FINAL THOUGHTS

The RE-searchers approach (and other critical dialogic and inquiry-based approaches) point to a version of the subject that is flexible enough to adjust to the changing landscape of religions and worldviews. The approach takes knowledge seriously by inducting pupils of any age into critical discussions relating the nature of knowledge, what can be known and who can know it. Such epistemic concerns are central to the academic study of religions and worldviews. Whilst I believe that this is a sufficient justification for adopting this approach to teaching the subject, the transferability of these skills to some of the challenges of modern life (such as interrogating the reliability of sources of information in the news, on social media and that is produced by AI systems) adds an additional warrant for investigating the merits, affordances and implementation of the approach.

REFERENCES

Ahs, V., Poulter, S. & Kallioniemi, A. 2016. 'Encountering worldviews: Pupil perspectives on integrative worldview education in a Finnish secondary school context.' *Religion & in Education*, 43(2): 208–229.

BBC News. 2022. *St Austell religious leaders object to Earth Goddess statue.* August 21st 2022 Available at: St Austell religious leaders object to Earth Goddess statue - BBC News.

Beaven, E. 2009. *Vicar takes down 'scary' crucifix.* 8th January 2009. Available at: Vicar takes down 'scary' crucifix (churchtimes.co.uk).

Commission on Religious Education [CoRE]. 2018. *Religion and Worldviews: The Way Forward. A National Plan for RE (Final Report).* London: Religious Education Council of England & Wales.

Dossett, W. 2019. 'Religious education and worldviews.' *British Association for the Study of Religions. Bulletin*, 134: 7–9.

Freathy, G. 2016. 'The RE-searchers approach: A quick start guide with exemplar units of work and activities.' Available at: https://www.reonline.org.uk/teaching-resources/re-searchers-approach/approach/ [accessed 27.03.23]

Freathy, G., Freathy, R., Doney, J., Walshe, K. & Teece, G. 2015. *The RE-searchers: A New Approach to Religious Education in Primary Schools.* Exeter: University of Exeter. Available at: https://www.reonline.org.uk/teaching-resources/re-searchers-approach/approach/ [accessed 27.03.23]

Freathy, R., Doney, J., Freathy, G., Walshe, K. & Teece, G. 2017. 'Pedagogical bricoleurs and bricolage researchers: The case of religious education.' *British Journal of Educational Studies*, 65(4): 425–443. DOI: 10.1080/00071005.2017.1343454

Freathy, R. & John, H. C. 2019. 'Religious Education, Big Ideas and the study of religion(s) and worldview(s).' *British Journal of Religious Education*, 41(1): 27–40.

Freathy, R. & John, H. C. 2019. 'Worldviews and "Big Ideas": A way forward for religious education?' *Nordidactica - Journal of Humanities and Social Science Education*, 2019: 4

Hatton, C. & Aitken, V. 2018. 'Keeping the flame alive: Legacies of Heathcote's practice across the Tasman.' *Drama Australia Journal*, 42(2). doi:10.1080/14452294.2019.1585 932

Heathcote, D. & Bolton, G. 1995. *Drama for Learning.* Portsmouth NH: Heinemann.

Larkin, S., Freathy, R., Doney, J. & Freathy, G. 2019. *Metacognition, Worldviews and Religious Education: A Practical Guide for Teachers.* 1st edition. London and New York: Routledge

Ofsted 2021. 'Research review series: religious education: A review of research into factors that influence the quality of religious education (RE) in schools in England.' Research *Review* Series*: Religious* Education - GOV.UK. Available at: www.gov.uk [accessed 30.03.23]

Ofsted 2022. 'Guidance school inspection handbook.' Available at: https://www.gov.uk/government/publications/school-inspection-handbook-eif/school-inspection-handbook [accessed 11.07.22]

Phillipson, N. & Wegerif, R. 2016. *Dialogic Education: Mastering Core Concepts through Thinking Together.* 1st edition. London: Routledge

Sayers, R. 2011. 'The implications of introducing Heathcote's Mantle of the expert approach as a community of practice and cross curricular learning tool in a primary school,' *English in Education*, 45(1): 20–35. DOI:10.1111/j.1754-8845.2010.01084.x.

Sherwood, H. 2022. *Rishi Sunak to become first British PM of colour and also first Hindu at No 10.* 24th October 2022. Available at: Rishi Sunak urges Hindus to stick to lockdown rules at Diwali | Diwali | The Guardian

Sherwood, H. 2016. *Robot monk to spread Buddhist wisdom to the digital generation.* 26th April 2016. Available at: Robot monk to spread Buddhist wisdom to the digital generation | Buddhism | The Guardian

SECTION 3

DEVELOPING PRACTICE

CHAPTER 11

ISLAMOPHOBIA AND A RELIGION AND WORLDVIEWS APPROACH

Kate Christopher and Lynn Revell

In this chapter, we discuss the nature of Islamophobia and explain why it is important that teachers can challenge Islamophobia in the classroom while at the same time supporting the right of young children to ask critical questions about Islam. We show how a Religion and Worldviews approach to teaching about Muslim communities and ideas associated with Islam supports teachers to engage with complex and sensitive ideas in ways that are appropriate for younger pupils. Using examples of resources and ideas for lessons that focus on a range of issues from the poet Rumi to immigration and Muslim lives in Birmingham we show how teachers can draw on substantive knowledge and personal knowledge as well as ways of knowing in relation to Islam and Islamophobia.

In this chapter we will explore the following areas:

1) What is Islamophobia?
2) What are the educational reasons for teaching about Islamophobia to pupils between the ages of 3–11?
3) How can a Religion and Worldviews approach allow teachers to teach Islamophobia in ways that are critical and creative?
4) Some practical examples using the Poet Rumi and Muslim lives in the city of Birmingham.

At the end of the chapter, you will find 'Notes for teachers'; a summary of ideas to be shared with colleagues or for your own records.

WHAT IS ISLAMOPHOBIA?

Islamophobia is an issue that many schools want to address but are unsure how to approach the multiple challenges of this complex area. Schools with a commitment to equality, tolerance and pluralism seek to combat racism and prejudice, often through

DOI: 10.4324/9781003361480-14

RE, but Islamophobia remains a difficult area for many teachers. Teaching about a form of racism or prejudice raises questions around exploring controversial issues, freedom of expression and critique, and a desire to promote respect and tolerance in society. Teaching about a religious tradition does not raise these problems in the same way. However, the answers to understanding Islamophobia do not lie in a study of Islam, but outside the Muslim world. There is often confusion about what Islamophobia is, so we start with a definition of Islamophobia. We will build on this understanding with practical advice for teachers.

Islamophobia can involve physical and verbal abuse, exclusion and discrimination. The Runnymede Trust defines Islamophobia as fear, hatred or hostility towards Islam, Islamic culture and Muslims (Runnymede Trust 1997). Barry van Driel, editor of the Journal *Intercultural Education* says Islamophobia is 'an irrational distrust, fear or rejection of the Muslim religion and those that are perceived as Muslims' (Van Driel 2004: 6). Islamophobia can result in violence and exclusion, but also behaviour which is more subtle and ambiguous. It is important for teachers to recognise Islamophobic patterns or tropes, and what lies beneath them. This way the similarities between upsetting and confusing individual events can be seen and a pattern can become visible. This is the beginning of assisting pupils to make sense of what they see, whether in school, in the media, in society, now and in the future.

Many teachers, aware of Islamophobia in their schools or communities, respond by presenting a positive and non-threatening model of Islam. A great deal is made of the beauty of Islamic artefacts and architecture and of the linguistic, cultural, intellectual and social contribution of Islam to the world. However, these strategies on their own fail to address the cause of Islamophobia because they do not show the roots and nature of Islamophobic thinking. We will suggest some ways that teachers can both explore Islamic art, culture, diversity and creativity and encompass a consideration of the contexts Muslims have to navigate in a later section.

DOES ISLAMOPHOBIA MEAN THAT PUPILS CAN'T CRITICALLY ENGAGE WITH ISLAM?

It is essential that teachers understand the nature of Islamophobia. Teaching about Islamophobia is not the same as teaching about Islam. Some teachers worry that a critical engagement with ideas connected to Islamic beliefs or cultures is Islamophobic. What is meant by 'critical engagement'? This does not mean being 'critical' of or 'criticising' Islam or Muslims. It means exploring beliefs, arguments or ways of seeing within Islam in a way that allows pupils to bring their own interpretations and ideas to the picture. This can be described as pupils engaging their 'critical faculties'. For example, older pupils might discuss whether Islamic athletes should fast when sporting events occur during Ramadan, or discuss a situation where two Muslim individuals are weighing up whether to have a flu jab, when the jab is not halal. Pupils will learn about different Muslim views regarding these scenarios, but will also bring their own ideas to the conversation. Younger pupils could look at mosques or art from different Islamic cultures and talk about what is different and what is similar. They could be introduced to a Muslim persona doll who describes the similarities and differences between his own and his friend's Muslim faith (see Chapter Nine, 'Visits and Visitors'). Pupils will encounter rich information and hear

■ **Table 11.1** Definition of Islamophobia developed from Allen 2012

'Othering 'ideology – 'us' and 'them'	'Us' and 'them' perpetuated	Discriminatory and exclusionary practices
An ideology that perpetuates meanings about Muslims and Islam that presents it in myriad ways as the Other. That is values and practices associated with Islam are understood as alien and essentially different from the values and norms of 'our' society and culture.	This ideology is sustained and perpetuated through narratives, legislation, political language and the creation of identities that define themselves against Islam.	Exclusionary practices that disadvantage, prejudice or discriminate against Muslims and Islam.

what a range of different Muslims are saying, and when they can bring something of their own perspective to the conversation they will be critically engaging.

Chris Allen argues that if the term 'Islamophobia' is to have any real use we need to be clear what it is about Islam that causes a 'phobic' response. He argues that although it is an enormously problematic and complex term it has three parts, see Table 11.1, which is developed from Allen's work (Allen 2012).

This is a definition of Islamophobia that rests on a view of Islam as fundamentally at odds with Western values and culture. Islam is not merely different in the way that customs associated with Buddhism or Hinduism may seem different to Western culture and norms, but threatening and aggressive. The hostility towards Islam is rooted in the fact that it has become a symbolic enemy, the polar opposite of the positive values and customs we associate with 'our' own culture. We will return to the model of Islamophobia proposed by Allen in the section on ideas and strategies for engaging with Islamophobia.

1) **What are the educational reasons for teaching about Islamophobia to younger pupils?**

Is the primary classroom a suitable place to address Islamophobia? In this section we will present arguments to provide answers to this question covering 'othering' and power. You will find these arguments in the 'teacher's notes' at the end of the chapter for your use with colleagues, parents or school leaders.

'OTHERING' AND EXCLUSION

Lying behind Islamophobia, as well as other forms of exclusion, such as misogyny or homophobia, are patterns of 'othering'. Robin Richardson from *Insted*, an organisation focusing on race and diversity in education, argues that the causes of Islamophobia are to be found not in Islam but in the way we define our communities and identities by excluding, marginalising and subjugating others. He states,

> The task of challenging Islamophobia through education ... does not primarily require teaching about Islam. Rather, it primarily requires teaching about Islamophobia. And, more generally, about colour and cultural racism, and about

the causes of these. The causes do not lie in the characteristics of the Other, and certainly not in the characteristics of the Other's religion. Rather, they lie in the culture, history and practices of ourselves.

(Robin Richardson, www.insted.co.uk)

Fekete (2009) outlines negative views of Islam common in the Western world. They are:

- Islam subjugates women through dress codes (wearing the veil, niqab etc), marriage (the Qur'an, allows men to marry four wives), arranged marriages and confining women to private spaces.
- Islam is an innately intolerant religion and one that is prone to religious fundamentalism.
- Islam is an innately violent religion and prone to extremism.

(Fekete 2009)

Does this mean Muslims only have themselves to blame when it comes to Islamophobia? In addressing this question, an understanding of 'othering' is crucial. It is not that Islam or Muslims are more misogynistic, intolerant or violent than any other religion or culture, it is that Islam is presented as 'other', or alien or different, to Christian, European values and society, whatever Muslims actually do, think and say.

These ideas are important for Western society not because of what they say about Islam but because of what they say about Western culture and attitudes. In 1978, Edward Said coined the phrase 'Orientalism' to describe the way in which Western thinkers demonise and caricature the East, or the 'Orient'. In RE we can see Orientalist images and prejudices in textbooks (Revell 2012) and even in Agreed Syllabuses (Panjwani and Revell 2020).

Islamophobia as an ideology legitimises the notion that Islam and Muslims are irreconcilably different from Christian, European culture and values. Teaching about ideologies is a challenge for teachers of young pupils because it can rely on rather abstract notions. Learning about such things as the 'other' and the power of a dominant worldview is something children will better understand as they grow, but the seeds can be sown when they are young.

The legitimacy of the idea of the 'other' relies to a large extent on isolation of groups and communities from one another. We can only see others as alien and attribute abhorrent qualities to them when we never question ourselves or our own communities and when our views of the 'other' are never challenged. Creating spaces for dialogue between groups is a recognised mechanism for building relationships between groups but when it is used creatively it can also encourage individuals to consider their own identity.

One creative approach to dialogue has been developed as part of a project to bring together people from different cultural and religious backgrounds. Julia Ipgrave analysed the email exchanges of primary aged pupils from an inner city, multicultural school in Leicester and the more homogeneously white schools in Leicester as part of the Building E-Bridges model. The project did not ask children to form friendships but to "provide insights for their partners into the religious and cultural groups to which they belonged…" (Ipgrave 2009). The focus on specific areas of their lives meant that children were expected to think about their identities so that they could explain it to others. Ipgrave found that when some children looked at what set them apart from others, in other words becoming aware of their own outlook, the tone of their communications became respectful and more tentative.

The REDco project (Religion in Education. A Dialogue or a factor of conflict in transforming societies of European Countries) found that even though children express tolerance towards others in abstract discussions they are less likely to do so at a practical level. Projects where communication between groups of children takes place can be embedded as part of a whole school approach to dialogue. Teachers could exchange guest speakers or visits to mosques for opportunities to engage with Muslim and non-Muslim children, perhaps from other schools or local areas (see Chapter Six concerning the potentially negative effects of visits and visitors). This approach could help children become aware that everyone has a worldview, including themselves. This could be the first step to an understanding that will last a lifetime, that the creation of 'others' is a widespread phenomenon in all human societies. To learn about these patterns is a valuable, some might say crucial, part of a child's education. It can help them to unlock all sorts of behaviours and attitudes, at school, in their community and in their future lives. This is part of our world and shapes so many aspects of society; who we listen to, who we respect, who can do what job, and, conversely, who is silenced, ignored and overlooked. Although it can be unsettling, an exploration of othering and power allows children to become aware of their own worldview and how it is maintained, as well as how other groups are imagined – whether in terms of neighbourhoods, religions, cultures, nations and so on. This is an important dimension of pupils' growing understanding of the world.

Power

Islamophobia is not just a collection of stereotypical assumptions about Islam. It is a form of power. Islamophobia relies on mechanisms and practices that exclude and discriminate. It is an ideology which is enacted through behaviours, rules, legislation and formal and informal codes of practice. To make sense of Islamophobia in the classroom is to assist pupils in making sense of how power is enacted on groups and individuals. The notion of 'othering', discussed above, is ultimately an enactment of power; where one worldview and way of living is rendered alien and somehow wrong in relation to a dominant worldview and way of living (Elton-Chalcraft 2009). Despite being challenging for the teacher who may feel underequipped to tackle such a slippery, abstract and potentially explosive topic, giving children the ability to detect power in society is a crucial part of their education.

2) **How can a Religion and Worldviews approach address Islamophobia in ways that are critical and creative?**

A Religion and Worldviews approach offers a radically different perspective on teaching about beliefs, religiosity and values. In Chapter Two of this volume 'Teaching RE Creatively', Ruth Flanagan and Linda Whitworth provide a comprehensive introduction to some of the debates about Religion and Worldviews, as well as suggesting ways a Religion and Worldviews approach can contribute to creative teaching. There are many different interpretations of worldviews. For us there are two guiding principles, the first is that a worldviews approach to teaching starts with people and the second is that pupils should have the opportunity to ask questions from different perspectives and subject disciplines.

Starting with people is important because it means that when we talk about religion or beliefs in the classroom our lessons are grounded in the experiences and practices of real people who live in real places and navigate real issues. This focus on real people means that the teaching can take account of personal and biographical factors but it also means that we avoid the trap of referring to beliefs in the abstract or of 'essentialising' beliefs. Essentialising is when we attribute a timeless and uniform quality to something. This might sound innocent enough, especially as the teacher must simplify information about religion and belief in order for pupils to grasp the key ideas, but the danger is a tendency to assume that *all* Christians believe something in the same way, or *all* Jews feel the same way about a festival or custom. Essentialism opens the door to sweeping generalisations and stereotypes. Many teachers of RE are in the habit of avoiding such generalisations. In our approach to Religion and Worldviews we take this habit one step further by always making sure that, where possible, we include the particular history, culture, era or geography when we explore people and their beliefs. In terms of Islamophobia, the need to avoid essentialising is doubly important because essentialisation is a key part of Islamophobia. Many people are hostile towards Muslims and Islam because they attribute the same qualities, beliefs and characteristics to all Muslims in all times and places. While it is legitimate for people to critique Islam and to express disbelief or even a lack of respect for traditions or practices associated with Islam, it is inaccurate and unfair to make such critiques on the basis that all Muslims always behave in this way or uphold this view.

WAYS OF KNOWING AND CHALLENGING STEREOTYPES

An Islamophobic ideology must be communicated throughout society in order to become a part of the everyday language of a society. Representations of Islam and Muslims that identify them as 'alien' or 'un-British' in the popular media, the news, textbooks and stereotypes are all central to this process. To delve into the ways Islamophobia is perpetuated in society is to show pupils how Islamophobic stereotypes are reproduced, and also how stereotypes generally are reproduced. A Religion and Worldviews approach encourages pupils to consider their own awareness of the way they look at the world as a way of disrupting stereotypes they may hold about Muslims.

Making stereotypes visible enables pupils to recognise and challenge them when encountered in conversation, in school or the media. Resources like 'Show Racism the Red Card' (https://www.theredcard.org/) adopt a popular approach to stereotypes. It offers pupils a range of images of different 'sorts' of people all wearing head coverings; a nun, a bridal veil, a sporting cap, a hoodie, a crash helmet, turban, hijab etc. Children are asked questions about why people wear head coverings. The aim of the activity is to show pupils that the common image (or stereotype) of Muslim women wearing hijab might be inaccurate or stereotypical and questions are designed to disrupt possible assumptions around Muslim head coverings. It points out that nuns also wear a hijab in much the same way as many Muslim women and asks readers to consider how they think society would react if somebody ripped off a nun's head covering in the street, as happens to Muslim women wearing the hijab.

■ **Table 11.2** The veiled Muslim woman

Assumptions/stereotypes	What this suggests about Western non-Muslim women
She is forced to wear the veil against her will.	Western women are free to choose how they dress.
She is regarded as second class even within her own culture and community.	Western women are regarded as equals.
Her dress is the product of a culture that is old fashioned and informed by ideas that are no longer accepted in modern democracies.	Western dress is modern and embodies the freedom and equality of Western women.
Her veil marks her out as someone who chooses not to 'fit in', as someone that sets her apart from the mainstream.	That Western society permits her to wear her veil signifies Western tolerance of others different from ourselves.

Activities like the above are useful because they can prompt pupils to reconsider the way they view the world and to question 'facts' that they held to be true, such as that only Muslim women cover their heads for religious reasons, or that in European society it is unusual for people to wear head coverings. It is also important to avoid sweeping claims about Muslim women and the hijab. Women from some Muslim countries do not widely adopt the hijab, such as Turkey. Women in other countries may feel they are compelled to cover their hair, whatever their own choice, such as Iran. Contextual, cultural and geographical differences can add a richness of understanding as well as avoid stereotypes and essentialism. Teaching about stereotypes can be developed further for older children by exploring what the stereotypes of Muslims or Islam are meant to communicate. The core of Islamophobia is the idea that Islam and Islamic societies are inherently different and inferior to Christianity and Christian societies. Pupils could suggest their reasons why a Muslim woman in a headscarf is seen in a negative light, whereas white, European women in various head coverings passes without mention. Of course, language about 'stereotypes' is another way of talking about 'othering'.

Look at this more detailed breakdown of stereotypes or assumptions that could apply to a Muslim woman in hijab (Table 11.2).

This is certainly a complex task and will need some support from the teacher. However, allowing pupils to see not just the assumptions lying behind stereotypes of 'others', but *what that says about the dominant culture,* is an incredibly powerful mode of thinking that will unlock layers of understanding over time (see Figure 2.5, p. 29).

FITTING IN AND EXCLUSION

Through simple techniques you can bring to pupils' attention some of the ways Muslims can be excluded in society. Some practices that exclude Muslims may not appear as discriminatory because they apply to everyone, however the reality is that they adversely affect Muslims disproportionally.

Invite pupils to discuss why schools have a school uniform that must be worn. It is usually justified on grounds of equality, erasing income differences and creating a sense of community. Yet normalised Western dress codes affect Muslims disproportionally because they reject dress which stands outside the Western norm, such as longer, looser garments and a head covering for females. A school uniform policy might appear neutral to some pupils, but in fact contain Western habits that might not sit comfortably with some Muslim families. This is a simple way of drawing pupils' attention to something they may never have thought of, which is the norms and assumptions beneath practices of the dominant culture.

Confronting Islamophobia in education means equipping pupils with skills so they can recognise the processes of exclusion, and potentially challenge it (Ramarajan and Runell 2007). Deliberately working towards pupils' ability to recognise othering, exclusion, the impact of stereotyping and the exercise of power in society can aid the development of these skills. A first step to enabling children to engage with the neutral appearance of some of these practices is providing them with skills of critical reflection and personal knowledge (OFSTED 2021) so that they consider their positionality and worldview in relation to the ideas underpinning Islamophobia.

Teachers can select processes, codes, guidelines or incidents that act as exclusionary processes as a way of encouraging pupils to engage and understand the way exclusion works. Pupils often discuss uniforms and dress codes in RE, PSHE and Citizenship education. They may be familiar with the symbolic nature of uniforms and the role they play in creating a shared identity.

There are numerous examples of exclusionary practices that have the effect of singling out Muslims. For example, in 2013 two 14-year-old Muslim boys were placed in isolation in their Lancashire school for a month because they refused to shave off their beards. The head teacher, Mr Xavier Bowers said the school 'had standards to maintain' (Williams 2013) and that wearing beards was not a religious activity in Islam. The purpose of introducing this incident to pupils is not to generate a discussion about whether the school has the right to ban Muslim boys who wear beards or whether beards are a part of Muslim practice. The aim of these lessons would be to encourage pupils to interrogate the way codes of practice can sometimes exclude different groups.

Pupils can discuss the questions in Figure 11.1 in relation to each uniform and evaluate the different approaches taken by schools.

Pupils could discuss the following questions about uniform in school:

A. The head teacher said that the school needed to maintain standards. What standards could he have been talking about?
B. In what ways could the wearing of beards lower standards?
C. Look at the list below, are any forbidden in your school's uniform policy?
D. What is the purpose of a uniform/dress code in a school?
E. If you wanted to write a uniform code that was inclusive, what reasons would you have for banning things. Look at the list below, would you ban any of them?

| More than one ear piercing | Tattoos | Not wearing uniform at all | Wearing a turban |
| Wearing a beard | High-heeled shoes | Coloured hair | Wearing trainers |

■ **Figure 11.1** Uniforms.

3) Practical examples – Rumi and Birmingham

In this final section we present two examples of learning materials which allow pupils to explore Islamophobic norms in different contexts; in translations of the poet Rumi and in exploring the lives of Muslims in Birmingham. We will also discuss how to introduce contextual explorations of Muslim lives with younger pupils, sowing the seeds for exploring Islamophobia as a context with older pupils.

In applying two worldviews' principles to your planning and teaching, which embrace content, complexity and diversity, you are guarding against abstraction and essentialism. Islamophobia is a context many Muslims in the Western world must navigate. When pupils are naturally engaging with contexts to Muslim lives, an exploration of Islamophobia is possible. It is not an add-on, it is part of a complex and growing understanding of the world. For example, if pupils are learning about Muhammad Ali, they will encounter issues of racism and Islamophobia present in the Southern USA in his time, as he had to. These are contexts to Muhammad Ali's life, as much a part of his life as his athletic talent and his Muslim faith.

As we have shown in the preceding sections, Islamophobia is a type of othering in society, it involves exclusion and alienation. Muslims in the West are associated with being different, whatever they actually do, and however comfortable they feel as part of British society. Islamophobia is an external context to Muslims and Islam, understanding Islam will not yield an understanding of Islamophobia. The norms of Islamophobia, that is othering and alienation, themselves have to be explored to make sense of this dynamic. This is true of other forms of group-based exclusion. When it comes to exploring Islamophobia in the classroom, children need to have the opportunity to explore wider social, economic or cultural contexts. In this section we will show some examples where this could be done in a way that is engaging and age-appropriate for the primary school.

PROGRESSION

You might be reading this with some alarm if you teach young children. We suggest that with young children we can sow the seeds so that they expect to explore contexts as a normal part of learning about people and places in RE, including painful topics like Islamophobia. A Religion and Worldviews approach enables young children to establish a confident knowledge base focussed on concrete lives that are historically and geographically located. Instead of starting with beliefs in the abstract, start with a person; learn about their time and place, language, culture, convictions and community, as well as the stated beliefs of the group they belong to. In our first example we start with the poet Rumi for children aged from four to seven. This opens the door for an exploration of how Rumi's poetry has been altered in the Western world for children age, seven to 11. which is an opportunity to see Islamophobic norms in action.

In our second example we take a geographical and cultural look at the city of Birmingham and why many Muslim families migrated there (as well as Sikh and Hindu families of South Asian heritage). This paves the way for an exploration of Islamophobia in cricket against the backdrop of the city of Birmingham. As you can see, the examples chosen offer a nuanced understanding of Muslim lives lived in a time and place, as well as the way Islamophobia manifests in that particular context. Islamophobia may be based on stereotypes and othering, but it is not found in the abstract. Just like Muslim lives, Islamophobia should be examined in real-world contexts. Wider learning points about power and exclusion can be drawn from specific case studies.

EXAMPLE 1A: RUMI AND DRAGONS (AGES 3–7)

You will find these examples ready for teaching on this link: https://www.reonline.org.uk/resources/islam-as-a-worldview/

The description below is based on these practical resources.

Jalal al-Din Muḥammad Rumi lived in the thirteenth century within the Persian empire and is one of the world's greatest poets. He was from a devout Muslim family, originally from Iran, who moved to Konya, in present-day Turkey. He studied Islamic law and the Qur'an. He discovered Sufism, a mystical path of Islam, and combined his deep knowledge of the Qur'an and Islamic law with the mystic's search for God. His poetry is rich and beautiful, with Islam and the Qur'an at its heart. As you can see from the resources, young pupils do not start with Sufi beliefs, they start with dragons, although in the course of their learning pupils will find out about Sufi beliefs and practices. Pupils look at dragons from three Islamic cultures: Persian, Ottoman and Central Asian. Pupils compare the ways the dragons are represented. They look at a map showing the Silk Road trading route, identifying the region each dragon comes from. This is an age-appropriate way to place Islam and Muslims in a time and place. Pupils read poetry by Rumi about love. They think about love for themselves, designing emojis. They learn how Rumi loved his friend, Shams, and was sad when he went away. Rumi connected his love for Shams to his love for God. This provides a further example of how young children can explore rather abstract ideas about the mystic's search for God through concrete examples of people.

You may be wondering what this has to do with Islamophobia. For this young age group, we do not directly address Islamophobia, but instead acclimatise children to exploring a context to Muslim lives. Teachers of younger children can sow the seeds so that pupils are used to considering complexity, context and different ways of seeing the world in RE, as we can see in the second example below.

EXAMPLES 1B: TRANSLATIONS OF RUMI (AGES 7–11)

This introduction to Rumi, his poetry and his mystical path constitutes the building blocks of progression to the material for older pupils; how translations of Rumi for a Western audience erase Islamic references. Pupils will find out how popular Rumi is in the Western world through examples: Beyoncé's daughter is named after the poet, his poetry has been tweeted by Ivanka Trump, tattooed on Brad Pitt and recited at a Coldplay concert. Pupils then compare translations of Rumi which remove religious references to translations which retain them and discuss if the meaning has been changed or lost. Pupils will read the views of a modern translator of Rumi, Sharghdazeh, who sees the erasure of Islam from Rumi's work as Islamophobic and a form of cultural colonialism. Pupils then have the chance to consider for themselves if they are witnessing the Western alienation of Islam and or simply the interpretation of writing for a new audience. This is an example of how Islamophobic patterns can be made visible, but can also be slippery and complicated. As Muslim lives are not lived in the abstract, neither is Islamophobia found in the abstract, although there are repeated patterns of Islamophobia as discussed in this chapter; the othering and alienation of Islam and Muslims. In exploring the removal of Islam in modern English translations of Rumi's poetry, a hidden power form becomes visible and can be investigated.

EXAMPLE 2A: BIRMINGHAM (LOWER PRIMARY)

Find this resource here: https://padlet.com/REth1nk/sxe0jq7724upjuam

This format allows teachers to choose the most appropriate content from a wide range and use or adapt the suggested teaching activities. This resource is not about a person or a group, but a city. The city of Birmingham, Britain's second city, is extremely diverse, with many communities from a South Asian background. In fact '44% of Birmingham's population have a migrant background, half of whom were born overseas' (Bloomfield 2019: xiv). You may be wondering as you read these ideas whether the topic has strayed away from RE. As noted, we are working within a Religion and Worldviews approach where geography, food, art and sport can all be part of RE, because they are all part of peoples' lives. Beliefs are not found in the abstract: they are embedded in peoples' lives. This is what we mean by the first Religion and Worldviews principle – that it starts with people.

Using this resource teachers can design a progression pathway from younger to older children, choosing the most suitable content and activities for their class. Some examples for children between three and five are given below:

■ Choose information about one or two women who migrated to Birmingham from India or Pakistan. Tell their stories. Look at all three countries on a map, trace the journey. Talk about the means of transport they would have taken; was it a boat or a plane? How long would it have taken? Compare the weather and geography of India and Pakistan to England and talk about what would have been different for the women.

This learning can open up understanding for children about migration, cultural diversity and a multicultural society.

■ Find out about the Balti curry, which originates in Birmingham, bring some for children to try (South Asian-heritage families might support you here). Try cooking your own Balti in Food Tech. Through learning about the Balti curry, find out about South Asian movement to the UK. Talk about what it might be like to move to a completely new culture and land. Some children in the class might have experienced this themselves.

This learning can open up conversations about peoples' similarities, differences and shared experiences.

■ Learn about Edgbaston cricket ground in Birmingham. This is an important national cricket ground and is also a central feature of the city. Many people play cricket in Birmingham, lots of them from South Asian backgrounds. In fact, cricket is the favourite game in Pakistan, where many Birmingham Muslim families originate from and have strong ties with. Take the children outside to play some cricket. Talk about sports and games that the children themselves love. This learning could pave the way for conversations about playing games with other people. As long as you all know the rules, can anyone play? Talk about playing with people who might speak different languages or like different things. This discussion could then extend to a conversation about difference, diversity and connections in a multicultural society.

Exploring food, migration pathways and cricket may seem outside the usual RE curriculum. We promote a Religion and Worldviews approach because it allows this contextualising view to be taken where real Muslim lives lived in a real city, in this era, are explored.

EXAMPLE 2B: BIRMINGHAM AND CRICKET (7–11)

Using the same resource, the learning described above could progress to more political, contextual explorations of life in Birmingham, including Islamophobia. Questions of cultural difference, identity and history in the city of Birmingham can be explored through cricket. This is a concrete 'hook' upon which to hang nuanced and complex information. This also allows pupils to see how communities and identities are ethnically and religiously fluid, how this dynamism is part of what it means to live in modern Britain.

- Explore the challenges experienced by Moeen Ali, a world-famous Muslim cricketer from Birmingham, as an international athlete who publicly professes his faith. Pupils can learn about discrimination has he faced, especially around wearing a beard. Through this example othering of Islamic customs in the West is made visible.
- The enormous popularity of cricket in India and Pakistan is a good introduction to talking about empire and the ties which connect the subcontinent with Britain. It was the British invaders who introduced cricket to the subcontinent. A focus on cricket opens up a wider conversation about the realities of colonialism and their ongoing impacts, such as racism in British cricket.

- Make exclusion visible by learning about the 'Ramadan League' at Edgbaston. This is a measure to encourage young Muslims who are fasting at Ramadan to attend cricket sessions after their 'iftar' meal at night, or after the fast is broken. This is an example of how minority communities can feel excluded at particular times, but also how measures can be taken which include and welcome people.
- Learn about Abtaha Maqsood, a Muslim hijabi-wearing woman who plays cricket for Birmingham. Through Abtaha's story, pupils can explore the particular intersections of stereotypes, assumptions and exclusion faced by Muslim women in the UK.

CONCLUSION

One of the most terrible things about Islamophobia is that in many ways it is an 'acceptable racism' (Fekete 2009). Islam is perceived to be so illiberal, such a threat to democratic or Western values that some people feel that hostility towards Islam and Muslims is understandable and, in some cases, even justified (Morey and Yaqin 2011). It is true that teaching Islam is not the same as teaching about Islamophobia but RE teachers and specialists in schools have a particular responsibility to confront the ideology behind Islamophobia and expose many of the myths, stereotypes and misrepresentations about Islam in the media and in textbooks. We may share a commitment to equality and fairness with other teachers, but as specialists in the teaching of religion we are best placed to inform the teaching of those values with a deep and rigorous understanding of the significance of Islam and Muslims in today's world.

Teacher's Notes

WHAT IS ISLAMOPHOBIA AND WHY SHOULD IT BE EXPLORED IN THE PRIMARY CLASSROOM?

This page of teacher's notes is a summary of the ideas presented in 'Islamophobia and a Religion and Worldviews Approach' by Kate Christopher and Lynn Revell. The notes are to furnish teachers' conversations, curriculum design and CPD.

WHAT IS ISLAMOPHOBIA?

Islamophobia can involve physical and verbal abuse, exclusion and discrimination. Islamophobia is fear, hatred or hostility towards Islam, Islamic culture and Muslims. Islamophobic attitudes are not based on what Muslims actually do, but a mistrust or rejection of the *idea* of Islam from a Western, European, Christian perspective. Islamophobia rests on a view of Islam as fundamentally at odds with Western values and culture

TEACHING ABOUT ISLAMOPHOBIA

Teachers can recognise Islamophobic patterns and understand what lies beneath them. They can bring these insights to their pupils and help reveal an unfortunate but important aspect of our world.

Teaching about Islamophobia is not the same as teaching about Islam. Islamophobia is generated outside Muslim communities and lives. A basic Islamophobic pattern is to view Islam and Muslims as essentially different from the values and culture of the West.

This view of Islam and Muslims is sustained and reproduced through media, stories, ways of thinking and in language and assumptions. The idea of Islam as alien to Western culture leads to behaviours that exclude and disadvantage Muslims in Western society.

Adopting two guiding principles of Religion and Worldviews can enable pupils to explore topics such as Islamophobia in the RE classroom. Firstly, start with real people and explore the contexts of their real lives. Secondly, give pupils opportunities to look through different lenses and ask different sorts of questions about the information they explore.

The following ideas all help the teacher to understand Islamophobia. To explore these ideas in the classroom, find concrete examples where the exclusion and alienation of Muslims can be made visible.

THE 'OTHER'

Islam is presented as 'other', or inherently different, to Christian, European values and society. Islam seems to act as the mirror image for how the Christian West sees itself, whatever real Muslims in the West actually do, think and say.

POWER

The process of creating 'others' in society is ultimately an enactment of power. One worldview, identity or way of living is represented as alien in relation to a dominant worldview and way of living. To make sense of Islamophobia in the classroom is ultimately to help pupils to make sense of how power is enacted on groups and individuals.

ESSENTIALISM

Presenting beliefs in the abstract, detached from people or context, is called essentialism. It is the idea that all members of group possess 'essential' qualities, whoever they are and wherever they live.

Islamophobia rests on essentialism; essentialism allows assumption about what all Muslims think and feel to be made. Taking the time to explore the context and particulars of Muslim lives guards against essentialism.

STEREOTYPES

Stereotypical images and language are forms of 'othering' and essentialism. Stereotypes reduce an individual to a simple set of ideas or assumptions. Teaching about stereotypes can be developed further for older children by exploring what the stereotypes of Muslims or Islam are meant to communicate. The core of Islamophobia is the idea that Islam and Islamic societies are inherently different and inferior to Christianity and Christian societies.

RESOURCES

Many of the resources discussed in this chapter are free and available on-line.
http://www.cps.gov.uk/assets/rara_ppts/classroom_activities_and_pupils_worksheets.pdf
http://www.unesco.org/new/en/education/resources/in-focus-articles/fighting-islamophobia
-in-schools/
http://media.education.gov.uk/assets/files/pdf/i/dept%20advice%20template_smscadvice
nov13.pdf
http://unesdoc.unesco.org/images/0021/002152/215299e.pdf
http://www.re-sillience.org.uk/indexphp/en/materials
http://www.srtrc.org.org/
http://instead.co.uk

REFERENCES

Allen, C. (2012) *Islamophobia*. Farnham: Ashgate.

Bloomfield, J. (2019) *Our City: Migrants and the Making of Modern Birmingham*. London: Unbound.

Elton-Chalcraft, S. (2009) *It's Not Just about Black and White, Miss. Children's Awareness of Race*. Stoke on Trent: Trentham.

Fekete, L. (2009) *A Suitable Enemy*. London: Pluto Press.

Ipgrave, J. (2009) The language of friendship and identity: Children's communication choices in an interfaith exchange. *British Journal of Religious Education*, 31(3), pp. 213–225.

Independent (2013) Racist Bullying: Far right agenda on immigration being taken into classrooms. Available at http://www.independent.co.uk/.

Morey, P. and Yaqin, A. (2011) *Framing Muslims*. London: Harvard University Press.

Ofsted (2010) *Transforming Religious Education*. Available at http://ofsted.gov.uk

Ofsted (2021) Research review series. Religious education. https://www.gov.uk/government/publications/research-review-series-religious-education/research-review-series-religious-education.

Panjwani, F. and Revell, L. (2020) Teaching about Islam: From essentialism to hermeneutics. In *The Forgotten Dimensions of Religious Education*. Eds. Gert Biesta and Patricia Hannam, pp. 85–98. London: Brill.

Ramarajan, D. and Runell, M. (2007) Confronting Islamophobia in education. *Intercultural Education*, 18(2), pp. 87–97.

Revell, L. (2012) *Islam and Education*. Stoke on Trent: Trentham.

Runnymede Trust (1997) *Islamophobia a Challenge for Us All*. London: Runnymede Trust.

Show Racism the Red Card. Available at https://www.theredcard.org/.

Smyth, G. (2012) Islamophobia. In *Teaching Controversial Issues in the Classroom*. Eds. Paula Cowan and Henry Maitles, (pp. 165–175). London: Continuum.

Van Driel, B. (2004) *Confronting Islamophobia in Educational Practice*. Stoke on Trent: Trentham.

Vygotsky, L. (1978) *Mind in Society*. Harvard: Harvard University Press.

Williams, R. (2013) Available at https://www.telegraph.co.uk/news/religion/10352453/Muslim-schoolboys-banned-from-lessons-for-refusing-to-shave.html.

CHAPTER 12

DEVELOPING PRACTICE – WHAT WE TEACH AND WHY

Sally Elton-Chalcraft

This final chapter is aimed at developing your practice. and should be particularly useful for teachers leading RE. I consider not only *how* to teach RE creatively, but also ask the reader to consider *what* they teach and *why*.

This chapter aims to help you:

- Appreciate that there are different RE curriculums – both in the UK and worldwide – and that worldviews have been grouped (Eastern/ Western/non-theistic).
- Understand diversity within, as well as between, religions – taking Global Christianity as an example.
- Learn about humanism as a worldview and be aware of the opportunities and pitfalls of planning thematically – using 'rites of passage' as an example.
- Consider the opportunities and pitfalls of comparing worldviews and how to use debates effectively.
- Use the 'Subject knowledge and confidence' audit to gauge your own competencies and areas for development.
- Understand the importance of widening the scope of the RE curriculum.

Children have little influence on what and how they are taught (Devine 2003). This volume has suggested creative approaches for RE, many of which involve giving the children more ownership of their learning.

Chapter 12 outlines how policy can influence practice, however, in many countries the RE teacher is still able to maintain some degree of autonomy in the classroom.

For many primary school RE lessons, what is taught is usually selected by the RE subject leader (if there is one, even though this is a requirement in the English context). The RE content in English schools depends on how the subject leader has interpreted the agreed syllabus. Sometimes ideas from continuing professional development sessions are included in the RE curriculum and sometimes advice from the county or diocesan RE adviser (if there is one) is drawn on. In many international contexts, it is the religious leaders who dictate subject content; occasionally the views of the staff at their school inform the RE content. So, unlike most other primary school subjects which are compelled to

DOI: 10.4324/9781003361480-15

adhere to governmental directives, RE has a lot more flexibility concerning the choice of what to teach, particularly in the British context. Recently in the British context, adherence to the locally agreed syllabus is the statutory requirement in terms of breadth, choice of belief systems studied, and so on – although this may change as the subject evolves. Aided schools and academies have their own requirements determined by governors. This chapter argues that children deserve to understand that a variety of belief systems exist. They do not necessarily need to know about all of these in detail (and neither should the teacher feel obliged to have wide-ranging knowledge). However, I argue that children have a right to be introduced to a variety of belief systems, be offered opportunities to engage in appraisal of these belief systems and understand how adherents view the world. In some countries, RE is not part of the curriculum (for example, in France and Spain religion is a matter left to a child's family and philosophical study is important in the French curriculum (Weiss 2011)). In England, despite various major overhauls of the curriculum, RE has maintained its place in the basic curriculum, as acknowledged in the comprehensive Cambridge Review of Education (Alexander 2010) and by OfSTED and CORE 2018. In this chapter, I explore the importance of introducing children in the primary phase to puzzling questions through a variety of different belief stances. In the English context, each county's agreed syllabus usually suggests children explore belief systems practised in their local community with a choice of studying several of the six major world religions. I aim to challenge the teacher to widen her/his perception of belief systems, in both community and faith schools alike. I argue that the choice of which belief systems to study and which to leave out is itself determining a child's outlook. So, children can be helped to understand that beliefs and values often underpin actions and, consequently, the actions and beliefs/values which may underpin them can be subject to scrutiny. The teacher's or school's choice of which belief systems to explore with the children and how these belief systems are presented may have an impact on the child's negative or positive perceptions of that belief system. This is explored in other chapters (Prescott, Chapter 4; Elton-Chalcraft, Brown and Yates, Chapter 3; Revell and Christopher, Chapter 11). In this chapter, I give examples of a variety of belief systems which are 'on the margins' and not often explored with primary children, often with legitimate reasons such as teachers' lack of subject knowledge. I hope that this chapter will persuade teachers to take a risk (one of the characteristics of creativity) and include some of these examples in their RE. The chapter offers practical examples of teaching and learning from outside the canon of the six major world religions (Buddhism, Christianity Church of England and Roman Catholicism, Islam, Judaism and Sikhism), about which much has already been written (multiple RE Today publications; Cooling 2020; Mogra 2023; Flanagan 2020). As well as being introduced to a wide range of different belief systems, children also need to learn how to 'respectfully disagree' with beliefs that are different from their own (Blaylock 2007:4). Finally, the chapter ends by discussing a teacher's mindset and reappraising the rationale behind the choice of religions/belief systems to be studied. Does a teacher's mindset reinforce or challenge a dominant worldview of 'acceptable' and 'dodgy' religions/belief systems?

CHOICE OF BELIEF SYSTEMS TO STUDY

Most agreed syllabi require children to learn about two or three of the six major religions: Buddhism, two branches of Christianity, Hinduism, Islam, Judaism and Sikhism. In the

QCA (2004) Non-Statutory National Framework which was used as a template for many agreed syllabi, the breadth of study includes 'Christianity, at least one other principal religion, a religious community with a significant local presence, where appropriate, and a secular world view, where appropriate' (2004:25 and 27). However, there is no suggestion for which combination of belief systems to cover. I would argue that these belief systems can be categorised into three groups:

- The 'Eastern' religions of India, Dharmic (Buddhism, Hindu Traditions and Sikhism)
- The 'Western' semitic religions, Abrahamic (Christian traditions, Islam and Judaism)
- 'Other' belief systems/worldviews ('secular' belief systems such as Humanism; atheism; smaller numbers religions such as Baha'i and Paganism)

The debate about what should be taught in RE is discussed by Lewin and Orchard in their blog listed in the *After RE project* (Lewin and Orchard 2023) where they also highlight that the 'what', the 'how', and the 'why' are inseparable. The CoRE report (2018) calls for teachers to consider subject knowledge, pedagogical knowledge and personal knowledge. The RE teacher's curriculum should "contain *collectively enough* substantive knowledge to enable pupils to recognise the diverse and changing religious and non-religious traditions of the world" but Lewin and Orchard pose the question what is meant by "collectively enough" (2023). They suggest this is not superficial but 'sufficiently inclusive'. But how do we decide what's what? This idea of substantive knowledge underestimates the extent to which *what* we see depends on *how* we look at it which is what I attempt to unpick below.

The six Eastern and Western religions are the most commonly taught in primary schools – although in practice Islam, Judaism and the Christian tradition of Catholic and Church of England are the most popular. I would argue that it is important for primary children to have some understanding of at least one Western and one Eastern religion plus one 'other' belief system, particularly those which are becoming more prevalent in today's society, such as humanism. I have argued elsewhere that our curriculum has been, for some time, white, Western, patriarchal (male-dominated) and Christian in outlook (Elton-Chalcraft 2009). Curriculum 2014 was not any less biased, and so it is left to the teacher to ensure children are receiving a more balanced diet – although the CoRE (2018) have produced a framework which goes some way to redress the imbalance as described in Chapter 2. Scoffman (2013), in his book Teaching Geography Creatively (in the same series as this volume), also asks teachers to encourage a wider perspective. Scoffman (2013:689) calls for children to view maps of the world from alternative viewpoints, i.e. Australia at the top in an attempt to challenge dominant thinking and develop locational awareness. Similarly, in RE, I consider it important for children to have some understanding of the main world religions, the six itemised earlier, but they should also at least be made aware of the existence of other belief systems – even if these are not studied in detail. This lack of awareness of worldviews outside their own context is not just a British issue. In some countries Religious Education focuses on the prevalent religion – mainly Christianity in Europe, and also particular denominations. For example, in Germany parents choose Katholische (Catholic) or Evangelische (Protestant) Religion classes for their child, while Ohne Religion (no religion) classes cater for the minority of children who are

Muslim, another faith or have parents who wish to opt out of the mainstream Katholishe or Evangelishe faith nurture RE. Franken (2021) discusses RE in Europe and explains that different kinds of RE happens in different kinds of schools different countries depending on the degree of alignment between the Church and the state (usually in Europe it is Christian faith which is aligned). So, for example "non-denominational RE is common in nations characterised by 'mutual independence' between the (Catholic) church and the state" whereas countries with *no* RE in state schools occur "where state and church are separated" (Franken 2021:417).

In the following sections I suggest activities and invite the teacher to make children aware of global Christianity and less familiar Christian denominations. Second, I present approaches for teaching about humanism alongside some of the Eastern world religions.

GLOBAL CHRISTIANITY

In a topic on 'Jesus' in Christianity, the children may be learning about the Jesus of history, the Christ of faith, and the Jesus of experience (Teece 2001). I would encourage the teacher to think about this not only from the perspective of the Church of England but also from less mainstream denominations of Christianity such as Unitarians, many of whom do not view Jesus as fully divine (God's son) – although this could be quite controversial for many mainstream Christian children and their families who think of Jesus as the son of God. Also, the children could investigate images of Jesus from around the world. I understand that many busy primary teachers may lack confidence in teaching RE in the first place and have little knowledge of the main denominations of Christianity, never mind the less well-known ones (Elton-Chalcraft 2020). After all, Christianity is a global religion with over two billion followers under many different branches of Christianity (Global Atlas 2023). However, teachers can widen their scope of what to teach and introduce the children to a variety of beliefs over the course of their seven years in primary school. This can be achieved by simply thinking about use of language: for example, avoiding 'we believe x, y and z' rather than 'many Christians around the world believe x, y and z'. Also, a more global perspective can be attained by using pictures from around the world. Margaret Cooling (1998), Faces of Jesus (RE Jesus 2014) and the RE Today publication Picturing Jesus (Blaylock 2004) are useful resources.

LESS WELL-KNOWN DENOMINATIONS IN CHRISTIANITY

Most teachers may be familiar with the denominations of Christianity called Anglicanism (Church of England) and many teachers may also have knowledge of Catholicism, because many primary schools have a Church of England or Catholic foundation. Yet many teachers have scant knowledge of the history of the Christian church and the variety of denominations and branches of Christianity in existence today. The BBC website has a helpful introduction; see Table 12.1.

Many Christians, including many Catholics and Anglicans (Church of England), believe Jesus is the son of God, whereas some Christians do not, for example Unitarians. Jehovah's Witnesses are not listed by the BBC as a Christian denomination because they are not recognised as part of mainstream Christianity by some denominations; they are listed elsewhere on the site as a branch of Christianity. While there is no expectation for

■ **Table 12.1** Denominations and branches of Christianity

Examples of different denominations and branches of Christian traditions which are listed on the BBC website under subdivisions of Christianity, available at http://www.bbc.co.uk/religion/religions/christianity/

- The Armish
- Baptist churches
- Christadelphians
- Church of England (Anglicans)
- Church of Scotland
- Coptic Orthodox Church
- Eastern Orthodox Church
- Exclusive Brethren
- Methodist Church
- Opus Dei
- Pentecostalism
- Quakers
- Roman Catholic Church
- Salvation Army
- Seventh-Day Adventists
- United Reformed Church

Considered as a Christian based religious movement, available athttp://www.bbc.co.uk/religion/religions/witnesses/

- Jehovah's witnesses

the children, or indeed the teacher, to have detailed knowledge of all the denominations listed in Table 12.1, I would argue that an awareness of the number of different denominations is important. Christianity might be better described as Christian traditions. Believers from these different denominations, while having some ideas in common (for example the existence of Jesus and his character as a positive role model), may disagree in their doctrines (beliefs) and ways of worship. For example, Eastern Orthodox Christians place great emphasis on using the senses to enhance worship, with artwork, iconography, music and incense playing a central role in services, whereas Quaker meeting houses are plain, and simplicity characterises their meetings. So, the purpose of RE is to encourage the child to understand religion from the believer's perspective. In this chapter, I argue that there is not one 'perspective' but a myriad of different and in some cases, opposing perspectives, as in the case of Christians. This may seem very daunting for the busy primary teacher who has to engage with subject knowledge in a range of primary school subject areas (science, geography, history, mathematics etc.) as well as RE. However, as I outlined at the start, there is not an expectation that the children or teacher should be experts, but rather that they have some knowledge of the diversity within a religion and not focus solely on the most common or dominant aspect. Lewin et al (2023) helpfully articulate how RE teachers should approach RE curriculum development in their article about the After Religious Education project.

■ **Table 12.2** Using a 'problem-solving model' to investigate worship in different Christian traditions

---

Problem solving: Lessons 1 and 2

In groups

Imagine you are the managers of a satellite station (ten years in the future) and you have one room, with a very large storage cupboard, which can be used for worship on two days of the week. The station has 200 workers made up of Christians from each of the five denominations.

Your team have to plan how the room would be used and furnished for each of the two days

Create a five-minute illustrative presentation for the satellite station owners explaining how you will meet the needs of each group of Christians in the satellite crew

Which presentation meets the needs of the crew most effectively – why?

Investigation and knowledge sharing: Lessons 3 and 4

Find out about your denomination/tradition of Christianity and how people worship

e.g.

Day of worship

What happens at worship

Pictures of the spaces used for worship and their significance

Create an informative PowerPoint about "Worship in …."

Share your findings with other groups

What are the similarities and differences?

Which presentation meets the needs of the crew most effectively – why?

The lesson ideas in Table 12.2 offer an example of how to engage children in a community of enquiry to investigate the characteristics of a variety of different denominations within Christianity. In pairs or threes, Year Five and Six children could use the internet to research worship in five contrasting Christian denominations Quaker Society of Friends, Church of England, Seventh-Day Adventist, Eastern Orthodox and Catholic. They could investigate these different denominations in groups using a problem-solving model (see Table 12.2). For more information about effective group work see Baines et al. (2008).

HUMANISM

Humanism is gaining in popularity as secularism (non-religious belief systems) becomes more prevalent in many countries. Between 2011 and 2021, those identifying as having 'No Religion' increased in England and Wales by over eight million, from 25% to 37% (ONS 2021). During the same period, the number of people identifying as Christian in England and Wales dropped by 5.5 million to 46.2% of the population (ONS 2021). If teachers are to provide children with a broad understanding of what it means to be human, then atheistic belief systems should be included as part of the curriculum. Sims (2011) explains that some faith representatives disagree with the inclusion of humanism in the school curriculum. Nevertheless, it is becoming increasingly common for children to investigate 'other' belief systems including humanism. According to the British Humanist Association (2023), humanists:

▨ Think for themselves about what is right and wrong, based on **reason and respect for others**.

▨ Find **meaning, beauty and joy in the one life we have**, without the need for an afterlife.

▨ Look to **science instead of religion** as the best way to discover and understand the world.

▨ Believe people can use empathy and compassion to **make the world a better place for everyone**.

Many notable figures are among its followers, including Professor Brian Cox (presenter and writer of TV science programmes), Sir Jim Al-Kalili (presenter, scientist and president of the Humanist Society), Steven Fry (actor) and Philip Pullman (writer). Humanism can be studied in RE during a topic such as 'Journeys', where children look at stages in a person's life. Sometimes referred to as rites of passage, the different stages throughout our lives are often accorded significance by religious ceremonies or secular practices which can be explored by children. The British Humanist society provide a wealth of free resources for inclusive assemblies and Religious Education (British Humanist association 2023).

Journeys and rites of passage

Whereas in the past many families would have drawn on church, synagogue, temple, gurdwara and so on for such ceremonies, many folks in Britain today are now looking elsewhere. The Humanist Society offers a list of officiates/ celebrants who can work with families to custom-design ceremonies. The approach to studying life stages (see Table 12.3) advocated by the following lesson ideas draws on shared human experience, traditional belief systems and individual patterns of belief from the Westhill project (Rudge 2000:88).

Activity: Children could begin by considering their own life journey, recording this in an imaginative way either as a cartoon, a timeline with peaks and troughs or a nonlinear mind map (Buzan 2014). The way they choose to record their life journey will be an interesting discussion point, as will what they choose to record. In the next lesson, the children can explore an aspect from a belief system; the example explores a naming ceremony from a humanist perspective. Throughout the topic, children would reflect on the impact of belief on action how an adherent makes sense of the world. They would also be invited to reflect more deeply on their own attitudes and beliefs and how these impact action. See Table 12.4 for 'Naming Ceremony' lesson ideas for Key Stage 1. A similar format could be adapted for use with any age group and any rite of passage e.g. with Year Three and Four a humanist wedding ceremony can be compared with Hindu traditions. Again, the emphasis is on the child understanding what a couple might be feeling about getting married. In Hinduism, the second stage in life, Grihasta or householder, emphasises the earthly roles of earning an honest living and being a good parent and partner. The children could discuss what they want to achieve when they grow up. Children could imagine (imagination being one of the four features of creativity outlined in NACCCE 1999:29) the thoughts of a Hindu couple preparing for their wedding day. The children could investigate why certain rituals are undertaken the meaning behind the seven steps in the Hindu marriage ceremony (life-power, wealth, happiness, offspring, a long-wedded

■ **Table 12.3** Using the Westhill model (Grimmitt 2000) of shared human experience, individual patterns of belief

Key questions 'shared human experience':
Who knows someone who has had a baby recently?
(Practically every child will have some acquaintance with a classmate who has a new sibling).
What 'rituals' happen when a new baby is born ('ritual' = events/ceremonies/occurrences)
Class discussions could include what rituals accompany a new baby – e.g. sending greetings cards and presents, visitors congratulating the family etc the theory behind this is shared human experience where children 'share' some knowledge and understanding of common practice. Hopefully a variety of practices will be raised by the children which can be discussed respectfully.
Key questions 'traditional belief system'
What happens during a humanist ceremony to welcome a new baby?
Children can use internet sources to find out about humanist ceremonies and role play interviews between parents and the humanist celebrant.
Source https://humanism.org.uk/ceremonies/find-a-celebrant/
http://www.inspirationalceremonies.co.uk/humanist-namingCompare the similarities and differences between ceremonies with which they are familiar. Encourage the children to 'get into the role' of being a humanist parent and why they might want to have a humanist naming ceremony for their child.
Key questions 'individual patterns of belief'
What would you include in a humanist naming ceremony?
Plan and act out the ceremony, choosing the readings and songs.
Why did you design your naming ceremony this way?
Evaluate why they have made those choices. Compare the similarities and differences between ceremonies with which they are familiar. Hopefully a variety of practices will be raised by the children which can be discussed respectfully – avoid comparing in terms of better or worse, like or dislike – rather discuss similarities and differences.

■ **Table 12.4** Extract from a humanist celebrant's website

Many parents feel that they want to celebrate and share their joy of having a child with family and friends but do not feel that they want a traditional christening or religious ceremony. This may be because they do not hold any religious beliefs themselves or because they want their child to be able to choose their own beliefs when they are older.

Humanist ceremonies are non-religious and therefore have no worship or fixed rituals. They are appropriate for anyone who would like a non-religious ceremony. The only guideline is that they do not include any religious content such as prayers or hymns. However, it is possible to have a moment of quiet reflection during the ceremony to enable people with religious beliefs to have a private prayer.

Why choose a humanist ceremony (2013) Taken from http://www.inspirationalceremonies.co.uk/humanist-naming

life and life companionship, and the prosperity of the children). It is important for children to learn about civil partnerships as well as heterosexual marriage. Stonewall has plenty of resources to support teaching (www.stonewall.org.uk); for example, their colourful 2014 'Different families same love' poster could be used as a stimulus for discussion.

However, teachers ought to note that rites of passage are themselves a 'construct'. Not all cultures and religious believers have the same framework for marking out specific rituals. There are a variety of different sacraments, rituals and stages in life which are marked in some way by humans all over the world. In some RE resources, a thematic approach is suggested. The teacher can use the pictures and text for primary children to compare rituals and customs from a range of belief systems about birth ceremonies, initiation rituals and so on. This can be an exciting and engaging way for children to appreciate the similarities and differences between and within various belief systems. A note of caution is needed because usually the rites of passage are the four mentioned in Table 12.5 namely birth, initiation, marriage and death. Yet, in some belief systems there are many other important stages, also described in Table 12.5.

When engaging in a thematic study, comparing one belief system with another, it is important to encourage children to look at similarities and differences and to avoid asking which they like best, as I discuss later.

COMPARING BELIEF SYSTEMS: 'RESPECTFULLY DISAGREEING'

It is important to avoid asking children which is the best/correct/accurate belief. Instead, children should be encouraged to justify their opinion about a particular aspect of the belief system in comparison to another belief system, with reference to evidence they have collected. They can then express their opinion in a fair and balanced manner, 'respectfully disagreeing' (Blaylock 2007) if appropriate. It is not expected that primary RE should encourage children to blindly accept a belief system's doctrine and practices in an uncritical way (see Chapters One and Two of this volume). Rather children can be shown how to draw on evidence about a belief system, look at life through the believer's lens and critically examine in a respectful manner. The 2010 Equality Act requires schools to ensure they are places of equality and diversity with no discriminatory practice (Equality Act 2010). Thus, it is important for teachers to have a clear understanding of what is and is not allowed to be articulated in the classroom. In the next examples, Tables 12.6, 12.7 and 12.8, the children are asked to engage in a debate about whether they think 'belief in the afterlife makes humans live a better life'. Some children who have strong religious views might agree, drawing on their own religious convictions. Other children will disagree, possibly drawing on secular worldviews such as the humanist stance. The RE classroom allows a teacher to provide a safe, secure space for children to investigate different viewpoints and offer children an opportunity to debate contrasting views. In the following debate lessons children can first investigate differing views, for example Muslim, Christian and humanist, Table 12.7. They can work effectively in groups using ideas from Baines et al. (2008) and Table 12.2, which outline strategies for successful debates.

Activity: A humanist funeral ceremony and humanist beliefs about death can be explored with Years Five and Six using a debate (see Tables 12.6, 12.7 and 12.8). While

■ **Table 12.5** Different rites of passage in different religions/worldviews

Teaching point:

Take care NOT to use ONE framework and compare all the religions through this one, different religions and denominations within these religions have different rites of passage/sacraments/stages; for example.

The Rites of passage usually discussed in 'outdated' RE resources revolve around the **four Church of England ceremonies:**

I.   Birth
II.   Initiation
III. Marriage
IV.   Death

However, in **Catholicism there are seven sacraments** (not four rites of passage). Also not all Catholics encounter each

i.   Baptism
ii.   Eucharist
iii. Reconciliation
iv.   Confirmation
v.   Marriage
vi.   Holy orders
vii. Anointing of the sick (last rites)
(http://www.americancatholic.org/features/special/default.aspx?id=29)

In **Hindu tradition there are four main stages to life**, (but these do not map exactly with the four rites of passage of Anglicanism or the seven Catholic sacraments)

I.   Student, age 12–24
      Brahmacharya Ashrama
II.   Householder, age 24–48
      Grihastha Ashrama
III. Senior Advisor, age 48–72
      Vanaprastha Ashrama
IV.   Religious Devotion, age 72 & onward
      Sannyasa Ashrama
      (http://www.hinduismtoday.com/modules/smartsection/item.php?itemid=5333)

Also, in Hindu tradition there are 16 Samskaras or rituals for the pure and healthy development of a Hindu's mind and body, five of which relate to pregnancy and birth.(http://www.vmission.org.in/hinduism/samskaras.htm)

but these do not map exactly with the four rites of passage of Anglicanism, or the seven Catholic sacraments, or the four stages of life in Hindu tradition)

Humanism provides **ceremonies for three life stages**

I.   Naming ceremonies
II.   Wedding ceremonies
III. Funerals

◼ **Table 12.6** Debates – bad and good practice

BAD practice: Encourages dangerous inflammatory opinions	Good practice: Acceptable critical debating skills
Allowing children to express feelings and preferences uncritically e.g. *I like this belief* *This belief is best* *I think this belief is rubbish*	Encouraging children to defend their opinion critically and respectfully with reference to what they have observed, read, heard etc *I think this belief makes more sense because x, y, z* *I do not agree with this stance because of a, b, c*

some teachers might have reservations about holding a debate, I would argue that, if conducted respectfully, it will provide children with an opportunity to explore different religious claims in a safe environment (see Table 12.6 of good and bad practices). A debate should not be an excuse for children to express preferences 'I like this belief best', 'I think that belief is rubbish', even though many television programmes and chat shows delight in such activity. Rather the teacher needs to educate the children to voice their opinions in a critical way.

It is acceptable to challenge a viewpoint if the challenge is expressed in a measured, defensible and respectful manner. For more information on debating skills see www.ehow

◼ **Table 12.7** Knowledge underpinning a debate

Most Humanists do not believe in life after death, They believe:	Most Muslims believe if they have lived a good life they will go to heaven, They believe:	Most Hindus believe if they have lived a good life they will return in another form. They believe :
'in the absence of an afterlife and any discernible purpose to the universe, human beings can act to give their own lives meaning by seeking happiness in this life and helping others to do the same.' https://humanism.org.uk/humanism/	'in the Day of Judgement when the life of every human being will be assessed to decide whether they go to heaven or hell.'http://www.bbc.co.uk/religion/religions/islam/beliefs/beliefs.shtml	'that the soul passes through a cycle of successive lives (samsara) and its next incarnation is always dependent on how the previous life was lived (karma).'http://www.bbc.co.uk/religion/religions/hinduism/beliefs/moksha.shtml

◼ **Table 12.8** Example of a debate for upper key stage two

Does belief in an afterlife make humans live a better life?	
YES: Belief in an afterlife makes humans live a better life	NO: Belief in an afterlife does not necessarily make humans live a better life

.co.uk/how_8694557_teach-debate-children.html. As well as the teacher's pedagogic knowledge of how to facilitate a successful debate, the children will need to enhance their subject knowledge for it to work effectively. Boden (2001) argues that subject knowledge is crucial to enhancing creativity. So, before the debate ensure all the children have some knowledge of several stances for example from each of the three belief systems mentioned at the beginning of this chapter, Western, Eastern and 'Other' (see Table 12.7). Groups of children can present information about their belief system in a five-minute presentation (possibly using PowerPoint) and then panellists can engage in debate. Once children have a secure knowledge having listened to the presentations, the debate can begin. See Table 12.8 for an example question.

In order to facilitate creative strategies in Religion and Worldviews learning which is wide ranging the teacher may understandably have concerns about their own subject knowledge. Throughout this chapter, I have emphasised the importance of widening the scope of RE to ensure learners are exposed to a range of religions and worldviews.

RELIGION AND WORLDVIEWS AUDIT OF SUBJECT KNOWLEDGE

It might be helpful to consider your own subject knowledge and understanding of a range of religions and worldviews by undertaking an audit like the one in Table 12.9. For further support and resources to help with your understanding of RE, please visit https://www.teachre.co.uk/wp-content/uploads/2019/07/IMPORTANT-Subject-knowledge.pdf. This audit has been ostensibly taken from here and the resource has some really good links to resources, endorsed by the National Association of Teachers of Religious Education (NATRE). See also chapter 2 and Smalley (2018) and Taves (2019) for comments on the idea of Worldviews.

It is also important to understand that some people may not align to one specific worldview. In her review of RE from 1971 to 2018, Cush (2021) has argued that it is important to not consider a binary of religious versus non-religious. Cush sees a change in direction in the UK context where individual belief systems are valued and studied as opposed to an objective interrogations of a single belief system seen as a monolithic entity. So, children can learn that being an agnostic Christian, a Pagan Buddhist, a Jewish humanist and a liberal Muslim might all be considered valid stances, because humans might not subscribe exclusively to one worldview (also see Bråten 2021; Barnes 2015; Kueh 2017).

WHY IT IS IMPORTANT TO WIDEN THE SCOPE OF RE

Throughout this chapter, I have attempted to convince the reader to widen your perspective and introduce children to a range of belief systems, diversity within belief systems, and the lived experience of humans who might adopt different elements from different belief systems. The underpinning rationale of such a mindset towards RE is to acknowledge diversity while at the same time considering the implications of that diversity (see also Sheehan and Elton-Chalcraft 2023). Having an informed understanding about Religion and Worldviews, namely being religiously literate, is important in order to detect distortions presented in the media as Waggoner (2023) points out. Christian privilege,

Table 12.9 RE Audit of RE subject knowledge and levels of confidence

Core components – subject knowledge and understanding	Current knowledge and confidence	Record of knowledge development through personal development e.g. reading/ courses etc

Diversity in religion and worldviews

- Recognise diversity within each religion and worldview
- Understand how not to perpetuate stereotypes – using language such as 'some' or 'many'
- Aware of relevant curriculum requirements e.g. in UK the Commission on RE's Report (CoRE, 2018).
- nderstand the National Entitlement (CoRE,2018,pp10-11) and reflect on both personal and institutional worldviews

The Abrahamic faiths
(Christianity, Islam and Judaism)

- Have a basic understanding of these faiths and some of the main differences between them
- Have an understanding of the range of beliefs within each faith (e.g. different denominations/Christian traditions)
- Have an understanding of how to explore these faiths through narratives, e.g. the biblical narrative for Christianity and Judaism
- Understand and are aware of key terms in these faiths:
- Christianity: Trinity, Incarnation, Salvation, Kingdom of God, Church, Sacrament, Word of God
- Islam: Tawhid, Ummah, Revelation, Iman, Khalifa, Ibadah
- Judaism: Covenant, Messianic Age, Chosen People, Shema, Torah, Atonement

The Dharmic faiths
(Hinduism, Buddhism, Sikhism)

■ Have a basic understanding of these faiths and some of the main differences between them

■ Awareness of the concept of a cyclical worldview

■ Are aware of and understand the role of narrative in the Hindu, Buddhist and Sikh Traditions

■ Have an awareness of the relationship between Hindu and Sikh worldviews, the significance of equality in Sikh traditions and consideration of whether the Buddhist worldview is a religious one

■ Understand and are aware of key terms in these faiths:

■ Buddhism: Buddha, dharma, samsara, dukkha, metta, sangha

■ Hinduism: dharma, karma, samsara, moksha, avatar, ahimsa

■ Sikhism: Ik Onkar, Sewa, Hukam, Sikh, Khalsa, Guru Granth Sahib

Non-religious worldviews
(Humanism and atheism)

■ An awareness and understanding of the humanist world view

■ An awareness of and understanding of an atheistic world view alongside the concept of uncertainty and agnosticism

The interdisciplinary nature of RE

■ An awareness that concepts taught in RE can also be engaged with and taught in other curriculum subjects when coupled with white privilege, can lead to the 'diminishment of minoritised groups'. RE can provide opportunities for informed discussions about LGBTQ+ issues in the context of 'the internal diversity of religious traditions' understanding that 'there is more than one way to interpret sacred texts, and in a pluralistic society… difference of opinion can be addressed with civility' (Waggoner 2023:2).

A skilled RE teacher can facilitate discussions around questions such as:

■ How far does my freedom extend when it is based upon sincerely held religious belief?
■ What happens when it runs up against a fellow citizen's freedom that is also held by sincere belief, be it based on religious or secular grounds?
■ How do we decide a way forward?

(Waggoner 2023:2)

This book attempts to provide support for all teachers in answering such questions. In Chapter Three, we asked you to assess your mindset (Table 3.1) to ensure that whichever belief systems are investigated and whichever pedagogical approaches are adopted, the teaching and learning will be fair, will be balanced and will subscribe to relevant legislation (e.g. the 2010 Equality Act in the UK). There are numerous resources to support the teacher (a few are listed in the 'Additional resources' section of this chapter). However, Warner and Elton-Chalcraft (2022) argue that some schools may be tempted to abide by the letter of the law but not the spirit of the law. Thus, some schools, albeit unwittingly, would be exhibiting 'dysconscious' racism (King 2004) that is affirming the high status of the majority culture (in RE this could be thought of as white, male-dominated Anglicanism and Catholicism) and lowering the status of minority cultures (in RE this could be denominations such as Seventh-Day Adventism, which has a large proportion of black adherents, Unitarianism, Quakers etc.). In this chapter, I have attempted to redress this balance by encouraging the teacher to engage in study of minority religions and atheist belief systems.

Another important point to acknowledge is the binary approach which separates religious and non-religious. There has been a move towards a non-binary approach particularly in the work of professor Denise Cush who interrogates the statement Buddhism is not a religion but paganism is (2020, 2021). Bråten (2021)draws on the work of Ann Taves calling for a new language for certain parts of human activity related to meaning-making rather than relying on the binary the implication for teachers being that instead of talking with children about religious or non-religious rather we should be encouraging children to think about how humans make sense of their world and what beliefs they hold. So, some people may adhere to one belief system, others may draw on a range of belief systems creating their own distinct worldview. Also, teachers need to be aware of debates which suggest that a binary approach – thinking of religious non-religious is not a helpful distinction, so using the term 'worldviews' can be helpful.

In this chapter, I have tried to convince the primary teacher to branch out and include references to a broad range of Religions and Worldviews, but I realise that it is impracticable to investigate more than a few in detail with the children and finding resources may be problematic. At every opportunity, I would encourage teachers to provide a chance for children to investigate alternative perspectives to the white, Western, patriarchal (male-dominated) Christian view which, I would argue, dominates our current curriculum, as we argued in Chapter 3. A creative strategy for challenging racism is using persona dolls (Brown 2008; Elton-Chalcraft 2005; and also Chapter 9 in this volume). A persona doll with children aged three to eight years, for example Jeetinder, a Sikh doll, can be used by the class teacher to explore issues of prejudice and discrimination (see Chapter 9; Elton-Chalcraft 2005). In these final two chapters in this section of the book, Lynn Revell and Kate Christopher (Chapter 11) discuss teaching Islam in a fresh and anti-racist way.

So, in the final chapters we challenge the teacher to be creative about the what, why and how in RE teaching and learning. As Chapter 1 of this volume explained, RE should not be boring and easy (for example a task filling in missing words and drawing a picture) Such an activity would be chosen by a teacher unwilling to get involved in the risky business of conflicting belief systems. Rather, RE can be taught creatively as a transformative subject encouraging children to challenge their own perspectives, which might at times be uncomfortable, but it can also liberate children to discover new ideas and perspectives and enrich their present and future lives.

In this book we have tried to present creative, exciting and challenging Religion and Worldviews education which, we hope, will provide all learners with the knowledge, understanding and skills to think deeply about their own humanity, their destiny and the beliefs of others which might be similar or different to their own. If we can achieve this teaching for diversity, and ability to help learners see things from another's perspective, then hopefully our world can be filled with wise and creative people, who understand mutual respect and can challenge discrimination. Teachers have the power (and responsibility) to create such a world, hopefully the chapters in this book will support us to do so.

REFERENCES

Alexander, R. (2010) *Children Their World Their Education: Final Report and Recommendations of the Cambridge Primary Review*. London: Routledge.

Baines, E., Blatchford, P. and Kutnick, P. (2008) *Promoting Effective Groupwork in the Primary Classroom: A Handbook for Teachers and Practitioners*. London: Routledge.

Barnes, L. P. (2015) Humanism, non-religious worldviews and the future of religious education. *Journal of Beliefs and Values*, 36(1), 79–91. https://doi.org/10.1080/13617672.2015.1013816.

Blaylock, L. (2004) *Picturing Jesus: Worldwide Contemporary Artists*. Birmingham: RE Today Publications.

Blaylock, L. (2007) *Inclusive RE*. Birmingham: RE Today Services.

Boden, M. (2001) Creativity and knowledge. In Craft, A., Jeffrey, B. and Leibling, M. (eds.), *Creativity in Education*, 95–102. London: Continuum.

Bråten, O. M. H. (2021) Non-binary worldviews in education. *BJRE*. DOI: 10.1080/01416200.2021.1901653.

British Humanist Association (2023) Home page. Available at www.humanism.org.uk , accessed 14 May 2023.

Brown, B. (2008) *Equality in Action*. Stoke-on-Trent: Trentham Books.

Buzan, T. (2014) Mind mapping. Available at www.tonybuzan.com/about/mind-mapping, accessed 18 April 2014.

Commission on Religious Education (2018) *Final Report: Religion and Worldviews: The Way Forwards. A National Plan.* London: Religious Education Council of England & Wales. Available at https://www.commissiononre.org.uk/wp-content/uploads/2018/09/Final -Report-of-the-Commission-on-RE.pdf.

Cooling, M. (1998) *Jesus through Art.* London: Religious Moral and Educational Press.

Cooling, T. (2020) Worldview in religious education: Autobiographical reflections on the commission on religious education in England final report. *British Journal of Religious Education.* https://doi.org/10.1080/01416200.2020.1764497.

Cush, D. (2021) Changing the game in English religious education: 1971 and 2018. In *Religious Education in a Post-Secular Age: Case Studies from Europe*, 139–156. Available at https://link.springer.com/chapter/10.1007/978-3-030-47503-1_8.

Cush, D. (2020) Time for a change? An analysis of the major issues in English religious education emerging from the work of the commission on religious education 2016–2018. In Lankshear, D. and Francis L. J. (eds.), *Religious and Values Education: Contextual Challenges.* Oxford, Bern, Berlin, Bruxelles, Frankfurt am Main, New York and Wien: Peter Lang.

Devine, D. (2003) *Children Power and Schooling* .Stoke-on-Trent: Trentham Books.

Elton-Chalcraft, S. (2005) Anti racism an attainment target for primary RE. Available at http://open.tean.ac.uk/bitstream/handle/123456789/623/Resource_1.pdf?sequence=1, accessed 20 April 2014.

Elton-Chalcraft, S. (2009) *It's Not Just Black and White, Miss: Children's Awareness of Race.* Stoke-on-Trent: Trentham Books.

Elton-Chalcraft, S. (2020) Student teachers' diverse knowledge and experiences of religion – Implications for culturally responsive teaching. *Journal of Higher Education Theory and Practice, 20*(6), 35–54.

Elton-Chalcraft, S, Revell, L. and Lander, V. (2022) Fundamental British values: Your responsibilities, to promote or not to promote? Ch 15 In Cooper, H. and Elton-Chalcraft, S. (eds.), *Professional Studies in Primary Education* (4th ed.). London: Sage. Available at https://us.sagepub.com/en-us/nam/professional-studies-in-primary-education/book273439.

Equality Act (2010) Equality Act 2010 guidance available at https://www.gov.uk/guidance/equality-act-2010-guidance#overview accessed 20.01.24

Flanagan, R. (2020) Worldviews: Overarching concept, discrete body of knowledge or paradigmatic tool?. *Journal of Religious Education, 68*, 331–344. https://doi.org/10.1007/s40839-020-00113-7.

Franken, L. (2021) Church, state and RE in Europe: Past, Present and Future. *Religion & Education, 48*(4), 417–435. DOI: 10.1080/15507394.2021.1897452.

Global Atlas (2023) World Map with Countries available at https://gisgeography.com/world -map-with-countries/ accessed on 20.01.24

Grimmitt, M. (ed.) (2000) *Pedagogies of RE* Great Wakering: McCrimmon.

King, J. (2004) Dysconscious racism: Ideology, Identity and the miseducation of teachers. In Ladson-Billings, G. and Gillborn, D. (eds.), *The Routledge Falmer Reader in Multicultural Education*, 71–83. Abingdon: Routledge Falmer.

Kueh, R. (2017) Religious Education and the 'knowledge problem'. In Castelli, M. and Chater, M. (eds.), *We Need to Talk about Religious Education*, 53–70. London: Jessica Kingsley.

Lewin,D. Orchard, J., Christopher, K. & Brown, A. (2023) Reframing curriculum for religious education, *Journal of Curriculum Studies*, 55(4): 369–387, DOI: 10.1080/00220272.2023.2226696

Lewin, D. and Orchard , J. (2023) What's 'what' in RE: Relating the what, the why and the how of curriculum content. Available at What's 'what' in RE: Relating the what, the how and the why of curriculum content. — After Religious Education and Project — After Religious Education, accessed 14 May 2023.

Mogra, I. (2022) Social justice and care for the world–adopting a critical view in religious education. *Journal of Religious Education*, 1–13. Available at https://link.springer.com/article/10.1007/s40839-022-00184-8 accessed 13 April 2023.

Mogra, I. (2023) *Religious Education 5–11 A Guide for Teachers*. Abingdon: Routledge

NACCCE (National Advisory Group for Creative and Cultural Education) (1999) All our futures: Creativity, culture and education. Available at: http://www.cypni.org.uk/downloads/alloutfutures.pdf, accessed 20 February 2014.

Open Access. Available at https://articlegateway.com/index.php/JHETP/issue/view/314 and PDF at https://articlegateway.com/index.php/JHETP/article/view/3130.

QCA (2004) Non-Statutory National Framework available at http://www.mmiweb.org.uk/publications/re/NSNF.pdf accessed on 20.01.24

REjesus (2014) Faces of Jesus. Available at http://www.rejesus.co.uk/site/module/faces_of_jesus/, accessed 18 April 2014.

Rudge, J. (2000) The Westhill project: Religious Education as maturing pupils' patterns of belief and behavior. In Grimmitt, M. (ed.), *Pedagogies of RE*, 88–112. Great Wakering: McCrimmon.

Scoffman, S. (2013) *Teaching Geography Creatively*. London: Routledge.

Sheehan, H and Elton-Chalcraft, S. (2023) Helping beginning religious education teachers plan effective and engaging lessons. In Sheehan, H. (ed.), *Mentoring Religious Education Teachers in the Secondary School* Abingdon: Routledge. Available at https://www.taylorfrancis.com/chapters/edit/10.4324/9781003191087-14/helping-beginning-religious-education-teachers-plan-effective-creative-lessons-helen-sheehan-sally-elton-chalcraft.

Sims (2011) Blackburn schools to teach Humanism in RE. Available at http://blog.newhumanist.org.uk/2011/03/teaching-humanism-in-re.html, accessed 12 January 2014.

Smalley, P. (2018) *Response to the Commission on Religious Education's Final Report, Religion and Worldviews: The Way Forward*. National Association of the Standing Advisory Councils on Religious Education. Available at https://nasacre.org.uk/file/nasacre/1-166-response-to-core.pdf.

Taves, A. (2019) From religious studies to worldview studies. *Religion*. DOI: 10.1080/0048721X.2019.1681124.

Teece, G. (2001) *A Primary Teacher's Handbook to RE and Collective Worship*. Oxford: Nash Pollock.

Waggoner, M. (2023) 50 Years of *religion & education*: The continuing imperative of religious literacy in a time of division. *Religion & Education*, *50*(1), 1–2. DOI: 10.1080/15507394.2023.2187975.

Warner, D. and Elton-Chalcraft, S. (2022) Teaching for race culture and ethnicity awareness and understanding Ch 14. In Cooper, H. and Elton-Chalcraft, S. (eds.), *Professional*

Studies in Primary Education (4th ed.). London: Sage. https://us.sagepub.com/en-us/nam/professional-studies-in-primary-education/book273439.

Weiss, O. (2011, March) Reflections on the REDCO project. *British Journal of Religious Education*, *33*(2), 111–126.

World Atlas (2023) Largest Christian denominations in the world. Available at https://www.worldatlas.com/articles/christian-denominations-by-the-numbers.html, accessed 14 May 2023.

Websites

After Religious Education.

Available at https//:www.afterre.org, accessed 14 May 2023.

British Humanist Association (2023) Home page. Available at www.humanism.org.uk , accessed 14 May 2023.

Office for National Statistics ONS (2021) Religion England and wales census 2021. Available at https://www.ons.gov.uk/peoplepopulationandcommunity/culturalidentity/religion/bulletins/religionenglandandwales/census2021, accessed 14 May 2023.

Resources about civil partnerships.

Available at http://www.stonewall.org.uk/at_school/education_resources/default.asp, accessed 12 March 2014.

Show Racism the Red Card. Available at http://theredcard.org/uploaded/SRtRC%20Education%20Pack%202012.pdf.

World Atlas (2023) Largest Christian denominations in the world. Available at https://www.worldatlas.com/articles/christian-denominations-by-the-numbers.html, accessed 14 May 2023.

INDEX

For Product Safety Concerns and Information please contact our EU
representative GPSR@taylorandfrancis.com Taylor & Francis Verlag GmbH,
Kaufingerstraße 24, 80331 München, Germany

Printed and bound by CPI Group (UK) Ltd, Croydon, CR0 4YY
08/06/2025
01897005-0020